Anonymous

Contemplations and Meditations

for the feasts of the Blessed Virgin and the saints according to the method of St.

Ignatius. Second Edition

Anonymous

Contemplations and Meditations
for the feasts of the Blessed Virgin and the saints according to the method of St. Ignatius.
Second Edition

ISBN/EAN: 9783337335724

Printed in Europe, USA, Canada, Australia, Japan

Cover: Foto ©Lupo / pixelio.de

More available books at **www.hansebooks.com**

✠

A. M. D. G.

CONTEMPLATIONS AND MEDITATIONS

FOR THE

Feasts of the Blessed Virgin and the Saints

ACCORDING TO THE METHOD OF ST. IGNATIUS

Translated from the French by
A SISTER OF MERCY

REVISED BY REV. W. H. EYRE, S.J.

SECOND EDITION

London: BURNS & OATES, Limited
New York, Cincinnati, Chicago: Benziger Brothers.
1898

Nihil Obstat.

    W. H. EYRE, S.J.

Imprimatur.

    ✠ WILLIAM BERNARD,
       Bishop of Birmingham.

INTRODUCTION.

AFTER having offered to pious souls four volumes of Meditations, according to the method of St. Ignatius, on the Life and Mysteries of our Lord Jesus Christ, it seemed natural to consecrate at least one volume to the Feasts of the Blessed Virgin and the Saints. Among the latter, we have chosen first those whose devotion is the most widespread, as the Apostles, the Founders of Religious Orders, etc.; second, those who, having lived in times nearer to our own, and having sanctified themselves in common and ordinary positions of life, seem to present models more within our reach. May these holy friends of God deign to bless this little work consecrated to their glory! Above all, may the august Virgin Mary, whom they recognise as their Queen, deign to procure for those who shall use it those graces of light and of unction which, in communicating to us the knowledge of the Christian virtues, may inspire a love of them and make their practice easy!

These Meditations are suited for the Feasts of the Blessed Virgin. But persons desirous of making use of them during the month of Mary can commence with the 1st Meditation, on the Immaculate Conception, and end with the 32nd Meditation, on Our Lady of Perpetual Succour.

CONTENTS.

FIRST PART.

	PAGE
I. The Immaculate Conception of the Blessed Virgin	1
II. The same Subject	5
III. The same Subject	7
IV. The Nativity of the Blessed Virgin	10
V. The Holy Name of Mary	13
VI. The Presentation of the Blessed Virgin in the Temple	15
VII. The Hidden Life of the Blessed Virgin	18
VIII. The Purity of Mary	20
IX. Mary is Given in Marriage to St. Joseph	23
X. The Annunciation of the Blessed Virgin	25
XI. The Visitation of the Blessed Virgin	28
XII. The same Subject	31
XIII. The same Subject	33
XIV. The Divine Maternity of Mary	35
XV. The Purification of the Blessed Virgin	38
XVI. The same Subject	40
XVII. The Seven Dolours of the Blessed Virgin	43
XVIII. Compassion of the Blessed Virgin	46
XIX. The same Subject	48
XX. The same Subject	50
XXI. The Apparition of Jesus Risen to His Holy Mother	52
XXII. The Interior of the Blessed Virgin	54

		PAGE
XXIII.	The Assumption of the Blessed Virgin	57
XXIV.	The same Subject	59
XXV.	The same Subject	61
XXVI.	Mary's Greatness	64
XXVII.	The Joy of Mary	66
XXVIII.	On the Holy Heart of Mary	69
XXIX.	The same Subject	71
XXX.	The same Subject	74
XXXI.	On Devotion to the Blessed Virgin	76
XXXII.	For the Feast of Our Lady of Perpetual Succour	79
XXXIII.	For the Feast of Our Lady of Martyrs	81
XXXIV.	For the Feast of Our Lady of Peace	84
XXXV.	For the Feast of Our Lady of Mount Carmel	87
XXXVI.	For the Feast of Our Lady of the Angels	89
XXXVII.	For the Feast of Our Lady of the Holy Rosary	91
XXXVIII.	For the Feast of Our Lady of Victory	94

SECOND PART.

I.	For New Year's Day	97
II.	For the Feast of St. Genevieve	99
III.	For the Feast of St. Peter's Chair	102
IV.	For the Feast of St. Agnes	104
V.	For the Feast of the Conversion of St. Paul	106
VI.	For the Feast of St. Francis de Sales	108
VII.	For the Feast of the Martyrs of Japan	110
VIII.	For the Feast of St. Matthias	112
IX.	For the Feast of St. Joseph	114
X.	Second Meditation for the same Day	117
XI.	Third Meditation for the same Day	119
XII.	For the Feast of the Patronage of St. Joseph	121
XIII.	For the Feast of St. Benedict	123
XIV.	For the Feast of St. Mark the Evangelist	125
XV.	For the Feast of SS. Philip and James	127

CONTENTS.

	PAGE
XVI. For the Feast of the Finding of the Cross	130
XVII. For the Feast of the Apparition of St. Michael	132
XVIII. For the Feast of St. Barnabas	134
XIX. For the Feast of St. Francis Regis	137
XX. For the Feast of St. Aloysius	139
XXI. Second Meditation for the same Day	141
XXII. Third Meditation for the same Day	144
XXIII. For the Feast of the Nativity of St. John the Baptist	146
XXIV. For the Feast of St. Peter	148
XXV. For the Feast of the Commemoration of St. Paul	151
XXVI. For the Feast of St. Vincent of Paul	153
XXVII. For the Feast of St. Mary Magdalen	155
XXVIII. For the Feast of St. James the Great	158
XXIX. For the Feast of St. Anne	161
XXX. For the Feast of St. Ignatius of Loyola	163
XXXI. Second Meditation for the same Day	165
XXXII. Third Meditation for the same Day	168
XXXIII. For the Feast of St. Dominic	170
XXXIV. For the Feast of St. Philomena	173
XXXV. For the Feast of St. Jane Frances de Chantal	175
XXXVI. For the Feast of St. Louis, King	177
XXXVII. For the Feast of St. Augustine	180
XXXVIII. For the Feast of the Exaltation of the Cross	182
XXXIX. For the Feast of St. Matthew, Apostle	184
XL. For the Feast of St. Michael and of all the Holy Angels	186
XLI. For the Feast of the Guardian Angels	189
XLII. For the Feast of St. Francis of Assisi	191
XLIII. For the Feast of St. Francis Borgia	193
XLIV. For the Feast of St. Teresa	196
XLV. For the Feast of St. Luke, Evangelist	198
XLVI. For the Feast of St. Raphael, Archangel	201
XLVII. For the Feast of SS. Simon and Jude	203
XLVIII. For the Feast of the Blessed Alphonsus Rodriguez	205

		PAGE
XLIX.	For the Feast of All Saints	208
L.	Second Meditation for the same Day	210
LI.	Third Meditation for the same Day	213
LII.	For the Commemoration of All Souls	215
LIII.	For the Feast of the Holy Relics	218
LIV.	For the Feast of St. Stanislaus	220
LV.	Second Meditation for the same Day	223
LVI.	For the Feast of the Dedication of a Church	225
LVII.	For the Feast of St. Cecilia	227
LVIII.	For the Feast of St. Catherine	230
LIX.	For the Feast of St. Andrew	232
LX.	For the Feast of St. Francis Xavier	235
LXI.	For the Feast of St. Thomas, Apostle	238
LXII.	For the Feast of St. Stephen	241
LXIII.	For the Feast of St. John the Evangelist	243

CONTEMPLATIONS AND MEDITATIONS.

FIRST MEDITATION.

THE IMMACULATE CONCEPTION OF THE BLESSED VIRGIN.

"From the beginning and before the world was I created."

Preparatory Prayer. Grant, O my Divine Lord, that, during this meditation, all the thoughts of my mind, all the affections of my heart, and all the operations of my soul may tend purely and solely to Thy service and to the glory of Thy Divine Majesty.

Come, Holy Ghost, fill the hearts of Thy faithful, and kindle within them the fire of Thy love.

Send forth Thy Spirit and they shall be created.

And Thou shalt renew the face of the earth.

Let us pray.

O God, Who, by the light of Thy Holy Ghost, didst instruct the hearts of the faithful, give us, by this same Holy Spirit, a love and relish of what is right and just, and the constant enjoyment of His comforts, through Jesus Christ our Lord. Amen.

Hail Mary, etc.

1st Prelude. Figure to yourself the adorable Trinity contemplating with love Mary immaculate, and offering her to the admiration of the Angels.

2nd Prelude. Immaculate Virgin, who wast, even

before thy conception, the object of the love of God and of the hope of man, obtain for me, from thy Divine Son, the pardon of my so many infidelities, and the grace to profit at length by His gifts and favours.

1st Point. Mary was, from all eternity, the object of the delight of the Almighty.

God, in Whose sight all time is present, had determined, from all eternity, on the creation and birth of Mary. From all eternity He had prepared, in the treasures of His power, the singular graces with which He willed to favour her; moreover, foreseeing from all eternity the perfect fidelity of this holy Virgin, He was well-pleased in her, on account of His anticipated vision of her perfections and her greatness. Like unto Mary, I also have been in the eternal mind of God. Before the world was created He thought of me, and prepared for me the means of sanctification, choosing me in a special manner to be born in the bosom of the true Church, to be brought up in the Catholic faith, and to receive a multitude of special graces, each more precious than the preceding ones. But, alas! far from being to Him, as Mary was, an object of joy and delight, I offered nothing but ingratitude and offences without number in His holy sight. How comes it that so much unworthiness has not dried up for me the source of so many graces? Ah! it is because the Blood of Jesus and the prayers of the Immaculate Mary have moved the Divine mercy in my favour; it is because the Sacred Heart of my Saviour and the immaculate heart of His blessed Mother have been opened for me, that I might offer their merits to God in compensation for my own extreme indigence.

2nd Point. Mary, from the beginning of the world, was the object of the hope of mankind.

The Lord had destined Mary to concur, as far as it was possible to a pure creature, to the mysteries of our salvation. Promised to the world from the beginning, as the mysterious woman who was to crush the head of the infernal serpent, she was, conjointly with her Divine Son, the object of the predictions of the Prophets, of the figures of the old Law, and of the desires of the Patriarchs. At length the moment is come, she is given to us; like unto the beautiful rainbow that our Lord showed to Noe after the deluge, the sign of peace and pledge of hope, Mary appears before us, conceived without sin and full of grace. The splendour of the Sun of Justice is still concealed from us; but she receives from it its rays, and shows herself resplendent with beauty. What hopes are not awakened at her appearance! It is through her that the Messias is about to be given to us: it is in her chaste womb that He will clothe Himself with our flesh, and draw forth the Divine Blood destined to wash away our crimes; through Mary, also, He will henceforth receive our prayers, and she, the new ark of the covenant will unite Heaven to earth, by rendering Jesus propitious unto us, and transmitting unto us His benefits. O Mary! could my heart ever suffice to show forth the gratitude and love with which this first mystery of Divine love ought to inspire me?

Colloquy with Mary Immaculate. Let us render her profound homage of veneration and love. Let us offer to the Divine Majesty all the glory which the most blessed Virgin rendered Him from the first moment of her conception. Let us unite ourselves to this pure offering, and ask, through the intercession of our Divine Mother, for the grace to be henceforth faithful in putting to profit all the benefits of the Lord.

Resolutions. To watch carefully over my heart, in order to preserve it in purity. To follow faithfully all the inspirations of grace.

Offering of the Resolutions. My God, I offer Thee these resolutions. Unless Thou deignest to bless them, I cannot be faithful to them. From Thy goodness, then, I hope to obtain this blessing, which I ask of Thee in the name and through the merits of Jesus, my Saviour.

Holy Virgin, Mother of my God, and also my Mother, my good Angel and holy Patron Saints, obtain for me the grace to keep these resolutions with perfect fidelity.

Spiritual Bouquet. O Mary, conceived without sin, pray for us who have recourse to thee!

Prayer. O God, Who, in preserving the most holy Virgin from the stain of original sin, hast prepared for Thy Son a worthy dwelling in the womb of the immaculate Virgin, we beg of Thee, that having preserved her from all sin, through the precious merits of the death of this same Son, that Thou wouldst also vouchsafe, through her intercession, to grant us the grace to be united to Thee, purified from all our sins. Through Jesus Christ our Lord. Amen.

Examen of the Meditation. Did I carefully prepare the points of my meditation, and resolve on the fruit I would draw from it? Did I recall it to my mind before I went to sleep? Did I, from the moment of awaking, occupy myself with it, to the exclusion of every other thought? Did I place myself as I ought to do in the presence of God? Did I make the preparatory prayer and the preludes? Did I preserve a becoming reverence in my attitude? Have I not passed lightly from one point to another? Have I reflected on the mystery before me with a sincere desire of profiting by it? Have I made the Colloquies, asking for grace to practise the virtue that God set before me? Have I made resolutions for the day, determining on the opportunities when I would reduce them to practice? Have I made a spiritual bouquet?

SECOND MEDITATION.

THE SAME SUBJECT.

"As the lily among thorns, so is my beloved among the daughters of Adam."

Preparatory Prayer, page 1.
1st Prelude, page 1.
2nd Prelude. Grant me grace, O Lord, to honour worthily the mystery of the Immaculate Conception of Mary, and to imitate, as closely as I possibly can, the perfect correspondence with grace of this most holy Virgin.

1st Point. Mary was conceived without sin.

It belonged to the glory of the Incarnate Word to preserve from original sin the Mother He had made choice of. If the thrice holy God exacted from the Israelites so many purifications when they erected a temple to Him; if every part of this temple was to be sanctified and consecrated with so much care and so many ceremonies, how much more necessary was it that Mary, the living sanctuary of the Incarnate God, should be exempt from every spot and stain!

This holy Virgin, in consequence, was immaculate in her Conception. This has always been the pious belief of the Church, and has been defined lately as an article of faith. What a signal privilege! Sprung from a guilty race, Mary is preserved, by an unparalleled miracle, from the general corruption. She is a flower of benediction sprung from a withered stem; and whilst the rest of mankind, even the most holy, are forced to exclaim, with David: " I was conceived in iniquity, and in sins did my mother conceive me," Mary, like a beautiful lily among thorns, presents to the Adorable Trinity a pure soul and virginal flesh, which corruption was never to reach, a heart exempt from every stain, whose entire affections divine love alone shall replenish. Holy and immaculate Virgin, how is my heart filled with joy at the sight of this glorious privilege! But this mystery ought to excite within me very many most different sentiments: it reminds me of the grace of my baptism, by which God freed me, almost at the moment of my birth, from the slavery of sin: it reminds me, also, of the numberless faults which have stained the robe of my innocence. Ah! may the sincerity of my sorrow, and thy maternal protection restore to me this day its pristine brightness, and, aided by thy grace, may I preserve it unspotted to the last moment of my life!

2nd Point. Mary, from the first moment of her Conception, was overwhelmed with the most precious and most abundant graces.

The privilege of Mary's Immaculate Conception exempted her from the triple concupiscence which we bring with us when born into the world. Neither was her spirit to be subjected to ignorance, another consequence of sin. The most pure lights, the most delicate and noble sentiments, an upright will, ever inclined to good, were the happy lot of this Blessed among all creatures. But these gifts did not suffice for the love of God Almighty for her; they would not have distinguished her from Eve—our first mother—in her state of innocence. The august Trinity, having willed to contract with Mary the very closest alliance, enriched her with all the treasures of grace with which a pure creature could be favoured. All the riches of the wisdom and goodness of the Lord were exhausted, so to speak, in order to make of her a masterpiece of holiness, and the most perfect image of the holy humanity of Jesus. From the first instant of her existence, Mary surpassed in grace and perfection all the Angels and Saints together, so that there never has been, nor ever will be again, any creature so excellent and perfect. Incomparable Virgin, who could render thee the homage thou dost merit? Who will ever be worthy to attract thy notice, or to obtain thy mediation? Yet the Church calls thee the Refuge of Sinners, the Gate of Heaven, the Help of Christians. She teaches me that Jesus on the Cross gave thee to me as my Mother. Confidence in thee must then overpower every other sentiment within me; the more perfect thou art, the more powerful are thy prayers before God; and since thou art my Mother, I may hope for all, and obtain everything through thee.

Colloquy with Mary Immaculate. Let us congratulate her on the transcendent prerogatives with which she was favoured from the first instant of her creation, and, above all, on her perfect fidelity in putting to profit so many graces. Let us pray to her to obtain for us the pardon of our constant infidelities, and beg her aid in order that we may serve our Lord with all the perfection He demands of us.

Resolutions. To watch and pray, in order to preserve or recover purity of heart.

Offering of the Resolutions, page 3.

Spiritual Bouquet. "My Beloved is like the lily among thorns."

Prayer. O God, etc., page 4.

Examen of the Meditation, page 4.

THIRD MEDITATION.

THE SAME SUBJECT.

"Thou art all fair, my beloved, and there is no spot in thee."

Preparatory Prayer, page 1.
1st Prelude, page 1.
2nd Prelude. Holy and immaculate Virgin, obtain

for me the grace to imitate thy fidelity in corresponding with the designs of God, and in profiting by His gifts.

1st Point. The fidelity of Mary in corresponding with divine grace.

Mary, laden with the richest treasures of grace from the first moment of her existence, never allowed any delay or reserve to have place in her fidelity. The first movement of her heart was to raise itself to God by a most perfect act of love, and to offer itself to fulfil all the designs of His providence. From this moment she consecrated herself entirely to the service of her Creator, with an intention so pure and disengaged from self, that she had in view neither the merits she was to acquire, nor the fresh graces which her fidelity was to draw down on her, nor even the recompense to which she could lay claim. Her entire life was nothing but a continuation and consequence of this first act of abandonment. Constantly attentive to the inspirations of the Holy Spirit, Who dwelt within her, Mary knew no other care than to abandon herself in all things to the good pleasure of God; no other intention than that of glorifying Him; no other end than to do, through love, whatever was most conformable to His adorable Will. What inconceivable progress must not such holy dispositions have caused her to make in all virtues! The holy Fathers assure us that the graces with which she was loaded from the first instant of her conception never ceased, during her whole life, to make prodigious increase; so that it is impossible for any created intelligence to conceive the sublime degree of perfection to which she attained. Virgin, most faithful! in thus corresponding with the grace of God, thou didst prepare thyself without knowing it for His designs. I beg of thee, offer to Him thy abundant merits to supply for my continued infidelities, and deign to obtain for me the grace to begin at length to serve Him with ardour and generosity.

2nd Point. I ought to imitate the fidelity of Mary.

Mary is not only my Queen, my Advocate, and my Mother; she is still more my Model. She can say to me, as her Divine Son has said: "I have given you an example that you should do as I have done". I must therefore apply myself to imitate her. Without doubt, God does not expect from me those pure and exalted virtues of which a creature conceived without sin, and most richly endowed with all the treasures of grace, is alone capable. He does not demand of me, as of Mary, that, exempt from all stain of sin, I should pass through this life without contracting any imperfection, or being unfaithful to any one grace. He knows my weakness, and His designs over me are proportioned to the gifts He has bestowed on my soul; but what He does desire, and what I cannot refuse Him without injustice, is, that, after the example of Mary, I offer myself to accomplish His designs over me with an entire and generous will; what He does expect from me is, that I employ all the strength and all the powers that He has given me in corresponding with His graces; and, if human weakness causes me to commit some faults, that I hasten to repair them with contrition and love. Such are the dispositions He wishes to find habitually in my heart. I ought to renew them constantly, with all the fervour of my soul, since they are the only means of repairing my past infidelities; of pleasing the Sacred Heart of my Divine Saviour; of obtaining the fulness of His graces; of rendering myself fit for His designs; and of procuring for Him all the glory He expects from me.

Colloquy with Mary Immaculate. Let us offer her our heartfelt homage of love and veneration. Let us congratulate her on the plenitude of grace with which God has enriched her, and on her perfect fidelity in corresponding with it. Let us pray to her to obtain for us the grace to imitate her as closely as we possibly can. Let us lay before her, with confidence, all the weaknesses and miseries and wants of our soul, that so she may help us to overcome the obstacles which the corruption of our nature opposes to the accomplishment of our good desires.

Resolutions. To follow faithfully the inspirations of grace. To do all my actions for God.

Offering of the Resolutions, page 3.

Spiritual Bouquet. "Behold me ready to do Thy Will, O my God."

Prayer. O God of infinite clemency, Who, for the salvation of sinners and the help of the miserable, hast given to the blessed Virgin Mary a heart like unto that of Jesus, her Divine Son, and hast made it a source of sweetness and mercy, grant to those who honour this Immaculate Heart the grace that they may have, through her intercession and her merits, hearts according to the Sacred Heart of Jesus. Amen.

Examen of the Meditation, page 4.

FOURTH MEDITATION.

The Nativity of the Blessed Virgin.

"Who is she that cometh forth as the morning rising?"

Preparatory Prayer, page 1.

1st Prelude. Let us picture to ourselves the Angels surrounding the cradle of Mary, and with them contemplate, with respect and admiration, this Babe so highly privileged.

2nd Prelude. Holy Virgin, obtain for me the grace to know thee worthily, and to gather from this solemnity practical fruits of devotion towards thee.

1st Point. The birth of Mary glorifies the adorable Trinity.

Mary is just born, and already directs to Heaven the

homage of her adoration and love:—already the most perfect sentiments of submission to the Divine Majesty, gratitude for His benefits, and zeal for His glory, are admirably blended in her blessed soul, and cause her to produce the most perfect acts of love, praise, and thanksgiving. The looks of the adorable Trinity, which, since the fall of Adam, had seen nothing on the earth but corruption and sin, can fix, at length, with delight on a holy and perfect creature, who will never forfeit the grace and beauty with which she is adorned. God the Father beholds once more in her His divine image, effaced by sin in the rest of mankind; the Spirit of grace, banished from almost every soul, beholds in her soul a temple worthy of His infinite holiness: He reposes with delight in a heart so docile to all His impressions. God the Son beholds in this incomparable Virgin so many virtues that He longs to call her His Mother. Oh! what glory must such a holy life procure God in every moment, since, from the very commencement, it was so pure and perfect! What a subject of joy for me to see the Divine Majesty so worthily honoured by the masterpiece of His hands! But I must not limit myself to sterile affections; Mary is a model proposed for my imitation; if I cannot pretend to equal her in sanctity and love, at least, like her, I ought to correspond with generosity of will and entire fidelity to the graces which are lavished on me.

2nd Point. The birth of Mary rejoices the Angels and prepares the way for the salvation of mankind.

The birth of Mary is the prelude and commencement of the blessings of the Lord. She is given to us as a pledge of the approaching advent of our Saviour, and already she announces it by the brilliance of the graces which are heaped upon her, as the morning rising announces the sun, being made bright with the strength of its shining. The Angels contemplate her with astonishment and respect: "Who is she," they exclaim, "that cometh forth as the morning rising?" Who is this sublime creature who, from her first steps in the career of life, is already raising herself up towards God by swift flights of the purest love, and who sheds brightest lustre, by the splendours of the virtues we see shine forth in her? Mankind ignores the treasure which is given to it. Men know not that this child born in obscurity is the new Eve, the true Mother of the Living, who comes to remedy all our evils, by giving us the Saviour promised to our Fathers; men are not aware that the mysterious woman, who was to crush the head of the serpent, is at length granted to the earth. If they knew it, with what joy would they not be penetrated! O Mary! this mystery, which was once concealed from the world, is not hidden from me to-day. I know that thou art my Mother, my Refuge, my Mediatrix with the Divine Majesty. I know that thou art the Help of Christians, the Refuge of Sinners, the Gate of Heaven, and the Dispenser of all the treasures of grace. Receive, then, all the homage of my heart, and grant that, through thy powerful intercession, I may reap the harvest of this holy solemnity.

Colloquy with the most Blessed Virgin. Let us congratulate her on the graces and heavenly gifts which God has heaped up together in her soul. Let us beg of her to apply to us the fruits of her birth by penetrating us with lively gratitude towards God, and a firm resolution to put to profit all His benefits.

Resolutions. To offer all my actions to God to-day, through love and gratitude. To enter frequently within my heart in order to unite its homage and acts of love to those of Mary.

Offering of the Resolutions, page 3.

Spiritual Bouquet. Heart of Mary, the most perfect and most faithful of all hearts, inflame my heart with the divine love which consumes thine.

Prayer. Remember, O most holy Virgin Mary, that no one ever had recourse to thy protection, implored thy help, or sought thy mediation, without obtaining relief. Confiding, therefore, in thy goodness, behold me a penitent sinner, sighing out my sins before thee, beseeching thee to adopt me for thy child, and to take upon thee the care of my eternal salvation. Despise not, O Mother of Jesus, the petition of thy humble client, but hear and grant my prayer.

Examen of the Meditation, page 4.

FIFTH MEDITATION.

The Holy Name of Mary.

"Thy name is as oil poured forth."

Preparatory Prayer, page 1.
1st Prelude, page 1.
2nd Prelude. O Mary! cause me to relish all the sweetness of thy name; may it be ever my consolation, my help, and my hope.

1st Point. The holy name of Mary merits my respect, my homage, and my confidence.

The holy name of Mary signifies *Queen* or *Mistress*. It is a name of power and grandeur, that causes hell to tremble, puts the demons to flight, commands the respect of the faithful on earth, and the veneration of the Angels in Heaven. It is, moreover, a name of clemency and love, for it also signifies *full of grace*, and gives us to understand two most consoling truths: the first, that Mary, full of virtues and merits, is all-powerful over the Sacred Heart of our Lord; the second, that in receiving the plenitude of grace, it has been given to her to distribute it, and that she bestows its treasures generously on all who have recourse to her. . . . "O holy Mary," says St. Francis, "Heaven and earth know no other name, after that of thy beloved Son, which procures for us mortals more graces, and which is more fitted to nourish our hope, and cause us to taste greater sweetness than thy name." " Happy is he who cherishes and respects thy name, O holy Virgin!" exclaims St. Bonaventure; "thy favour will support him in his troubles, and will produce within him abundant fruits." What then can I do more glorious for Mary, or more profitable for myself, than to invoke her name frequently with love and confidence? What can I do more in unison with that spirit of zeal, with which a truly Christian soul ought to be penetrated, than to excite others to have recourse to that most blessed name in their temptations and dangers, and to make use of it as a powerful weapon against the enemies of their salvation?

2nd Point. The holy name of Mary ought to be my refuge in all my necessities.

The holy name of Mary signifies "*Star of the Sea*," and this meaning presents me with fresh and most powerful motives of confidence. As long as I shall dwell on this earth, storms and tempests will threaten my soul. The world, in the midst of which I am obliged to live, is a sea full of rocks and dangers, and I bear within my heart passions which expose me every instant to a sad shipwreck. It is against these great dangers that Mary offers me her aid; if the false maxims of the world seduce me; if bad example drags me, for a time, out of the path of salvation; if, in consequence of my infidelities, I oblige the Sun of Justice to hide from me the brightness of His rays, Mary, the Star of the Sea, will cause her sweet and gentle light to shine before my eyes, reminding me that she is the Mother of Mercy; she will excite within me a salutary repentance, accompanied with the hope of pardon, and will lead me back to the paths of virtue. If the storms of temptation agitate my heart, if the clouds of diffidence and discouragement weigh down my spirit, Mary will cause the daylight to shine upon the shades of darkness, and will restore confidence and peace in my soul. O Mary! holy name, calling upon which no one ought to despair, be ever on my lips and in my heart, together with that of thy Divine Son. Remain with me during this life so full of afflictions and troubles; but, above all, be with me during that supreme moment which will decide my eternal lot, and obtain for me the grace of landing happily on the shores of my heavenly country.

Colloquy with the Blessed Virgin. Let us ask her to inspire us with a tender confidence in her intercession, and beg her powerful help in all our wants.

Resolutions. Often to pronounce with piety the holy name of Mary.

Offering of the Resolutions, page 3.

Spiritual Bouquet. "O Mary! under the protection of thy name, no one ought to lose confidence."

Prayer. O holy Mary! be to me all that is betokened by thy name. Mayst thou be honoured in Heaven, revered on earth, and dreaded in hell. Next to God, reign over all that is less than God, but above all reign over our hearts; be thou our consolation in our trials, our strength in our weaknesses, our counsel in our doubts, and, above all, our hope at the hour of our death. Amen.

Examen of the Meditation, page 4.

SIXTH MEDITATION.

THE PRESENTATION OF THE BLESSED VIRGIN
IN THE TEMPLE.

"Beware lest thou ever forget the Covenant with the Lord thy God, which He hath made with thee" (Deut. iv. 23).

Preparatory Prayer, page 1.
1st Prelude. Let us figure to ourselves Mary, three

years old, ascending the steps of the temple to offer herself to God within it.

2nd Prelude. O Mary! who didst offer thyself to the Lord with so much love and generosity, obtain for me the grace to consecrate myself to His service with the firm resolution of no longer refusing anything to His grace.

1st Point. Mary offers herself to God with all the fulness of her heart.

Let us consider Mary, the masterpiece of nature and grace, presenting herself before the altar of the Lord, and consecrating herself to Him for ever. Possessing, according to the belief of the holy Fathers, the perfect use of reason, enlightened by the purest rays of grace, and perfectly docile to the divine inspirations, she comes to offer herself entirely and unreservedly to the Divine Majesty; she renounces the comforts of her Father's home; she chooses the holy temple for her dwelling, and desires no other inheritance than the grace and love of her God. What reflections ought not the sacrifice of Mary to arouse within me!—a sacrifice so prompt, so entire, and so generous! God made me for Himself alone; from the first dawn of reason, He has deigned to ask for my heart by the secret inspirations of His grace; from that time, I also, like Mary, should have responded to His love by giving myself to Him. If I have not done so, if my many infidelities have delayed so far this so merited act of gratitude and submission, is it not time at least now that I should give back all to Him, Who has given all to me, by consecrating all the faculties of my soul and body to His service and glory?

2nd Point. Mary offers herself to God irrevocably and for ever.

It is much to give oneself to God without placing any reserve to the sacrifice; it is a great deal to immolate to the accomplishment of the Divine Will our dearest affections, our most lawful rights, and even our future hopes; yet, after such an act, all is not yet accomplished: inconstancy, so natural to the human heart, may cause a retractation, and after having given ourselves to God, we may withdraw from His divine will, to give ourselves up to our passions, and place ourselves anew under the cruel dominion of our invisible enemies. How often have I not gone through this sad experience! how frequently, after resolutions, which seemed of the firmest, to lead a fervent and regular life, have I not looked back and abandoned my good purposes! Ah! may the example of my most holy Mother this day reanimate my courage and arouse my languor! At this moment she is making the first step in the path of sacrifice; she is entering the way of the Cross; but it is to walk therein with a firm and constant step until her last sigh. Generous she is and faithful, because divine love inspires her; firm and unshaken in the holy course she has commenced, because she has placed all her confidence in the Lord; she will advance from virtue to virtue until she reaches the very summit of perfection. All the graces she will receive will bear their fruits in her soul; all her actions will be meritorious; all her days will be full. Oh! what glory will such a beautiful life procure for God, and what a magnificent reward will it not receive from Him in Heaven! . . . O Mary! if up to the present my life has been so different from thine, obtain for me that at least, from this moment, I may be constant in treading in thy steps, and may increase more and more in the fidelity I owe to God.

Colloquy with the Holy Heart of Mary. Let us venerate it as the most perfect holocaust of divine love, begging her to unite our offering to hers, and to rectify, by the application of her merits, all that is defective and imperfect in our own.

Resolutions. Often to renew the offering of myself to God, and to perform all my actions in a spirit of consecration and sacrifice.

18   CONTEMPLATIONS AND MEDITATIONS.

Offering of the Resolutions, page 3.

Spiritual Bouquet. "Beware lest thou ever forget the Covenant with the Lord thy God, which He hath made with thee" (Deut. iv. 23).

Prayer. Receive, O Lord, all my liberty without reserve; deign to accept my memory, my understanding, and my will. I have nothing, I possess nothing, which is not the gift of Thy bounty. I give back all to Thee; I abandon all without reserve to Thy will, that Thou mayst dispose of all as it shall please Thee. All that I ask of Thee is Thy grace and Thy love. With these I shall be rich enough, and I beg for nothing more.

Examen of the Meditation, page 4.

SEVENTH MEDITATION.

THE HIDDEN LIFE OF THE BLESSED VIRGIN.

"The beauty of the king's daughter is within."

Preparatory Prayer, page 1.

1st Prelude. Represent to yourself the Blessed Virgin Mary, occupied either in the work of her hands, or in the humble duties which she exercised in the house of God.

2nd Prelude. Virgin most prudent, obtain for me the grace to conceal, as thou didst, from the eyes of men all that might draw on me their praises, and to seek the approbation of God alone in the good which His grace may enable me to accomplish.

1st Point. Mary loved retreat and silence.

Mary, concealed from the eyes of men, and cherishing her prized retirement, is the model I ought continually to propose to myself. She knows that free intercourse with the world is full of dangers, that the strongest virtue is scarcely proof against the contagion of its vices and the seduction of its pleasures; and although full of grace, she distrusts herself and withdraws herself to a distance, out of the reach of all danger. What a beautiful lesson of humility, self-diffidence, and flight from the world! Again, another motive leads Mary to love her retreat; it is the powerful attraction she experiences for prayer, union with God, and the practice of those interior virtues, which only take root in the soul under the shade of recollection and silence. Why cannot I understand, as she did, the happiness of an interior and recollected soul? Why cannot I feel that to a certain extent I ought to esteem, desire, and seek after this life hidden in God with Jesus Christ, Who is the guardian of all graces, the source of all merits, and the fount of all spiritual sweetness? I have already meditated many times on this subject; I cannot be truly happy if my heart is not united to that of Jesus, and I shall never attain this so much-desired union unless I keep myself removed as much as I possibly can from all worldly distractions. When will it be that, dead to myself and unoccupied with all useless cares, I shall live for nothing but God alone, after the example of my holy Mother?

2nd Point. Mary loved obscurity, and sought to be forgotten by creatures.

It would have been too little for Mary to withdraw from the eyes of the world, if she had not endeavoured to conceal even from the holy companions of her retreat, the precious gifts with which grace had enriched her soul. The refinements of her love for God made her fear the poison of vainglory, and every motive capable of diminishing the value of her actions; thus she was extremely careful that all her actions should be simple and ordinary, and she avoided everything that would have distinguished her from others. How fruitful is this her example in salutary instructions! She teache: me in what that true humility consists, which spring: from the pure love of God; that simplicity which alway: takes by preference the most ordinary and direct road which keeps its eyes fixed on God alone; that complete purity of heart which rejects every motive foreign to the perfection of His holy love; in a word, that life hidden in God with Jesus Christ, which shines with a lustre all the purer in the sight of the Angels, as the veil is thicker which conceals it from the eyes of men With what resolutions ought this conduct of my holy Mother to inspire me! . . .

Colloquy with Mary in the Temple. Let us ask her to teach us how to practise those social and interior virtues, which are the foundation of all true Christianity and the only means of becoming united to God through love.

Resolutions. To perform all my actions solely through love of God. To conceal from the eyes of creatures all the acts of virtue I mean to practise to-day.

Offering of the Resolutions, page 3.

Spiritual Bouquet. "All the beauty of the king's daughter is within."

Prayer. Remember, O most holy Virgin, etc.

Examen of the Meditation, page 4.

EIGHTH MEDITATION.

The Purity of Mary.

"He that made me, rested in my Tabernacle" (Eccli. xxiv 12).

Preparatory Prayer, page 1.

1st Prelude. Again represent to yourself Mary in

the house of God; the august Trinity looks down on her from Heaven; a multitude of angels are deputed to guard her, and accompany her everywhere.

2nd Prelude. Spotless Virgin, obtain for me the grace to imitate, as perfectly as I can, thy perfect purity, that so I may give pleasure to the Sacred Heart of Jesus, thy Divine Son.

1st Point. Mary is the most pure of all virgins.

The purity of Mary is so perfect that it has not been granted to any human voice to celebrate it worthily, or to any created intelligence to conceive its excellence. The holy Scripture paints it under the most beautiful figures; at one time in compares Mary to the cedar of Libanus, whose wood is incorruptible and whose verdure is perpetual; at another time to the lily of the valley, which conceals its dazzling whiteness from the scorching rays of the sun. And again, Holy Writ puts into her mouth those words which describe so well the secret power by which she attracts and delights pure souls: " I gave a sweet smell like cinnamon, and aromatical balm; I yielded a sweet odour like the best myrrh" (Ecclesiasticus xxiv. 20). The Church finding herself, as it were, incapable of exalting as she could wish this incomparable purity, multiplies and, if we may use the word, heaps up expressions of admiration, one upon another. She calls Mary the Virgin of Virgins, alluding to the name of Holy of Holies, a title due to God alone; she calls Mary the Virgin most prudent, the Virgin most venerable, the Virgin most renowned, the Virgin most powerful, the Virgin most amiable, the Virgin most faithful, the Queen of Virgins. . . . How beautiful are these titles of my sacred Mother! How they ought to make me cherish the precious virtue which had so many charms in her eyes, and merited for her such singular privileges!

2nd Point. Mary is the Queen and the Mother of all pure souls.

Mary was the first who consecrated her virginity to

the Lord by her free and voluntary choice. She was the first who planted in the garden of her Spouse the beautiful lily of perfect chastity, which was, later on, to bear such ample fruits, and was to bring forth to the Lord so many chaste and pure souls. Thus the Royal Prophet had said, contemplating beforehand the glorious retinue of this Queen of Purity: "After her shall virgins be brought to the king" (Ps. xliv. 15). Yes, Mary, the Queen of all Christians, is especially the Queen of those souls who cultivate with care the precious virtue of purity; she watches over the pure with especial tenderness; removes from them the perils which might menace their innocence; sustains their weakness under the numberless attacks of their invisible enemies; preserves them from their own corruption; and maintains within them, in all its lustre, that delicate flower which the least breath is sufficient to tarnish. If I am anxious to please Mary, to merit her assistance, and draw down on myself her favour, I must strive to preserve a spotless purity, both of mind and heart, by exercising myself continually in the practice of humility, recollection in the spirit of mortification, vigilance over myself, and contempt for all the dangerous pleasures of the world.

Colloquy with the Blessed Virgin. Let us render her our homage of veneration and love as to the most holy of creatures, to our Mother, and to the most tender of mothers. Let us beg of her to increase within us the love for the most lovely of virtues, to perfect it within us, that so we may be pleasing to the Beloved, Whose delight is amongst the lilies.

Resolutions. To watch over all my senses, that I may preserve purity of heart. To observe carefully the rules of modesty.

Offering of the Resolutions, page 3.

Spiritual Bouquet. "He who loves cleanness of heart, shall have the king for his friend" (Prov. xxii. 11).

Prayer. O God of infinite clemency, etc., after Med. 3rd.
Examen of the Meditation, page 4.

NINTH MEDITATION.

Mary is Given in Marriage to Saint Joseph.

"The Lord guides me, nothing shall be wanting to me" (Ps. xxii. 2).

Preparatory Prayer, page 1.
1st Prelude. Represent to yourself Mary at the foot of the altar, where she receives Saint Joseph for her Spouse; behold also the holy Patriarch; everything in him breathes forth humility, purity, and union with God.
2nd Prelude. Grant me grace, O Lord, to draw from this meditation a spirit of entire abandonment to Thy Providence, and perfect fidelity in accomplishing Thy divine will.
1st Point. What were the designs of God in uniting the blessed Virgin to Saint Joseph?
Mary had consecrated herself to God from the age of three years, and a pious tradition teaches us that Saint Joseph on his part had pledged himself to perpetual chastity. Yet, both being instructed respecting the will of God, they did not hesitate to contract an alliance, which was to be so much the closer for being more holy and more pure. God willed, by this union, to give Mary a supporter, a consoler, and an aid in all her labours. He wished to conceal from men and from demons the mystery of the Incarnation of the Word, and to offer to Christians in the married state a perfect model of the virtues they should practise in that state.

These designs were concealed from Mary and Joseph; nevertheless, they submitted to the orders of Divine Providence without any human reasonings coming forward to oppose the simplicity of their obedience. How happy I should be if, more faithful in imitating their example, I knew how to despise the anxieties and restlessness of my own judgment and my own will, in order to give myself up entirely to the guidance and paternal care of a God Who is wisdom and goodness itself, and Who desires my happiness more ardently than I myself can wish it.

2nd Point. With what dispositions did Mary and Joseph contract this alliance?

If I examine the interior dispositions of Mary and Joseph concerning the step they take on this day, what perfections shall I not find in them! Mary, enlightened by the Holy Ghost as to the merit of him to whom God willed her to be united, gave him her heart and her hand, as she would have done in the case of the purest of all the Angels; she confided to him the treasure of her virginity, without the slightest fear arising in her soul. Joseph, on his side, received Mary from the hands of the High Priest as a sacred deposit that God had placed in his hands, and although he did not then appreciate, as he did later on, the immense treasures of virtue contained within the heart of his holy Spouse, he was already penetrated with a respect for her which partook of the most profound veneration. What beautiful and touching instructions are here presented to me! Joseph venerates Mary almost without knowing her. It is true that the modest deportment of this most holy Virgin, together with the impress of humility and gentleness on every feature of her countenance, are indications of her virtue: but the uprightness of heart, the charity and sincerity of the holy Patriarch have also a large share in this favourable judgment. Are the judgments I form of my neighbour always conformed to this great example? Mary gives her confidence to Joseph, and constitutes him the guardian of her purity; he is in consequence the special protector of all those who cherish this beautiful virtue. I ought then to honour and invoke him as my father and protector, and his name should be ever on my lips, together with those of Jesus and Mary, when I am earnest in resisting temptation.

Colloquy with Mary and Joseph. Let us offer them our homage of love and respect. Let us ask them to obtain for us the spirit of confidence and abandonment to Divine Providence, charity and esteem for our neighbour, and every other virtue of which their holy union offers us the model.

Resolutions. To despise all vain anxieties which tend to withdraw me from the path of abandonment to Divine Providence, in which I ought steadfastly to walk. To reject all thoughts and judgments unfavourable to others.

Offering of the Resolutions, page 3.

Spiritual Bouquet. "The Lord leads me, I shall want for nothing."

Prayer. Pater Noster, etc.

Examen of the Meditation, page 4.

TENTH CONTEMPLATION.

THE ANNUNCIATION OF THE BLESSED VIRGIN.

Preparatory Prayer, page 1.

1st Prelude. "The Angel Gabriel was sent from God into a city of Galilee, called Nazareth, to a Virgin named Mary. . . . And the Angel being come in said unto her: Hail, full of grace, the Lord is with thee. . . . Behold thou shalt conceive in the womb and shalt bring forth a Son. He shall be great and shall be called the Son of the most High, and the Lord God shall give unto Him the throne of David, His father; He shall reign over the house of Jacob for ever, and of His kingdom there shall be no end" (Luke i. 26-33).

2nd Prelude. Represent to yourself the poor and humble dwelling of Mary.

3rd Prelude. O Mary! Virgin most pure, perfect model of all virtues, obtain for me the grace to imitate thee as closely as my weakness will permit.

1st Point. The Angel Gabriel is sent to Mary. He salutes her; she is troubled at his visit.

Consider the persons, their words, and their actions. A profound silence reigns in the dwelling of Mary; the immaculate Virgin is prostrate before God, and absorbed in holy recollection. She prays, she hastens in desire the moment of the Incarnation of the Word, and of the salvation of mankind. Suddenly she is surrounded by a heavenly light; an Angel appears before her. He salutes her: " Hail, full of grace, the Lord is with thee". He says to her: " Blessed art thou amongst women". Mary is troubled; the prudent Virgin thinks within herself, whence comes the flattering salutation which alarms her humility? Oh! how pure must that heart be in which the words even of an Angel excite a chaste fear! How worthy is it to become the sanctuary of the incarnate Word! Heart of Mary, give me some share in thy dispositions, since I am so often honoured by the visit of this thrice holy God, and nourished with His sacred Flesh.

2nd Point. The Angel announces to Mary that she is to be the Mother of God.

Listen to the words. " Fear not, Mary, for thou hast found grace with God. Behold thou shalt conceive in thy womb, and shalt bring forth a Son. He shall be great, and shall be called the Son of the most High, and the Lord God shall give unto Him the throne of David, His father. He shalt reign in the house of Jacob for ever. And of His kingdom there shall be no end." The moment so long called for by thy sighs and ardent prayers has at length arrived, O Mary; the Desired of all Nations is about to become incarnate, and He has chosen thee to be His Mother. He only awaits thy consent:—canst thou hesitate a single instant? No, Mary hesitates not, but her answer is a refusal, if in becoming the Mother of God she must cease to be a Virgin. " How shall this be done?" she asks, and she brings the objection of her vow of virginity. O Mary! how greatly does the delicacy of thy virtue endear thee to Him, Whose delight is to be among the lilies! Virgin most holy, who will give to me to imitate, as closely as my weakness will enable me, this ravishing virtue of which thou art the most perfect model?

3rd Point. Mary gives her consent, and the mystery of the Incarnation is accomplished within her.

Consider the same persons, their words and actions. The Angel makes known to Mary, how by a special privilege and miracle without example, our Lord wills to render her virginity fruitful. " The Holy Ghost shall come upon thee, and the power of the most High shall overshadow thee. And therefore the Holy that shall be born of thee shall be called the Son of God." Reassured by these words, Mary answers: " Behold the handmaid of the Lord; be it done to me according to thy word" (Luke i. 35-38). At the same instant the mystery of the Incarnation is accomplished; the Son of God becomes incarnate in her virginal womb; she adores Him within her; her soul is filled with respect and admiration; she contemplates the Divine Majesty humbled, the God made man and annihilated, according to the expression of the Apostle Paul. Penetrated with astonishment and veneration, she humbles herself before Him, and produces the most sublime acts of praise, adoration, and thanksgiving. Holy and immaculate Virgin, deign to give me a share in the feelings which possessed thy soul at this moment, that I may also render to my Saviour a homage worthy of Him.

Colloquy with the Blessed Virgin. Let us venerate her as the Mother of God. Let us join in the adorations which she offers to the eternal Word become Man in her chaste womb. Let us beg of her to obtain for us, from this God Who emptied Himself out, perfect purity and profound humility.

Resolutions. To watch carefully over my heart in order to preserve its purity. To practise some acts of humility to-day, in honour of the annihilation of the Word.

Offering of the Resolutions, page 3.

Spiritual Bouquet. "The Word was made flesh." "Hail, Mary, full of grace."

Prayer. We fly to thy patronage, O holy Mother of God; despise not our petitions in our necessities, but deliver us from all dangers, O ever glorious and blessed Virgin.

Examen of the Meditation, page 4.

ELEVENTH CONTEMPLATION.

THE VISITATION OF THE BLESSED VIRGIN.

Preparatory Prayer, page 1.

1st Prelude. "Mary, rising up, went into the hill country with haste, into a city of Juda" (Luke i. 39).

2nd Prelude. Represent to yourself the rugged and mountainous roads which Mary traversed in order to reach the house of her cousin: then the house itself of Elizabeth.

3rd Prelude. Obtain for me, O Mary, the grace to imitate the virtues of which thou dost give me the example in the mystery on which I am about to meditate.

1st Point. Mary sets out on her journey, and hastens to her cousin.

Consider the persons and the actions. Mary, impelled by the Spirit of God, sets out on her journey to visit Elizabeth. Let us watch her on her way. What perfect modesty! What profound recollection! She bears Jesus within her, and her soul is closely united to our Divine Saviour. She walks with a firm step, notwithstanding the difficulty of the road. Charity and zeal support her courage; no objects which she meets on her way are capable of attracting her notice, much less of fixing her attention; she is occupied with Jesus alone.

2nd Point. Mary enters the house of her cousin; John the Baptist is sanctified, and Elizabeth is filled with the Holy Ghost.

Consider anew the persons. Mary, full of grace and sweetness; Elizabeth, who advances towards her full of respect.

Consider the actions. Mary anticipates her relative and is the first to salute her. John the Baptist, purified from the stain of original sin by the presence of Jesus and Mary, exults with joy in his mother's womb. Elizabeth herself is filled with the Holy Ghost. O Jesus! O Mary! what blessings and graces you diffuse in every place which you honour with your presence. Oh! when will my soul become pure enough to be your habitual dwelling?

Listen to the words—" Blessed art thou amongst women," Elizabeth exclaims, " and blessed is the fruit of thy womb. And whence is this to me, that the Mother of my Lord should come to me? For, behold, as soon as the voice of thy salutation sounded in my ears, the infant in my womb did leap for joy. And blessed art thou that hast believed, because those things shall be accomplished that were spoken to thee by the Lord " (Luke i. 42-45). What reply will Mary make to such congratulations? Gratitude inspires her; she proclaims in her sublime canticle the mercies of the Lord: "My soul," she exclaims, "doth magnify the Lord, and my spirit hath rejoiced in God, my Saviour, because He hath regarded the humility of His handmaid". Then, humbly losing sight of herself in the thought of her own greatness, and not being able to find any expressions with which to exalt worthily the marvellous favours of which she is the object, she adds: "He that is mighty hath done great things to me, and holy is His name. His mercy is from generation to generation, to them that fear Him" (Luke i. 49-50). These praises of Mary ascend to Heaven as pure and sweet-smelling incense, because her heart is humble, grateful, and entirely loving. O my God! when shall my heart be in similar dispositions in Thy sight?

Colloquy with the Blessed Virgin. Let us congratulate her on the great things the Almighty has wrought within her; and above all, on her profound humility, which renders her ever more and more worthy of the favours of her God. Let us ask her to penetrate our soul with humble gratitude for the favours the Sacred Heart of our Lord has conferred upon us, and beg of her to obtain for us the grace to procure His glory and the salvation of souls in the intercourse He means us to have with others.

Resolutions. Often to call to my mind the benefits of God, and to return Him thanks for them. To keep myself closely united to Jesus, so that I may become an instrument for communicating His love and goodness to others.

Offering of the Resolutions, page 3.

Spiritual Bouquet. "He that is mighty hath done great things to me."

Prayer. Remember, O most holy Virgin Mary, etc.

Examen of the Meditation, page 4.

TWELFTH CONTEMPLATION.

THE SAME SUBJECT.

"Mary, rising up, went with haste into the hill country" (Luke i. 39).

Preparatory Prayer, page 1.

1st Prelude. Again, image to yourself the mountainous and rugged rocks which Mary traverses.

2nd Prelude. O Mary! whose heart was like unto that of thy Divine Son, obtain for me the grace to imitate Him after thy example.

1st Point. The zeal and generosity of the Sacred Hearts of Jesus and Mary in the mystery of the Visitation.

If Jesus, my Saviour, is the Model of the Predestined, and if, in order to please His Heavenly Father, I ought to study continually His Sacred Heart, seeking therein in all the mysteries and in all the actions of His life the motives from which He acts; the Heart of His most holy Mother also offers me an example I ought to imitate, if I wish to deserve eternal recompense. In fact, the Heart of Mary was so conformed to that of Jesus her Divine Son—it was always so intimately united to His—that I cannot, so to speak, separate these two hearts when I pay them my homage and strive to imitate them. What then do they teach me in this day's mystery? They present themselves to me abounding with generosity, zeal, humility, and meekness. The Sacred Heart of Jesus has scarcely come into existence when It burns to shed abroad the profusion of graces of which It is the Source. Jesus inspires His holy Mother to pay a visit to Zachary; and Mary who shares the zeal of her Son, Mary who knows the treasure she possesses within her, and who is conscious of the blessings of which she may become the instrument, hastens on her journey. Nothing can cool her ardour, neither the length or difficulties of the roads, nor the weakness of her sex, nor the delicacy of her frame; she sees nothing but the good of those souls that the Sacred Heart of her Son desires to procure through her means, and this consideration renders her insensible to everything else. Such ought to be my eagerness, my generosity, and my courage, when there is question of entering into the views of Jesus, and seconding His designs.

2nd Point. The humility of the Sacred Hearts of Jesus and Mary, in the Mystery of the Visitation.

The humility of the Sacred Hearts of Jesus and Mary, together with their incomparable meekness, is also manifested in this mystery in a manner well calculated to inflame my love for these two precious virtues. Jesus wills to sanctify His Precursor by His presence; but the state of abasement, as an infant, to which His love has reduced Him, places it out of His power, so to speak, to do this alone. Mary is required to carry Him to the house He wishes to bless. What humility in a God! Mary, faithful and attentive to these lessons of humiliation, forgets her own sublime dignity; she anticipates her relative's welcome, salutes her the first, tells her that she has come to congratulate her, and to serve her; as if the first congratulations were not due to her who, by all generations, shall be called Blessed; as if she whom all the Angels honour and serve as their Queen, owed her services to any creature whatsoever. Mary keeps an inviolable secret regarding the mysteries worked in her, but the Holy Ghost has published abroad her humility. Elizabeth salutes her as the Mother of God; then Mary, penetrated with gratitude, intones her beautiful canticle, and gives back to God all the glory of His gifts.

Colloquy with Jesus and Mary. Let us ask them to trace within us all their sentiments, all their dispositions, and all their virtues, and to make us worthy instruments of imparting their love to others.

Resolutions. To practise, on all occasions, humility and meekness towards others.
Offering of the Resolutions, page 3.
Spiritual Bouquet. "My soul doth magnify the Lord."
Prayer. Ave Maria, etc.
Examen of the Meditation, page 4.

THIRTEENTH MEDITATION.

THE SAME SUBJECT.

"And Elizabeth was filled with the Holy Ghost. And she cried out with a loud voice and said: Blessed art thou among women. And whence is this to me that the Mother of my Lord should come to me? For, behold, as soon as the voice of thy salutation sounded in my ears, the infant in my womb leaped for joy" (Luke i. 41-44).

Preparatory Prayer, page 1.
1st Prelude. To represent to yourself the house of Zachary; it is equally removed from worldly luxury and from sordid poverty.
2nd Prelude. O Mary! thou who hast been made the depository of all graces by thy Divine Son, obtain for me a tender confidence in thee, and a true zeal to propagate thy devotion.
1st Point. Mary is in our regard the Dispensary of the graces of her Divine Son.

Jesus, in choosing for Himself a Mother from among men, has formed the design of making her the channel of His graces and benefits in their regard. It was in order to make us comprehend this consoling truth that, a little later on, at the marriage of Cana, He will grant to her prayers the first of all His miracles in the order of nature; and it is to make us feel this still more sensibly that He again, to-day, works, through her means, His first wonders in the order of grace. Oh! how great is the power of Mary with Jesus! What graces are not bestowed on those who address themselves to this most blessed Mother! The eloquence of the Doctors of the Church never runs dry on this subject. St. Bernard calls Mary an Omnipotence of Supplication. St. Anselm fears not to advance that heavenly favours are sometimes obtained more easily by asking for them through Mary, than by addressing Jesus directly: and he assigns for this view these two reasons, so truly worthy of the tender and loving Heart of our Divine Master. Jesus loves His holy Mother; it is His desire that Christians shall honour her by every kind of testimony of respect, confidence, gratitude, and love; and it is in order to excite them strongly thereto that, on certain occasions, He grants more easily what is asked of Him through Mary than what is asked immediately of Himself. Moreover, this adorable Son knows that the heart of His well-beloved Mother, so conformable to His own, has, like Himself, an ardent love for all men, and finds its sweetest pleasure in showering blessings upon them. He places, therefore, in her hands the graces He designs for us, in order to double His own pleasure, if we may so speak, by sharing it with the heart of His holy Mother. Oh! how just, then, is the title these two hearts have to all the affections of my own!

2nd Point. What are the obligations which the power and goodness of Mary impose upon me?

Since it is through Mary we go to Jesus, according to St. Bernard; since other holy doctors have applied to her the words of Wisdom: *He that hath found me shall find life* (admirable words which teach me that the love of Mary leads infallibly to the love of Him Who came to give life to the world), I ought then to open wide my heart to receive this so pure, so sweet, so saving a love. But it is not sufficient for me to love Mary; the numberless benefits procured for me by this most blessed Mother impose on me a sacred debt of gratitude and zeal. I ought to endeavour to excite others to love her; I ought to spread her devotion, and sweetly to lead those souls over whom I have any influence to look on Mary as their Mother, to have recourse to her in all their wants; to merit her maternal protection by the homage of a pure and tender confidence. Oh! how much good may I not do in this way! How many graces may I not draw down on myself, and on those who are so dear to me!

Colloquy with the most holy Heart of Mary. Let us offer her all the homage of love, respect, and gratitude which we owe to her on so many titles. Let us beg of her to penetrate us with tender confidence towards her, and ardent zeal for her glory, in order that, in accordance with the designs of God, we may labour to propagate her worship, and so more surely gain souls to the Sacred Heart of Jesus.

Resolutions. To have recourse to Jesus through Mary. To induce others to confide in this most blessed Mother.

Offering of the Resolutions, page 3.

Spiritual Bouquet. "The Mother of God is my Mother."

Prayer. We fly to thy patronage, etc.

Examen of the Meditation, page 4.

FOURTEENTH MEDITATION.

The Divine Maternity of Mary.

Preparatory Prayer, page 1.

1st Prelude. Represent to yourself the stable of Bethlehem. Behold Jesus laid there in the manger, Mary and Joseph close to Him, the Angels and the Shepherds adoring Him.

2nd Prelude. Most holy and powerful Mother of God, obtain for me the grace to honour thy greatness worthily, and to merit thy protection.

1st Point. Mary is both a Virgin and a Mother.

Mary, in becoming the Mother of God, did not cease to be the purest of Virgins. From my earliest childhood I have believed in this, her glorious privilege; but it is so dear to her, that I am certain of pleasing her by meditating on it anew. Yes, Mary was always a Virgin, before, during, and after her Divine Maternity. This precious prerogative shone forth in her with the purest splendour. The Church, in the Litany, which, in honour of Mary, she daily puts into the mouth of her children, has taken pains to fix our thoughts in a special manner on this title of Mother ever Virgin. "Holy Mary," she says, "Holy Mother of God, pray for us." And then, as if she feared that this title of Mother of God should cause us to forget for an instant that she who bears it is the Virgin by excellence, she hastens to add: "Holy Virgin of Virgins, pray for us". Afterwards, unfolding, with that dignity which belongs to her, the admirable union of the Maternity and Virginity of Mary, she continues: "Mother of Christ, Mother of Divine Grace, Mother most Pure, Mother most Chaste, Mother Undefiled, pray for us". In effect, any single title would not have sufficed to explain the incomparable purity of Mary, a purity which in some sort elevates her virginal flesh to the rank of the pure spirits, and renders it worthy of giving birth even to the Son of God. How lovely this purity should appear to me! How eager I ought to be to imitate it as nearly as possible, with the grace of God!

2nd Point. The Divine Maternity is for Mary the highest point of elevation.

"O Mother of Christ, Mother of Divine Grace, pray for us," the Church says. How glorious are these titles! Jesus Christ, the Son of God, is eternal and all-powerful, like unto His Father. He is the Holy of

Holies, before Whom the purest Spirits prostrate with respect, and cover their faces with their wings. God, the Father, begets His Word from all eternity; Mary conceives Him, and brings Him forth in time; and, as in Jesus Christ the Godhead and the human nature assumed make but one and the same Person, this holy Virgin is truly the Mother of her Creator. What a dignity! "Holy Virgin," exclaims St. Bernard, "I know not in what words of praise to exalt the wonders wrought in thee, for He Whom the heavens cannot contain is enclosed within thy womb." But why has our great God willed to receive from Mary a body like ours, and subject to death? Because He came to merit for us, and to bring down from Heaven that grace which we had lost by sin. Jesus is the Author of Grace, and Mary is His Mother. "Mother of Divine Grace." It is through her He comes to us, and it is also through her that He loves to communicate to us the treasures of which He is the Source. What sweet and loving confidence ought to penetrate my heart when I invoke Mary under the precious titles of Mother of Christ and Mother of Divine Grace!

Colloquy with the Blessed Virgin. Let us offer her our homage of veneration, love, and confidence. Let us beg of her to increase within us a love for holy purity, and to obtain for us, from her Divine Son, all the graces we need to work out our sanctification.

Resolutions. To watch over myself carefully, in order to preserve purity of heart. To go to Jesus through Mary in all my trials and necessities.

Offering of the Resolutions, page 3.

Spiritual Bouquet. "Mother of Divine Grace, pray for me."

Prayer. Hail Mary, etc.

Examen of the Meditation, page 4.

FIFTEENTH MEDITATION.

PURIFICATION OF THE BLESSED VIRGIN.

" And after the days of her purification, according to the law of Moses, were accomplished, they carried Him to Jerusalem to present Him to the Lord " (Luke ii. 22).

Preparatory Prayer, page 1.

1st Prelude. Figure to yourself the Temple of Jerusalem, and behold therein Mary, Joseph, and the Child Jesus, Who is being presented to God Almighty.

2nd Prelude. Holy Virgin, obtain for me the grace to imitate the obedience, humility, and generosity of which thou dost give me such a touching example in the mystery on which I am about to meditate.

1st Point. The obedience and humility of Mary in the mystery of the Purification.

The Heart of Mary completely unveils itself in this day's mystery. Her love of obedience, her astonishing humility, manifest themselves in it in the most admirable and touching manner. The law of purification could not concern Mary : the Child she has given to the world was the fruit of her virginity, the Saint of Saints ; and by the terms of the law she was exempt from the obligation common to other mothers. But this holy Virgin cherished obedience too much to make use of her rights on such an occasion. Accordingly she went to the Temple, and accomplished to the letter all that the law of Moses prescribed. Her humility does not shine forth with less lustre than her obedience in such conduct. She is a Virgin, and this quality is so dear to her that she would have preferred it to the Divine Maternity, if that signal honour had interfered with it ; yet she is content to lose its glory in the eyes of the world, by bringing herself down to the level of ordinary women in the ceremony of purification.

Descended from the royal race of David, she veils and conceals her lofty rank under the externals of poverty; it is the offering of the poor only that she makes at the Altar to redeem her Divine Son; all in her is hidden and obscured; the beauty of the King's daughter is entirely within. Oh! how Jesus would delight in my heart if He found in it dispositions like unto those of Mary's heart. How pleasing would my homage be to Him if I were confirmed in these interior virtues, which, avoiding the eyes of the world, desire Him alone as witness, because His love alone is their beginning and their end! Heart of Mary, Heart of my Mother, form thy image within my heart, that so thy Divine Son may find me not quite unworthy of the special favours which He never ceases to heap upon me.

2nd Point. The generosity of Mary in the mystery of the Presentation in the Temple.

It would have been too little for Mary to submit to a humiliating law which lowered her in the eyes of men. Humility and obedience constituted the greatest delights of this holy Virgin: it was for her the sweetest of joys to humble herself thus. But her virginal Heart made a sacrifice on this day of which God alone could know all the bitterness. Mary offered her Divine Son to the Eternal Father. She was acquainted with the prophecies; she is not ignorant that she was devoting Him as a Victim to torments and to death; and, as if all that she had read in Isaias and David had not sufficiently enlightened her on this mystery of sorrow, Simeon adds to it a new prediction: "*A sword shall pierce thy soul,*" he says to this tender Mother, for "*this Child shall serve for a sign that shall be contradicted*". What bitterness must have penetrated the Heart of Mary at that moment! She redeemed her Divine Son, she received Him back from the hands of the High Priest; but the dreadful sacrifice had been accepted. It was to be offered up in due time, and all its horrors found place already in her maternal Heart.

Yet, far from refusing so much suffering, Mary adored the designs of the divine justice, and submitted herself to it in a spirit of generosity and love. Is it with similar dispositions that I accept the bitter chalice of suffering when it is presented to me? Is my heart, like that of my most holy Mother, always peaceful, submissive, full of resignation and love in the trials which I endure, and in those which I foresee? Heart of Jesus, Heart of Mary, fortify my heart, render it generous and pure, receive the offering I make of it, and accomplish in it all the designs of your love.

Colloquy with the Sacred Hearts of Jesus and Mary. Let us offer to them all the homage of respect, love, and gratitude which this day's mystery is so calculated to inspire us with. Let us ask of them the spirit of obedience, generosity, humility, and of all those virtues they wish to see within us.

Resolutions. To act for God alone. To sacrifice generously to Him the inclinations and repugnances which might oppose the accomplishment of His Divine Will.

Offering of the Resolutions, page 3.

Spiritual Bouquet. "Behold me ready to do Thy will, O my God."

Prayer. Receive, O Lord, etc., page 18.

Examen of the Meditation, page 4.

SIXTEENTH MEDITATION.

The same Subject.

"And Simeon said to Mary, His Mother, Behold, this Child is set for the fall and for the resurrection of many in Israel, and for a sign which shall be contradicted; and thy own soul a sword shall pierce" (Luke ii. 34, 35).

Preparatory Prayer, page 1.

1st Prelude. Represent to yourself anew the Temple of Jerusalem; behold Mary and Joseph, the Infant Jesus, and the holy and aged Simeon.

2nd Prelude. Heart of Mary, model of the most perfect generosity, obtain for me the grace to imitate thee.

1st Point. The generosity of Mary in the sacrifices she makes to God Almighty.

The feast of the Purification is essentially the feast of the generosity of Mary. In all the other mysteries of her life she receives, but in this she gives. She makes a sacrifice of the glory of her virginity, consenting to pass for an ordinary mother in the eyes of men. But that which costs her much more is the sacrifice which she makes of her Son to God, submitting to the divine decrees which condemn this Divine Son to die for the salvation of the world;—decrees whose severity she foreknew, together with their smallest details. This spirit of generosity with which Mary was filled, ought also to be mine. The sacrifices which my God demands of me will never equal those imposed on her. She must sacrifice Jesus, must consent to see him expire in the midst of torments; I, on the other hand, am sure of becoming united to this Divine Saviour, of glorifying Him, and of pleasing His Sacred Heart, in proportion to the courage I shall have in sacrificing my disorderly attachments and bad inclinations. How then can I refuse to go to the Temple, treading in the footsteps of Mary, there to unite my offering to hers?

2nd Point. The generosity of Mary in her submission to the decrees of Providence, as made manifest to her.

The holy old man Simeon, having taken the Child Jesus in his arms, says to Mary: "Behold, this Child is set for the fall and for the resurrection of many in Israel, and for a sign that shall be contradicted; and thy own soul a sword shall pierce" (Luke ii. 34, 35). These prophecies were nothing new to Mary. She was already aware of the torments and combats which awaited her Divine Son; but at this moment, when she offered Him to the Divine Justice, these words brought most vividly before her mind the prolonged succession of sufferings which she would have to undergo. Thus, this circumstance of her life is placed among the number of her Seven Dolours. When God, in some measure, raises a corner of the veil which conceals the future from me, and causes me to foresee trials which seem to me inevitable, my heart trembles with fear, and I would gladly escape from them. It is at such times I should have recourse to my most holy Mother, and pray to her to make my heart like unto hers. The heart of Mary, given over to the most afflicting trials, was always lovingly submissive to the Divine Will; her generosity was, moreover, full and entire. What a model for me! Undoubtedly, I can never copy it perfectly, but I ought, at least, to use my best endeavours to imitate it as closely as I possibly can.

Colloquy with the Blessed Virgin. Let us thank her for the painful sacrifices which she imposed on herself to procure our salvation. Let us pray to her to make us like unto her, by inspiring us with an ardent love for God and with great generosity in His service.

Resolutions. To refuse nothing to the interior inspirations of grace. Frequently to offer myself to God to do, in all things, His most Holy Will.

Spiritual Bouquet. " Behold me ready to do Thy will, O my God."

Prayer. Receive, O Lord, etc., page 18.

Examen of the Meditation, page 4.

SEVENTEENTH MEDITATION.

The Seven Dolours of the Blessed Virgin.

" Daughter of Jerusalem, thy grief shall be great as the sea."

Preparatory Prayer, page 1.

1st Prelude. Represent to yourself Mary in the Temple, where she listens to the prophecy of Simeon; or on the road to Egypt, whither she has to flee with her Divine Son; or at Jerusalem, where she seeks Him for three days; or on the road to Calvary; or at the foot of the Cross; or when the mangled Body of Jesus is placed in her arms; or, lastly, when she had to separate herself from Him and see Him shut up in the Sepulchre.

2nd Prelude. O Mother of love and sorrow! love has given thee the Cross, grant that the Cross may give me love.

1st Point. The extent and duration of the sufferings of Mary.

The Church offers Mary to our veneration and homage to-day, under the title of Our Lady of the Seven Dolours. This title recalls to my mind all the suffering of my sacred Mother:—sufferings which commenced at the moment when she consented to become the Mother of God, and lasted to the end of her life. Among the sorrowful mysteries in which Mary was chiefly concerned, seven special circumstances have been chosen and named the *Seven Dolours*. The number seven is, in the language of Scripture, a complete number; it specifies a whole to which nothing can be added; and it is particularly in this sense that Mary is called Our Lady of the Seven Dolours, which signifies Our Lady *of all Dolours*. In real truth, scarcely had she pronounced that *fiat* which made our Redemption sure than her sufferings commenced. The

Passion of Jesus Christ, which she knew beforehand through the Prophecies, was ever present to her mind. In lavishing her care on her adorable Infant, in nourishing Him with her milk, in receiving His tender and innocent caresses, she thought of the torments which were in store for Him; and the sword of sorrow, announced by the holy Simeon, seemed to pierce deeper and deeper into her heart. At length the fatal moment arrives; Jesus ascends Mount Calvary; Mary follows in the traces of His Blood, she is a witness of His torments, and sees Him expire in her immediate presence. Will the sufferings of her maternal heart finish with those of her Divine Son? No; long after His Ascension she must remain on the earth and be a witness also of the first persecutions and the first heresies that desolated the Church of God. Thus her entire life was but one tissue of sorrows, and replete with bitterness. O my Mother! the homage which you expect from me to-day is that of compassion, love, and imitation. Obtain for me the grace to render it unto you with all my heart.

2nd Point. The designs of God in the Dolours of Mary.

Why had Mary to drain the chalice of bitterness throughout the course of her whole life? Exempt from sin, distinguished among all creatures by privileges to which no other before or after her has ever pretended, or could ever pretend, ought she to be mixed up with the guilty children of Adam, and be fed like them with the bread of sorrow? The most important instructions are contained in this conduct of Almighty God in her regard. Ever since the Son of God willed to become a Man of Sorrows, suffering has become the royal road to glory, and the most precious treasure of souls inebriated with divine love. No one was ever to be so holy as Mary, so elevated in grace and in glory, so conformed to the likeness of Jesus Christ, the Head and Model of all the Elect. No one, consequently, was to have so large a share as herself in the sufferings and in the sacrifices of the Man-God. Jesus distributes the Cross according to the special designs of sanctification which He has concerning His elect; those He loves the most receive the most painful trials from His hand. When my Divine Lord gives me a share in His chalice, I ought as a consequence to accept it with love and thanksgiving as a pledge of His love, and as a powerful means of uniting myself to His Sacred Heart.

Colloquy with Mary the desolate one. Let us beg of her to teach us to love Jesus, to compassionate His sufferings, to esteem the Cross, and to carry it lovingly whenever He shall please to lay it on our shoulders.

Resolutions. To unite all that I shall have to suffer to-day to the Cross of Jesus and to the sufferings of Mary.

Offering of the Resolutions, page 3.

Spiritual Bouquet. O Mary! love has given thee the Cross, pray that the Cross may give me love.

Prayer. O Mary, the most desolate of all Mothers! what a terrible sword has pierced thy soul! Every blow inflicted on Jesus has fallen on thee, all His sorrows have crushed thee, all His wounds have torn thee; but above all the last farewell which He addressed to thee reopened all thy wounds, and when thou didst see Him yield His last breath, what supernatural strength did it not require to sustain thy soul! O Mother of love and of sorrow! teach me how to love and to suffer after thy example. Queen of Martyrs, give me a share in thy martyrdom. Love has given thee the Cross, pray that the Cross may give me love; and if in order to love we must suffer and die, obtain for me the grace to love all that comes to me from the Heart of God, even sufferings and death. Amen.

Examen of the Meditation, page 4.

EIGHTEENTH MEDITATION.

COMPASSION OF THE BLESSED VIRGIN.

"There stood beneath the Cross of Jesus Mary His Mother."

Preparatory Prayer, page 1.

1st Prelude. Image to yourself Mount Calvary, Jesus crucified, and Mary standing at the foot of the Cross with St. John and the holy women.

2nd Prelude. O Mary, Queen of Martyrs! make my heart sensible to the deep affliction of thy heart; may I renounce sin for ever, which was the sole cause of thy sorrows.

1st Point. Mary at the foot of the Cross experiences within her heart all the sufferings of her Divine Son.

Never can I form a correct idea of the bitter grief which filled the heart of Mary on Mount Calvary. Mary, the most tender of all Mothers, sees her Divine Son and her God fastened to the Cross; she stands beneath that Cross; the Sacred Blood of Jesus flows in her very sight; she witnesses all the torments He endures, not a single one of His sufferings can escape her attention. Alas! what a torture for her Immaculate Heart, whose sensibility is so acute, and whose love is so pure and ardent, to behold her Divine Son, the object of all her affections, covered with wounds, pierced with nails, torn with cruel thorns, and having for His bed of agony nothing but the wood of the Cross! It is at this awful time that the sword predicted by the holy old man, Simeon, is plunged into her heart, and pierces it through and through: then it is, according to the expression of the Prophets, that her grief is vast and deep as the sea. Shall I behold unmoved the inconceivable affliction of my ever blessed Mother? It is I who have been the cause of it: it is to expiate my sins that Jesus suffers and dies, and that

Mary shares all the rigour of His sacrifice. Awful sin! how could I ever give thee entrance into my soul? Shall I not now detest thee with all my heart, and do my very utmost to expiate thee?

2nd Point. Mary, at the foot of the Cross, consents to the sacrifice of her Divine Son, offers Him to His Heavenly Father, and receives us for her children.

Three circumstances add still further to the sufferings of the Heart of Mary. As the new Eve, she must participate in our Redemption, because our first Mother helped to bring about our fall, and because, before the Sacrifice of Jesus, God exacted the express consent of Mary. Yet more; Jesus is about to offer Himself both as Priest and Victim; He wills that this offering should pass through the heart of Mary; He wills that this afflicted Mother, standing at the foot of the Altar of His holocaust, should give her consent to all His sorrows, and offer Him willingly to the justice of His Father. Is even this sufficient suffering for her maternal heart? No, a crowning trial is yet required of her. Mary has adored the Divine Justice which exacted the immolation of Jesus; she has submitted to it, and consented to the sacrifice of her Divine Son, forgiving His torturers and murderers from her heart; but even at this moment, when the excess and acuteness of her grief seem to leave her scarcely the strength to forgive them, it is demanded of her to love them so greatly as to become their Mother, and to receive them in her heart in place of her only Son, Who is being snatched from her by their sins. O Mary! how truly art thou styled the Queen of Martyrs, the Mother of love and sorrow! How many tears my sins have caused thee! How truly generous thou hast been to me! What love and gratitude do I not owe thee!

Colloquy with the afflicted Heart of Mary. Let us render her our homage of veneration, gratitude, and love. Let us beg of her to make us truly sensible to the sorrows of Jesus and her sorrows, so that, being penetrated with grief at the remembrance of our sins, we may expiate them by sincere repentance.

Resolutions. Often to recall to mind the sufferings of Jesus and Mary, in order to excite ourselves to compunction.

Offering of the Resolutions, page 3.

Spiritual Bouquet. Heart of Mary transfixed with a sword of sorrow, enkindle within my heart, by thy intercession, the divine fire which consumes thy heart.

Prayer. O Mary, the most desolate, etc., page 45.

Examen of the Meditation, page 4.

NINETEENTH MEDITATION.

THE SAME SUBJECT—APPLICATION OF THE SENSES.

Preparatory Prayer, page 1.

1st Prelude. " There stood beneath the Cross of Jesus His Mother, with Mary of Cleophas and Mary Magdalen."

2nd Prelude. Represent to yourself anew the summit of Mount Calvary; Jesus crucified, and Mary at the foot of the Cross, with St. John and the holy women.

3rd Prelude. O Mary, Queen of Martyrs! make my heart truly alive to the deep grief of thine, and obtain for me to renounce sin for ever, for sin was the sole cause of thy dolours.

1st Point—Sight. Let us fix our eyes at times on Jesus fastened to the Cross, at times on Mary plunged in the most profound sorrow. The torments of Jesus are incomprehensible. He is suspended by the wounds in His feet and hands. His whole sacred body, now hanging on the Cross, has been most cruelly torn by His scourging; the long sharp thorns are buried in

His head; He cannot rest it without redoubling His sufferings. What dreadful tortures! And all these pains and sorrows are being renewed within the Heart of Mary. The afflicted Mother has her eyes fixed upon her beloved Son; not one movement of His escapes her notice. Oh! how her every look and feature reveal the bitter grief of her soul! But at the same time, how everything in her exterior manifests peace, resignation, and generosity!

2nd Point—Hearing. Let us listen, as far as we can, to the interior language of the afflicted Heart of Mary. It is to me it addresses itself. Reflect and see, it says to me, if there be a sorrow like unto my sorrow. Listen also to the words of Jesus Christ; they reveal His interior sufferings: "My God, My God, why hast Thou forsaken Me?" This touching complaint causes a fresh wound in the Heart of His desolate Mother. She also hears Him ask for something to drink, and she cannot even procure Him the most trifling relief. At length His last loud cry puts the finishing stroke to her grief, "All is consummated". O Mary! thy soul would at this moment have followed thy Divine Son, had not God miraculously sustained thy life to prolong thy martyrdom.

3rd Point—The Smell. The Spouse in the Sacred Canticles had said: "I will ascend to the mountain of myrrh and the altar of incense". Mary now carries out the mystic import of these words: she offers to God the incense of the Sacrifice of Jesus, alone worthy of the Supreme Majesty; but how bitter to her mouth is the taste of the myrrh! This incense, this myrrh, are the perfumes which are to draw me after Mary in the footsteps of Jesus crucified.

4th Point—The Taste. Mary opens her heart to me, and invites me to taste of the profound bitterness with which it is filled. Oh! how salutary is this bitterness! It purifies the heart, banishes from it all misplaced affection, disposes it to unite itself to that of

Jesus, to enrich itself with His merits, and to receive all the treasures of His grace and of His love.

5th Point—The Touch. How many objects offer themselves to my veneration! The Cross purpled with the blood of my Jesus; but above all, the adorable feet of my crucified Saviour, upon which, no doubt, Mary is pressing her virginal lips. She permits me also to apply my own.

Colloquy, Resolutions, Offering of Resolutions, Spiritual Bouquet, Prayer, Examen of the Meditation, all as in the preceding Meditation, page 48.

TWENTIETH MEDITATION.

The same Subject.

"O all you who pass by the way, attend and see if there be any sorrow like to my sorrow."

Preparatory Prayer, page 1.

1st Prelude. Again represent to yourself Mary standing at the foot of the Cross of Jesus.

2nd Prelude. Heart of Mary, the most tender, the most afflicted, and the most generous of all hearts, teach me to sanctify all my trials by uniting them, as thou didst, to the sufferings of my Divine Lord.

1st Point. The afflicted Heart of Mary is the consolation and support of those who suffer. If the Heart of Mary, so like unto that of Jesus her Divine Son, is penetrated with the most tender love for us, and if at all times we ought to have recourse to this most holy Mother with entire confidence, it is above all when we suffer that her love for us seems to assume a character more than ever sweet, and more than ever maternal. We have not, says St. Paul, a Mediator Who knows not how to compassionate our miseries, since, having become Man for us, He has Himself experienced them. These words may well be applied to Mary, in due proportion. Mary, whose soul was transpierced with sorrow on Calvary, knows what suffering is; and, above all, the suffering of the heart: she understands it well, and she soothes afflictions of every description when we address ourselves to her in order to obtain consolation, strength, and courage. O Mary! inspire me always with the thought of having recourse to thee in all my trials, and confiding them to thee; next to Jesus, thy Divine Son, be thou the dearest object of my confidence, and my sweetest consolation.

2nd Point. The afflicted Heart of Mary is the model of those who suffer.

What sublime and touching lessons the Mother of my Divine Saviour offers me when sorrowing at the foot of His Cross! She endures the most inconceivable of martyrdoms, but the calm submission of her soul cannot be troubled on this account. She lovingly accepts all her sufferings, and her heart, fastened to the Cross with the same nails which fasten her Divine Son to it, offers itself in union with Him as a victim for the glory of God and the salvation of mankind. The glorious titles of Disciple of Jesus Christ and Child of Mary, which I have the honour to bear, impose on me the obligation of copying within my heart the virtues of which this Mother of sorrows gave the example on Calvary. All the trials with which Divine Providence visits me have for their end to unite me to the Sacred Heart of my Divine Saviour, to procure His glory, and to draw down upon me His most precious favours. They are also sovereignly efficacious in bringing down the graces of salvation on souls which are very dear to me. I ought in consequence, after the example of Mary, to adore the divine decrees in the afflictions sent me, and, in accepting them, to join myself to Jesus crucified. O Mary!

obtain for me the grace to comprehend this great and important lesson, and to rule my conduct by it all the days of my life.

Colloquy with Mary suffering. Let us offer her our homage of veneration and love; let us beg of her to obtain for us the grace to unite our sufferings with those of the Sacred Heart of Jesus, and our trials to those of her own Immaculate Heart; practising faithfully resignation, patience, conformity to the Divine Will; suffering courageously for the glory of God, for the salvation of souls, and for our own sanctification.

Resolutions. To unite myself in all my sufferings with Jesus and Mary suffering.

Offering of the Resolutions, page 3.

Spiritual Bouquet. Heart of Mary, Consolation of the Afflicted, pray for me!

Prayer. O Mary! the most desolate, etc., page 45.

Examen of the Meditation, page 4.

TWENTY-FIRST MEDITATION.

The Apparition of Jesus Risen to His Holy Mother.

"According to the multitude of my sorrows, Thy consolations have given joy to my soul."

Preparatory Prayer, page 1.

1st Prelude. Retire in spirit into the solitary dwelling to which Mary withdrew after the burial of Jesus; behold your Divine Saviour risen again, and Mary transported with joy.

2nd Prelude. Heart of Mary, whose sorrows were abundantly recompensed by the joy thou didst experience on seeing Jesus risen again, obtain for me the grace to unite myself, as thou didst, to the Saviour of the World on Calvary, that so I may share one day in His happiness and glory.

1st Point. The sorrows of Mary on Calvary are abundantly recompensed by the joy which she experiences on seeing Jesus risen again.

The love of Mary for her Divine Son had been, on Calvary, the cause of her intense sorrow; now it is the mainspring of her joy. What happiness! What joy for Mary to see Jesus, the only object of her love, victorious over death and hell; to behold Him surrounded by Angels, who applaud His triumph; escorted by the souls of the just, whom He has just freed from Limbo; crowned with a glory which nothing can deprive Him of; established in a permanent state of beatitude, which renders Him incapable of suffering and of dying again! It is thus our Divine Master is pleased to indemnify her for the sufferings He has caused her. He had drunk all the bitterness of His chalice; He now inebriates her with the torrents of delights which He Himself enjoys. If I love this Divine Saviour—if I attach myself with Him to the Cross—I shall one day behold Him in the splendour of His glory, and His happiness will become my own.

2nd Point. The sorrows of Mary lasted only for a time; her joy will be eternal.

A reflection, well fitted to inspire me with a holy courage, ought naturally to present itself to my mind when I meditate on the immense joy experienced by Jesus and Mary on the day of our Blessed Lord's Resurrection. The sufferings of both had surpassed all that I could ever conceive, but they only lasted three and thirty years; and, as the author of the *Imitation of Christ* says: "All is little which passes with time". Jesus Christ has now taken possession of a new life—of a life as full of glory and happiness as the former had been of humiliation and sufferings. Mary already rejoices in His triumph; a few years more, and she will share it fully, and the pure delights in which her soul shall then be plunged will last throughout an endless eternity.

What is the longest life, were it passed entirely in the endurance of sorrows and trials, compared to the surpassing and everlasting happiness prepared in Heaven for the true friends of Jesus? The afflictions of this life are, for a Christian, the seed of future glory; our conformity in this world with Jesus suffering will be the measure of our union with Him in the next.

Colloquy with the Blessed Virgin. Let us congratulate her on the happiness which she experienced at the moment when Jesus risen appeared to her, and on that which she now enjoys in Heaven. Let us beg of her to obtain for us the grace to unite ourselves to Jesus suffering, by accepting for His love all the trials of this present life—a grace which will be a certain pledge of future happiness.

Resolutions. To unite all my sufferings to those of Jesus and Mary.

Offering of the Resolutions, page 3.

Spiritual Bouquet. "He that sows in tears shall reap in joy."

Prayer. Regina cœli lætare. Alleluia, etc., etc.

Examen of the Meditation, page 4.

TWENTY-SECOND MEDITATION.

THE INTERIOR OF THE BLESSED VIRGIN.

"The beauty of the King's daughter is within."

Preparatory Prayer, page 1.

1st Prelude. Represent to yourself the dwelling of St. John, where Mary passed in obscurity the remainder of her life after the Ascension of Jesus Christ.

2nd Prelude. Mother of fair love, obtain for me the grace to sanctify, as thou didst, all my actions, and every instant of my life, by the most perfect purity of intention and an ardent love for God.

1st Point. How useful Mary was in her solitude for the glory of God and the good of the Church.

Mary, after the Death and Ascension of Jesus Christ, had completed, it might be thought, the great task which our Lord had confided to her; and it only remained for her to go and receive in Heaven the reward of her heroic virtues, and of her long sufferings. But our Lord, Whose designs infinitely surpass our thoughts, judged differently. He willed that the Blessed Virgin, already so perfect, should continue to increase yet more in perfection, and should consume herself, night and day, with the ardours of the purest love. He willed to leave her as a support to the infant Church, and to teach us, through her example, how great is the power of a soul given to prayer, and the immense good which can be effected by its means in obscurity. In very truth, we had need of such a lesson, we who are so given to esteem nothing but what appears visible to the eye, and to regard only those as useful to the Almighty who are active and enterprising, or who, at least, employ themselves in functions of zeal. Mary, hidden in an obscure solitude, draws down the blessings of Heaven on the Gospel harvest, dispels the storms which would retard its progress; she is the adviser, the consoler, and the support of the Apostles and first Christians. Beyond all doubt, I can revere, admire, and imitate such an example at a distance only; but, at least, it should teach me that the love of obscurity, of humiliation, of an interior and recollected life, are the surest means for producing solid fruits for the glory of God, the salvation of souls, and my own sanctification.

2nd Point. The virtues that Mary practised in her solitude.

To know all the treasures and graces accumulated in the soul of our ever Blessed Mother, we should require an Angel to come and open for us this august sanctuary; or, rather, the perfections contained therein surpass the intelligence even of the blessed Spirits. God alone has ever known, and now knows, perfectly, all the riches hidden in Mary's virginal heart. Let us, however, endeavour to form to ourselves some slight idea of them, in order to animate us to love, honour, and imitate her. The heart of Mary, the sanctuary of the purest and most ardent love that has ever existed, multiplied unceasingly acts of that love. Her entire life, more strictly speaking, was but one continued act of love, which sleep itself was not able to interrupt; and this love was in her the mainspring of all her other virtues. Thus, all within her soul was purity, disinterestedness, zeal for the divine glory, tender charity for others, love of the Cross and of suffering, a perpetual spirit of sacrifice — in a word, conformity to, and perfect union with, the Sacred Heart of Jesus, her Divine Son. From these arose the modesty, meekness, sweetness, patience, and evenness of soul of which all her actions bore the impress. If I wish to imitate Mary, and desire that my life should be, after the example of hers, pleasing to our Lord and edifying to others, I ought, like her, to attach myself above all to the acquisition of these interior virtues, and especially of that pure charity which is the sole foundation of all true perfection.

Colloquy with the Blessed Virgin. Let us offer her our homage of veneration and love, begging her to retrace within our hearts, as perfectly as it shall be possible to do so, the virtues and perfections of hers, that so we may be useful in spreading the glory of the Sacred Heart of Jesus.

Resolutions. To exercise myself in the practice of interior recollection. To unite myself in all my actions to the Sacred Hearts of Jesus and Mary.

Offering of the Resolutions, page 3.
Spiritual Bouquet. " The beauty of the King's daughter is within."
Prayer. Remember, O most holy Virgin Mary, etc.
Examen of the Meditation, page 4.

TWENTY-THIRD MEDITATION.

The Assumption of the Blessed Virgin.

" Precious in the sight of God is the death of His Saints " (Ps. cxv. 15).

Preparatory Prayer, page 1.

1st Prelude. Image to yourself Mary at the moment in which, while giving back her beautiful soul to God, she seems to fall into a sweet sleep.

2nd Prelude. Holy Virgin, our refuge during life and our hope in the hour of death, obtain for me a happy death, which may put me in possession of eternal beatitude.

1st Point. The death of Mary was holy and peaceful.

All is calm and consoling in the happy departure of Mary, in that supreme hour in which the holiest persons tremble in the presence of Him Who judges justices, and before Whom the heavens themselves are not perfectly pure. She rejoices in a profound peace. What indeed could trouble the calm of her soul? Immaculate in her Conception, she has passed through life without contracting the slightest stain ; never have the gifts she has received remained sterile within her; she has accumulated merit upon merit. All her days have been full before the Lord. She has no judgment to undergo, nothing but recompense to expect ; no trouble can offer itself to her in this moment which is to be the last of her mortal career. This earth for her has long been a place of exile, an abode of captivity; Jesus, the only object of her love, has gone before her to the city of the Saints; she is going to join Him there, never more to be separated from Him. One day, like my most blessed Mother, I shall be on the point of appearing before my God; if I shall have imitated her example as far as my weakness has permitted; if my life has passed in innocence; if the virtues which the Sacred Heart of Jesus had a right to expect from me, have shone forth in my conduct; if the love of my adorable Lord has been the only love of my heart, death will lose all its horrors for me, and its approach will overwhelm me with joy. O Mary! prepare me thyself for so precious a death by guiding me to follow thy footsteps in the paths of fidelity and love.

2nd Point. The ardour of divine love was the sole cause of the death of Mary.

To die in the love of the Lord, that is, in the possession of sanctifying grace, is an end in every way most earnestly to be longed for; it is the death of all the just, and that which I may undoubtedly hope for myself, but which I should ask for every day with humble fear, since it is a pure gift of the divine bounty, and no one can merit it. To die through love—namely, to sacrifice life rather than forfeit the love of God—is an end still more precious; it is that of the martyrs; a precious death, which causes their souls to soar at once up to the bosom of God, and places their mortal remains on our altars. But to die of love is a death which infinitely surpasses the two first, and such was the death of Mary. The celestial ardours which consumed this holy Virgin caused her to experience an indescribable martyrdom; her heart could no longer bear up against their effects: at length, this divine fire consuming by a last effort the ties which still bound her to the earth, her beautiful soul gently separated itself from her body, and ascended to heaven like a pure flame or perfume of aromatic wood which has just been consumed by fire. Who could tell us all the ineffable delights which then flooded this perfect soul! No mortal tongue can describe such bliss, no mind can understand it; but a heart that loves Mary may form some slight idea of its sweetness, and rejoice in silence at the beatitude of this most holy Mother.

Colloquy with the Blessed Virgin. Let us congratulate her on her happy transit. Let us beg of her to obtain for us from the Sacred Heart of her Divine Son the grace of a holy life and of a happy death. Let us also ask the same favours for those dear to us.

Resolutions. To serve God with as much care and fidelity as if each one of my actions were to be the last of my life.

Offering of the Resolutions, page 3.

Spiritual Bouquet. "Precious in the sight of God is the death of His Saints."

Prayer. Ave Maria, etc.

Examen of the Meditation, page 4.

TWENTY-FOURTH MEDITATION—CONTEMPLATION.

The same Subject.

Preparatory Prayer, page 1.

1st Prelude. Recall to mind what tradition teaches us regarding the glorious Assumption of the Blessed Virgin. The sacred body of Mary, having been placed in a sepulchre, arose again on the third day, and the Angels coming to fetch their Queen carried her both in body and soul to Heaven.

2nd Prelude. Represent to yourself the tomb of Mary, and then the heavenly Jerusalem.

3rd Prelude. O Mary! obtain for me the grace of worthily celebrating thy triumph, and help me to surmount the difficulties in the practice of virtue by the thought of Heaven.

Consider the persons, the words, and the actions. The body of Mary reposes in the tomb. The Angels watch around it. Soon her holy soul comes forth to join itself again to the body; immediately the body is radiant with light; it is immortal and impassible, and possesses all the qualities of glorified bodies; yet her beauty, her brightness, and sweet majesty infinitely surpass those of all the Saints. Mary is borne in triumph up to Heaven. The choirs of the heavenly spirits who dwell before the throne of God are astonished and ravished at the splendour of her glory; seized with admiration, they exclaim: "Who is she that cometh up from the desert, flowing with delights, leaning on her beloved?" And truly her Divine Son is near her. He has gone forth to meet her, and He Himself presents her to His Heavenly Father. The august Trinity welcomes her with the highest praise; God the Father repeats once again the words in which He has already so often addressed her: "Thou art all fair, My beloved, and there is no spot in thee". The Holy Spirit says to her: "Come, My Spouse, come from Libanus, My beloved one; come and receive the crown destined for thy merits and thy virtues". God the Son seats her at His right hand, on a throne exalted above that of all the Saints. He deposits in her hands His treasures of grace; He wishes her to share His sovereign power. "Command, O My Mother," He says, "and all thy wishes shall be accomplished in Heaven and on earth." And Mary, penetrated with gratitude and love, exclaims once more in the fulness of her joy: "My soul doth magnify the Lord . . . because He hath regarded the humility of His handmaid. . . . All generations shall call me blessed. . . . He that is mighty hath done great things to me . . . holy is His name. His mercy is from generation to generation; unto them that fear Him." How shall I contemplate the triumph of my most holy Mother without following her in spirit to that happy abode ; without my desires and my hopes being elevated towards those eternal dwellings into which my God wishes one day to welcome me ? Oh ! how contemptible should the earth appear to me, when borne aloft on the wings of faith, I fly in the glorious future reserved for the children of God ! Oh ! how easy and sweet all the sacrifices, the struggles, and combats with which this miserable life is filled should seem to me when I contemplate so magnificent a reward !

Colloquy with the Blessed Virgin. Let us rejoice with her in her triumph, and congratulate her with all our heart. Let us pray to her to obtain for us a lively faith, a firm hope, and an ardent love, that so serving God fervently, we may find favour with Him, and merit His eternal rewards.

Resolutions. Often to reflect on the triumph of my holy Mother, in order to arouse my hope, inflame my courage, and animate myself continually to the practice of all virtues.

Offering of the Resolutions, page 3.

Spiritual Bouquet. " How contemptible this earth appears to me when I contemplate Heaven " (St. Ign.).

Prayer. Sub Tuum, etc.

Examen of the Meditation, page 4.

TWENTY-FIFTH MEDITATION.

The same Subject.

" Come from Libanus ; come and be crowned."

Preparatory Prayer, page 1.

1st Prelude. Transport yourself in spirit into Heaven ; behold Mary therein, seated on a brilliant throne, and crowned with a diadem whose brightness rejoices all Paradise.

2nd Prelude. Glorious Queen of the Universe, Sovereign Mistress of Angels and of men, may I worthily honour thee this day, and draw down on myself thy powerful protection.

1st Point. Mary is crowned the Queen of Angels and Saints.

Mary, while on earth, among all creatures most resembled Jesus, her Divine Son; like Him she had suffered; like Him she had loved; her pure and perfect virtues had reached the highest degree of conformity to those of the Man-God attainable by any creature. Now, her adorable Son distinguishes her magnificently, rendering her like unto Himself in the happy Kingdom of which He has taken possession. Jesus Christ has been acknowledged King in the day of His power and might; all nations have been given to Him as His inheritance, and at His adorable Name every knee bends, in Heaven, on earth, and in hell. He wills that His much loved Mother should participate in His glory and His sovereignty; Mary is declared Queen of Heaven and of earth; exalted above all the Saints, she sees at her feet all that is less than God, and receives the homage of the highest Seraphim and most sublime Intelligences. What greatness! This was due to the humility of Mary. Jesus had emptied out Himself, becoming obedient, even unto death; and His humiliations, as St. Paul remarks, have been the cause of His Glory. It was meet then that she who had followed Him more closely than any one else on earth in the paths of humiliation, should receive in the Heavenly City the most brilliant crown and the most like unto His own.

2nd Point. Mary reigns only to exercise a supremacy of mercy and clemency.

Mary is declared Queen of Heaven; but her power, far from inspiring any sentiment of fear, should cause the sweetest confidence to arise within us. She is a Queen, and in this character she disposes of all the treasures of her Son as she pleases; but she is at the same time a Mother, and the vast power which she possesses is only, in her hands, a means of making us happy. "Hail, O Queen and Mother of Mercy!" the Church sings in the holy Office. The majesty of this amiable Queen has nothing in it to alarm our weakness; if she is "terrible as an army in battle array," according to the expression of the Scriptures, it is only towards her enemies, whom she scatters by one look alone, as soon as her name is invoked. A powerful Queen, she shields us with her protection, enriches us with her heavenly gifts, obtains for us an easy access to our Sovereign Lord, Whose anger our sins would often provoke, did not her intercession render Him favourable to us, and induce Him to grant us, at her prayers, graces of conversion. Who would not be touched with such maternal goodness? Who would not lovingly lie prostrate before the throne of this amiable Sovereign? Who would despair of salvation having for Queen the Mother of Divine Grace, and for Mother the Queen of Mercy and of Peace?

Colloquy with the Blessed Virgin. Let us offer her our homage of love and veneration. Let us place ourselves under her particular protection, and beg of her to cause us to experience the sweet effects of her power, by obtaining for us every virtue pleasing to the Sacred Heart of her Son.

Resolutions. To have recourse to Mary in my wants with the most entire confidence.

Offering of the Resolutions, page 3.

Spiritual Bouquet. "Hail, holy Queen, Mother of Mercy!"

Prayer. Salva Regina, etc.

Examen of the Meditation, page 4.

TWENTY-SIXTH MEDITATION.

Mary's Greatness.

"He that is mighty hath done great things to me."

Preparatory Prayer, page 1.

1st Prelude. Represent to yourself Mary in Heaven exalted above all the Saints, the throne of God alone being above hers.

2nd Prelude. Venerable Virgin, most powerful Mother of God, deign to penetrate me with the most profound respect for thee, together with the most tender love and entire confidence.

1st Point. The greatness of Mary had its source in the admirable privileges which she received from the Almighty.

The Divine Wisdom has taken pleasure, if we may so speak, in uniting in Mary all that could render her most worthy of our veneration and homage. Conceived without sin, and exempt all her life from the least imperfections and even from the slightest inclinations to evil, this most pure Virgin offers to us the most perfect image of the holiness of God Himself, of that sanctity which the Angels adore, and before which they cover their faces with their wings, so greatly are they penetrated with respect and admiration. But the title of Virgin Immaculate is not the only one which renders Mary venerable before men and even before the Angels; she is the Mother of God, which glorious quality elevates her to a dignity so sublime that God alone can justly appreciate the greatness thereof. Indeed, this is an exalted dignity! To have borne within her Him Whom even the Heavens cannot contain; to have given birth in time to Him Who was engendered from all eternity by the Father; to have beheld Him submissive to her orders Whom the Angels obey; and, again, to possess in Heaven so much power over the heart of her Divine Son, that He can refuse nothing to her prayers! To find a higher dignity, where could we go to look for it? We should have to go to God Himself. Yes, God alone is exalted above Mary; never has there been, never will there be on earth or in Heaven glory to be compared with that of the Blessed Virgin. What a subject of joy for a heart that loves her!

2nd Point. The greatness of Mary had its source also in the sublime virtues which she practised.

It is related, in the holy Gospel, that a woman, filled with admiration at the lessons of life which proceeded from the words of Jesus Christ, exclaimed in a holy transport: "Blessed is the womb that bare Thee and the breasts that gave Thee suck!" To which our Divine Lord replied: "Yea, rather, blessed are they who hear the word of God and keep it!" These words contain an important instruction. They teach me that if it was glorious for Mary to give birth to the Son of God, it was still more glorious for her to be docile to the divine word, or rather that it was her perfect fidelity that drew on her the looks of our Lord, and rendered her worthy of His choice. Yes (and I cannot ponder this truth too deeply), Mary was less blessed in having been the Mother of Jesus Christ than she was in having imitated all His divine virtues. It was a less advantage for her to have fed Him with her milk than to have nourished herself with His most sacred word: and the source of the supreme happiness and sublime exaltation, in which she now rejoices in Heaven, was not so much the authority which she exercised over Him in His infancy, as the care which she took to humble herself after His example, and to drink with Him every day of her life of the chalice of sufferings and humiliations. What practical fruits ought I not to gather for myself from these considerations? They teach me that I also must seek for glory in the path of humiliations and sacrifices, and that the glorious title of a disciple of

Jesus Christ ought to be the motive of my fidelity and fervour here below, if I desire that it should be the source of my glory and happiness in Heaven above.

Colloquy with the Blessed Virgin. Let us offer her the most profound homage of respect, veneration, love, and confidence. Let us congratulate her on the glorious privileges with which she has been favoured, but, above all, on the exalted virtues which she practised. Let us ask her to lead us in her footsteps to the love of Jesus, and to the imitation of His Sacred Heart.

Resolutions. To unite myself in all my actions to the Sacred Heart of Jesus and to the Immaculate Heart of Mary.

Offering of the Resolutions, page 3.

Spiritual Bouquet. " Blessed are they who hear the word of God and keep it." " He that humbleth himself shall be exalted."

Prayer. Remember, O most holy Virgin, etc.

Examen of the Meditation, page 4.

TWENTY-SEVENTH MEDITATION.

THE JOY OF MARY.

" According to the multitude of my sorrows, Thy consolations have given joy to my heart."

Preparatory Prayer, page 1.

1st Prelude. Let me transport myself to Heaven in spirit, there to behold Mary enraptured with delights, and let me penetrate, as far as it may be allowed, the depths of her heart, there to taste all the sweetness of her peace and happiness.

2nd Prelude. O Mary! Mother of fair love, obtain for me the grace to attach myself like you to Jesus suffering, that so I may one day share in the ineffable happiness with which He rejoices His elect in the City of the Saints.

1st Point. The joy and consolation of Mary during her life on this earth.

Mary is called the Mother of Sorrows, and justly so, since on Calvary she shared the torments of her Divine Son ; and again, because during her entire life the sufferings which awaited Him were present to her maternal heart. Yet all these most galling bitternesses more than once gave place to consolations, all the more pure for the reason that they had been preceded by the most cruel sufferings. For example, we cannot doubt that the heart of Mary, so full of zeal for the divine glory and the salvation of the world, should not experience a very great joy when the Angel revealed to her that her days were accomplished, and that the Desired of all Nations was about to appear on the earth. The love which she felt for Jesus must also have made her sensible to the adoration which was paid to Him lying in the manger, by the Angels, the Shepherds, and the Kings. When this God-Man commenced His evangelical career, and the splendour of His miracles drew numberless crowds to follow Him, doubtless Mary could not behold without a secret joy such numbers attaching themselves to Him, and receiving His divine word with docility. But, above all, what must not have been her consolation, after the harrowing scene on Calvary, and the burial of her Divine Son, when the bright day of the resurrection arose to dissipate these gloomy scenes, and when she saw Jesus living, impassible and immortal, filled to overflowing with delights, and crowned with glory. A heart as loving as Mary's could alone conceive all the consolation and joy she then experienced. It is thus that the Master Whom we serve knows how, in certain times of trial, to dispense to those whom He tries most, such heavenly joys as make them forget in an instant the acutest sufferings. A skilful Director of souls, He knows how to measure and intermix the bitters with the sweets, that He may confirm in His love those who are His own, and lead them to the summit of perfection. Oh! how sweet it is, and how advantageous, to give ourselves up blindly to His guidance!

2nd Point. The joys and consolations of Mary in Heaven.

Three feelings had caused the sorrows of Mary when she lived on earth : her ardent zeal for the divine glory, which rendered her deeply sensible to offences against God ; her love for her Divine Son, which caused her at the time of His painful sacrifice to suffer herself all the tortures of crucifixion ; lastly, her tender love for mankind, which penetrated her with sorrow at the sight of the prodigious number of souls who fall daily into hell. To-day these three feelings have become for her so many sources of ineffable joy. A witness in the realms above of the homage paid to God, she drinks in prolonged draughts of the happiness of seeing Him loved by all the Angels and Saints ; her Divine Son, the object of her dearest affections, is seated in Heaven at the right hand of His Father ; she beholds the highest Seraphim acknowledging Him for their God ; she hears the canticles which the blessed eternally sing to His praise ; she sees Him reigning over all hearts. Her love for man causes her also to taste the sweetest consolations. The happy Mother of all the Elect, she rejoices in the happiness of each one as if it were her own, and her heart, which contains them all, experiences nothing but joy in the numberless objects of her love. O Mary! how justly was this happiness your due! Enjoy your endless beatitude, O my most holy Mother, I congratulate you upon it; but in the midst of so much delight, do not forget your child still an exile upon the earth, and exposed to the danger of being lost ; show yourself my Mother ; help me to reach Heaven, that I may share in your delights, and by doing this augment your glory.

Colloquy with the Blessed Virgin. Let us congratulate her on the happiness which she now enjoys in Heaven. Let us ask her to inflame our heart with divine love, so that sanctifying all our joys and all our sorrows, by close union with Jesus, we may one day deserve to possess eternal beatitude.

Resolutions. To unite all my sufferings and all my joys to those of the Hearts of Jesus and Mary. To thank God equally for both joys and sorrows.

Offering of the Resolutions, page 3.

Spiritual Bouquet. "They that sow in tears shall reap in joy." "The Lord leads me, nothing shall be wanting to me."

Prayer. We fly to thy patronage, etc.

Examen of the Meditation, page 4.

TWENTY-EIGHTH MEDITATION.

ON THE HOLY HEART OF MARY.

"He that finds me finds life."

Preparatory Prayer, page 1.

1st Prelude. Represent to yourself Mary stretching out her arms, and inviting you lovingly to her maternal heart, in order that you may find in it the virtues pleasing to the Sacred Heart of her Son.

2nd Prelude. Heart of Mary, Heart of my Mother! inspire me with the sentiments thou dost desire I should have for thee, and aid me to imitate the virtues of which thou art the perfect model.

1st Point. The Heart of Mary is worthy of my respect, of my love and confidence. My love for Mary, my confidence in her goodness, my zeal for her glory, and, above all, my eagerness to make her known and loved, ought to have no limits. We do not really love

Jesus Christ when we do not love His holy Mother, and our Divine Saviour accepts as offered to Himself the honour rendered to the Mother who gave Him birth. Oh! upon how many titles does she not merit my veneration and my love! The Heart of Mary is the sanctuary made choice of by God Himself, and which He has adorned with all virtues and with every gift of grace. It is the throne of virginity, the trophy of humility, the perpetual holocaust of divine love, the living and perfect image of the adorable Heart of Jesus. It is for me the Heart of the most affectionate of all Mothers; my model, my support, my mediatrix with the Sacred Heart of my Divine Lord. Oh! how greatly I ought to love and venerate Mary! How zealously I ought to exert myself that she may be glorified! With what confidence I ought to have recourse to her in all my wants and in all my trials!

2nd Point. It is through the Heart of Mary I ought to go to that of Jesus.

Called upon by my vocation to Christianity to copy in my soul the virtues of the Sacred Heart of Jesus; urged by the chosen favours with which He unceasingly overwhelms me, to devote myself to propagate His religion, to gain souls to Him, and to indemnify Him by my love for the outrages and ingratitude of sinners, I have to fulfil important obligations, for which I need great virtues; but in order to acquire these virtues, and correspond with the designs of our Lord, I possess a sweet, easy, and efficacious means: it is devotion to the holy Heart of Mary, and confidence in her. This most holy Mother knows better than any one the inclinations and desires of the Sacred Heart of her Divine Son. She only wishes to form me to the practice of the virtues which she has herself learned from this adorable Heart; she offers me her mediation for this end, and opens to me the treasures of grace which He has deposited with her. Who then can still retard my progress in perfection, and place any obstacle to the good which the Sacred Heart of Jesus desires to effect through me if I have recourse with confidence to Mary! O Heart of my loving and most holy Mother! cause me to experience more and more thy power and thy love; defend me against my enemies; sustain my weakness under every combat; teach me to imitate Jesus; lead me to His Sacred Heart, and obtain for me the grace never more to leave it.

Colloquy with the Holy Heart of Mary. Let us offer it our homage of respect, love, and veneration, as to the most perfect and most amiable of all hearts after that of Jesus her Divine Son. Let us pray to her to retrace within us all her virtues, and to procure us favour with the Sacred Heart of our Divine Lord, obtaining for us all the aids we stand in need of to glorify Him perfectly.

Resolutions. To have recourse to the Heart of Mary in my difficulties and trials, and often to ask her to lead me to the Heart of her Divine Son.

Spiritual Bouquet. "O Mary! show thyself my Mother!"

Prayer. Receive, O Lord, page 12.

Examen of the Meditation, page 4.

TWENTY-NINTH MEDITATION.

THE SAME SUBJECT.

"The beauty of the King's daughter is within."

Preparatory Prayer, page 1.

1st Prelude. Represent to yourself Mary in the solitude of Nazareth at the moment when the Angel saluted her "full of grace".

2nd Prelude. Heart of Mary, sanctuary of all heavenly gifts and of all virtues, obtain for me the grace to honour thee worthily, and to imitate as closely as possible thy fidelity in putting to profit the graces of our Lord.

1st Point. The Heart of Mary should be the object of my devotion.

Let us reflect on the immense plenitude of the graces with which the pure Heart of Mary was laden, and how worthy she was of having the gaze of God fixed upon her. From the first moment of her existence her most pure Heart was enriched with all heavenly gifts, with a magnificence which could not be approached by all the Angels and Saints together; from the first moment also Mary possessed the full use of her reason, and corresponded with so much fidelity to the graces with which she was enriched, that she made them bring forth a hundredfold; so that the graces she put to profit so well, unceasingly and ever freshly developed within her, rendering her an object of admiration to all the heavenly court. Oh! how greatly God delighted in that Heart which He had chosen for His own Tabernacle, in that august Sanctuary of all virtues, in that Holy of Holies from which arose continually the perfume of prayer, and in which the precepts of the Divine Law and the Sacred Manna of His word were kept with so much fidelity! If He deigns to attach value to our poor hearts, and shows Himself jealous of possessing them because He beholds in them some traits of His divine resemblance, what love must He not have for the most pure Heart of Mary, in which His image is so perfectly traced! Ah! I ought to rejoice at the glory which His most holy Mother will procure Him for all eternity. I ought to offer Him her perfect homage to supply for the imperfection of my own, and pray to her to cause my heart to bear some resemblance to her virginal Heart, that so I may not be quite unworthy of the love of my Creator.

2nd Point. The Heart of Mary ought to be the object of my imitation.

The Heart of Mary is like a sacred book open before me, from which I ought continually to gain instruction. Notwithstanding my profound unworthiness, our Lord has deigned to say to me, as to my most holy Mother: "My Child, give Me thy heart". He expects from my heart a fidelity worthy of His love and of His graces; He wishes to console Himself by its devotedness for the coldness and contempt of the greater number of Christians. I ought therefore to go to Mary to learn from her how I should receive the graces of Heaven, so that they may fructify within me. The Heart of Mary was always the most humble of all hearts; the heavenly gifts with which she was so highly favoured penetrated her with deep gratitude towards God; the more profound because she attributed all to His mercy alone. To humility and gratitude her Heart, so pure and delicate, always united the most complete fidelity. Fervent in the service of God, ever attentive to His will, generous and constant under the most painful sacrifices, this immaculate Heart offers me the example of the purest and most heroic virtues. Oh! how pleasing I should be to the Sacred Heart of my Divine Lord, if my heart were the faithful copy of that of my holy Mother!

Colloquy with the Immaculate Heart of Mary. Let us offer her our profound homage of veneration and love. Let us thank her for the numberless graces which she has obtained for us from her Divine Son. Let us entreat of her to reproduce her virtues within our hearts, and present us to the adorable Heart of Jesus.

Resolutions. To be lovingly attentive to the will of God in the least things, and above all to show myself very faithful in the accomplishment of the duties of my state.

Offering of the Resolutions, page 3.

Spiritual Bouquet. " O Mary, full of grace, make my heart like unto thine!"

Prayer. O God of infinite clemency, etc., page 10.
Examen of the Meditation, page 4.

THIRTIETH MEDITATION.

THE SAME SUBJECT.

" Within the Holy of Holies was a golden Altar, on which perfumes were continually burning."

Preparatory Prayer, page 1.
1st Prelude. Represent to yourself Mary, either in the Temple, where she was consumed with the love of God, or at the foot of the Cross, where she adopted us for her children; or in Heaven, where she ceases not to intercede for us before the Divine Majesty.
2nd Prelude. Most Holy Heart of Mary, ardent furnace of the purest love, I beg of thee to communicate to my heart the sacred fire which ever consumes thine.
1st Point. The love of the Heart of Mary for God.
God was pleased to unite in the Heart of Mary all the most perfect gifts of nature and grace. Never was there a heart so loving or so pure as the virginal heart destined to give life to the Sacred Heart of the God of Love: never was there a heart that knew how to love so perfectly or so ardently. This immaculate Heart preserved from all corruption, was not heavily weighted like ours; nothing could hinder it from raising itself to God, nothing could impede within it the activity of the ardours of divine love. Love is the life of every virtue. Mary, who possessed them all in a super-eminent degree, must, consequently, have been infinitely more inflamed than any of the Saints with this divine fire, which alone gives value to all the virtues. Mary, as the immaculate Virgin, and the most holy of all creatures, had for God a love above all loves; but,

when she became His Mother, this love increased so greatly, that, surpassing itself, so to speak, it attained a degree of strength and perfection that the divine intelligence alone is capable of conceiving. What intimate communications were then established between the Heart of the Son and that of the Mother! All the feelings of the Sacred Heart of Jesus passed through the Heart of Mary; it was the same love for the same Heavenly Father; the same zeal for His glory; the same horror for all that displeased Him; the same ardour to accomplish His holy will at the cost of every sacrifice. O Heart of my most holy Mother! teach me to copy, as thou didst, the image of the Sacred Heart of Jesus, that so my Divine Saviour may accomplish His designs concerning me in all their extent.

2nd Point. The love of the Heart of Mary for mankind.

The Heart of Mary, so conformable to that of her Divine Son, could not fail to be opened to those for whom our adorable Saviour came to give His blood and His very life. Our souls were so dear to her, that to deliver them from hell she hesitated not to give up her own Son to torments and to death, so that the words which Jesus Himself said of His Heavenly Father may justly be applied to her: " God so loved the world as to give us His only-begotten Son ". But it was, above all, at the foot of the Cross that the Heart of Mary was, in a more special manner, opened to us. Jesus, turning His dying eyes towards her, said to her, alluding to St. John, who, according to the teaching of the holy Fathers, represented us all: " Woman, behold thy son ". These words immediately effected what they signified. Mary accepted us as our Mother, and loved us as she loved her Divine Son. This love of Mary for us did not cease with her life; in Heaven this kind Mother still maintains all her love for us; she intercedes for us unceasingly, shields us with her protection, and favours us with a multitude of graces. Oh! who could measure or reckon up those she has obtained for me! I ought to pray to her to teach me to profit fully by them, and to make me worthy of the tenderness which she feels for me, and of the graces with which she loads me.

Colloquy with the loving Heart of Mary. Let us offer her our homage of love and veneration; thank her with profound gratitude for the numberless graces we owe to her; beg of her to obtain for us to imitate all her virtues, and consecrate ourselves to her virginal Heart, that she may present us to Jesus, and cause Him to look favourably on us.

Resolutions. To offer all my actions to-day to the holy Heart of Mary, through gratitude and love.

Offering of the Resolutions, page 3.

Spiritual Bouquet. "Heart of Mary, my hope and my refuge, inflame my heart with the divine love which ever burns in thine."

Prayer. Remember, O most holy Virgin, etc.

Examen of the Meditation, page 4.

THIRTY-FIRST MEDITATION.

On Devotion to the Blessed Virgin.

"Thou art, O most venerable Virgin, the only hope of sinners, and the pledge of the recompense promised unto us" (St. Augustine).

Preparatory Prayer, page 1.

1st Prelude. Image to yourself the most holy Virgin Mary, seated in Heaven on an exalted throne, looking down lovingly on those who invoke her.

2nd Prelude. Sacred Virgin, Mother of mercy and love, obtain for me the grace of a true devotion to thee, and help me to advance thy glory by endeavouring to make thee known.

1st Point. In what true devotion to Mary essentially consists.

It has been in the experience of all, that a true servant of Mary can never be lost; nothing can, therefore, be more solid, more precious, or more desirable than devotion to this Queen of Virgins; nothing can be more consoling than to possess it oneself; nothing more salutary than to spread it amongst others. In what does it consist? Only in three things, and all easily practised. To be devout to Mary we have but to honour her, to invoke her with confidence, and to love her. The imitation of her virtues ought to be undoubtedly the fruit of the perfection of our devotion to her; but we must not refrain from being devout to her although we may not have the courage to imitate her. This is the teaching of the Fathers of the Church, whose writings are the guide of our belief. Hence, the imperfect, nay, even the sinful, may aspire to the protection which Mary delights in affording to all who are devout to her. As we behold men and women, plunged in all kinds of disorders, maintain feelings of respect and love for their mother, and as we see these mothers, though grieving over their children when they go astray from the paths of virtue, yet ceasing not to love them, it may happen, and, in reality, it does happen every day, that sinners, and souls separated for many years from God, preserve their devotion towards Mary, and find in the love of this Mother of mercy a refuge in their miseries, and a means of conversion and salvation. Oh! how great an advantage it is, then, and how much in harmony with the spirit of zeal with which I ought to be animated, not only to penetrate myself, daily, more and more, with the sentiments of respect and love that I owe to the Mother of God, but also to make known and to propagate a devotion at once so easy and so profitable! O Mother most kind!

obtain for me the grace to labour to gain souls for thee; give efficacy to my words, to my example, and to my prayers. To draw souls to thee, O Mary! is to gain them for thy Divine Son, is to ensure their salvation.

2nd Point. What fruits may I promise myself from devotion to Mary?

Mary is the Mother of Mercy; her Heart, the perfect image of that of Jesus, is full of the most tender and ardent charity. What fruits may I not hope for from my devotion to her; above all, if this devotion extends so far as to cause me to attach myself, for love of her, to those virtues which are the dearest to her? Ah! if her maternal protection procures for the most abandoned sinners the graces of conversion, what will she not do for a soul whose desires are for perfection, and whose efforts all tend to procure the glory of God? Mary is my Mother, and the most tender of all Mothers; she has promised to love those who shall love her: "I love those who love me," she says in the Book of Wisdom. I am, then, sure of always finding in her, light, strength, and consolation. If I have grieved the Sacred Heart of Jesus by my infidelities to His grace, she will obtain my pardon: if temptations assail me, and difficulties alarm me, she offers me her help to triumph over all my enemies: if doubts, anxieties and interior darkness rob me of the light of Heaven, she is the star which shines in the midst of the night to enlighten me: if I wish to strive zealously to advance in virtue, she will uphold my efforts. O Mary, O my tender Mother! may I forget myself rather than ever forget to invoke thee in my necessities, to have recourse to thee in my weaknesses, but, above all, to honour thee with an unbounded love, an ardent zeal to make thee known, and a constant fidelity in rendering myself like unto thee by imitating thy virtues.

Colloquy with the Blessed Virgin. Let us pay her our homage of respect, veneration and love. Let us beg of her to increase within us devotion towards her, and to obtain for us a special grace to inspire others with this precious devotion.

Resolutions. To have recourse to Mary in my wants with the confidence and simplicity of a child towards its mother. To put to profit every opportunity of making known her Immaculate Heart, and of increasing devotion to it.

Offering of the Resolutions, page 3.

Spiritual Bouquet. "O Mary! show thyself my Mother."

Prayer. Remember, O most holy Virgin, etc.

Examen of the Meditation, page 4.

THIRTY-SECOND MEDITATION.

For the Feast of Our Lady of Perpetual Succour.

"Her protection shall encompass thee as a buckler, and thou shalt be in safety beneath her wings."

Preparatory Prayer, page 1.

1st Prelude. Represent to yourself Mary looking down from Heaven above on those who invoke her, and extending her hands over them to defend and protect them.

2nd Prelude. Most powerful Virgin, deign to fill me with the most lively confidence in thy maternal protection.

1st Point. The power of Mary to help those who invoke her.

Mary disposes as a sovereign of all the treasures of her Son, and there is no Christian—indeed, there is no one on earth—who has not received some signal favour from her. The holy Fathers, according to the metaphorical expressions which speak of Jesus Christ as the Head of the Church, and of Christians as the members of this mystical Body, have added that Mary is as it were the sacred Neck thereof; by these words giving us to understand that it is through her that the graces which we receive from our Divine Head are transmitted to us, and that not a single one of those graces reaches us without having first passed to us through her. It is a matter of experience that Mary has at all times given the most unequivocal signs of her unlimited power. There is no country, nor even we may say any Catholic province, which does not contain some pilgrim-shrine celebrated for the signal blessings received from this heavenly Queen; and who could name one single species of misfortune which she has not opportunely relieved, one only kind of favour which she has not obtained for those who have had recourse to her? With the most entire confidence I ought then to prostrate myself to-day before her, and claim that powerful protection under which we are shielded from all dangers and miseries. And should temporal trials be necessary for our sanctification, the aid of Mary is the means of our deriving from our trials an abundant treasure of merits and of virtues.

2nd Point. The goodness of Mary in helping those who invoke her.

"Come to Me, all you who labour and are burdened," said our Divine Saviour during His mortal life, "and I will ease and refresh you." From the highest Heaven Mary addresses the same words to those who are tried by afflictions, or who are exposed to any peril either of soul or body. No tender Mother is so careful to provide for the wants of her children, and even to anticipate their wishes with loving kindness before they think of having recourse to her. How many are there who, scarcely knowing her, have owed to her their conversion and salvation! How many despairing sinners have escaped, as it would seem, inevitable ruin, through her intercession! The experience of all ages justifies the confidence which St. Bernard testified for her when he said : "Remember, O most holy Virgin Mary, that no one ever had recourse to thy protection, implored thy help, or sought thy mediation, without obtaining relief". If such, then, is the goodness of Mary for all mankind, if even those who have most outraged her Divine Son find in her maternal heart an asylum and a refuge, provided they desire to be sincerely converted, what ought I not to expect from her loving heart, if, penetrated with the sentiment of my necessities, I offer my prayers to her with entire confidence?

Colloquy with the Blessed Virgin. Let us pay her our humble homage of respect, love, and confidence. Let us place ourselves under her special protection, begging her to defend us against the enemies of our salvation, and to help us to acquire every virtue pleasing to the Sacred Heart of her Divine Son.

Resolutions. To have recourse to Mary with filial confidence in every necessity.

Offering of the Resolutions, page 3.

Spiritual Bouquet. "Remember, O most holy Virgin Mary, that no one ever had recourse to thy intercession without obtaining relief."

Prayer. Remember, O most holy Virgin, etc.

Examen of the Meditation, page 4.

THIRTY-THIRD MEDITATION.

FOR THE FEAST OF OUR LADY OF MARTYRS.

"No one shall be crowned unless he strive lawfully."

Preparatory Prayer, page 1.

1st Prelude. Represent to yourself Mary in Heaven seated on a throne of glory; the Martyrs come and lay down their palms and crowns at her feet; she receives them with complacency, and looks down also from above on those who are still combating on this earth.

2nd Prelude. O glorious Queen of Martyrs! obtain for me the grace to imitate their combats by my generosity and devotedness in the service of thy Divine Son.

1st Point. The title of Queen of Martyrs is justly due to Mary, since she has suffered more cruel torments than all the Martyrs put together.

Mary, who was to surpass all the Saints in merit, and imitate more perfectly than they could Jesus crucified, has alone suffered incomparably more than all the Martyrs united together. It will be easy for me to understand this, if I consider, 1st, that it was within her heart that Mary, this Mother of love and sorrow, received all the blows which were to unite her in sacrifice with her Divine Son : her virginal heart, so refined and sensitive, felt the sufferings of Jesus crucified beyond all expression, and it cannot be doubted that Mary would a thousand times have preferred to be nailed to the Cross herself than to have beheld Jesus crucified upon it; 2nd, these tortures of the heart of Mary did not last simply for a few hours like the torments of the Martyrs; they commenced from the moment in which she consented to become the Mother of Jesus, for she foreknew from the prophecies all the details of the Passion of our Divine Redeemer, and those harrowing scenes were ever present to her soul; 3rd, Mary did not experience, as the Martyrs did, those interior delights which tempered, and even sometimes entirely removed, the feeling of their torments. As she was the perfect image of Jesus suffering, she drank in, as He had done, without the smallest alleviation, all the bitterness of His chalice ; like Jesus, she bore all the rigour of the blows of divine justice ; she foresaw the loss of a multitude of souls who would not profit by the fruits of the sufferings and death of their Saviour. And more than once, during the course of the cruel

Passion of her Divine Son, it was necessary that a strength more than human should support her miraculously. By a most just title, then, is this holy Mother honoured by the Church as Queen of Martyrs, and beholds in Heaven all these champions of the faith surrounding her throne and prostrate before her.

2nd Point. The title of Queen of Martyrs is justly due to Mary, since they owe their victories to her maternal protection.

Mary, the Mother of all the faithful and the Mediatrix between her Divine Son and mankind redeemed by His blood, is for us the channel of all graces, and, without deceiving ourselves, we may attribute to her assistance and to her prayers all the graces that we have received. She presided at the combats of the Martyrs, and she did this in a more special manner because she is the Refuge of those who suffer, and the Help of those who combat ; and because the Martyrs defended the glory of her Divine Son, which is infinitely dear to her. The title of Queen of Martyrs is, therefore, doubly due to her : but in honouring her to-day with the Church under this glorious epithet, I ought to gather from it some of the great truths which it recalls to my mind, and some practical fruits of sanctification. Mary suffered with Jesus, and her sufferings were the source of the happiness and glory in which she now rejoices. I ought then to embrace the Cross after her example, and unite myself in spirit to Jesus suffering, that so, when this life is over, I may rejoice in the love and possession of my adorable Saviour. Mary presided at the combats of the Martyrs, and her help caused them to gain the victory ; I ought, therefore, to have recourse to her in all my temptations and weaknesses, and to hope for all things through her maternal help. In this way I shall render her the service which her heart desires, for above all things she wishes to see me put her favours to profit and to imitate her example.

Colloquy with Mary, Queen of Martyrs. Let us pay her our homage of veneration, love, and confidence. Let us beg of her to obtain for us the grace to attach ourselves to Jesus Crucified, and to combat generously the devil, the world, and ourselves, that so the love of our Divine Saviour may triumph within us.

Resolutions. To have recourse to Mary in my temptations and in all my spiritual wants. To labour to overcome myself, so that I may become united to Jesus Crucified.

Offering of the Resolutions, page 3.

Spiritual Bouquet. O Mary, Queen of Martyrs, be my refuge and my strength!

Prayer. O Mary, the most desolate, etc., page 45.

Examen of the Meditation, page 4.

THIRTY-FOURTH MEDITATION.

For the Feast of our Lady of Peace.

" Justice and peace have kissed " (Ps. lxxxiv. 11).

Preparatory Prayer, page 1.

1st Prelude. Figure to yourself Mary in Heaven between Jesus and yourself, while she is praying Him to forgive your sins and bestow favours on you.

2nd Prelude. O Mother of grace and mercy, obtain for me, from the Sacred Heart of thy Divine Son, peace with God, peace with my neighbour, and peace with myself.

1st Point. Mary procures peace for repenting sinners by reconciling them with God.

When Mary was given to the earth, she made her appearance as a token of peace between God and man. Promised from the beginning of the world as the mysterious and powerful woman who was to crush the head of the infernal serpent, she was, from the first instant of her existence, an object of joy for the Angels, since they beheld in her a pledge of the approaching accomplishment of the promises of the Almighty, and of the deliverance of the human race. This Mother of love and mercy is still, to-day, for repenting sinners, a pledge of hope and clemency. If they invoke her most sweet name, calm quickly takes the place within them of the movements of fear and of grief which previously agitated them; a secret unction, acting upon their souls, gives them to understand that Mary truly exercises, in union with Jesus, her Divine Son, the office of peacemaker between God and His creatures. Have I not experienced this myself? Have I never felt how greatly a guilty heart, but which is grieved at its faults, feels itself strengthened and consoled in remembering that Mary is the Advocate of sinners? O Mother of clemency! may these precious reminiscences remain with me for ever, in order to excite my gratitude; but, above all, may they induce me to suggest to others the salutary thought of themselves experiencing thy maternal goodness towards all and thy power with God.

2nd Point. Mary obtains for the just the peace which Jesus promised to His true followers.

If the title of Queen of Peace is justly due to Mary on account of her goodness to sinners who return to God, not less does she merit this title on account of the precious favours she obtains for the souls of the just. One who truly loves Mary, who honours and invokes her, and, above all, strives to imitate her, enjoys the sweetest peace. "I leave you My peace, I give you My peace," said Jesus to His Apostles. He delights in placing this precious peace, as well as all His other gifts, in the keeping of His ever-blessed Mother, that she may bestow it as she pleases on His faithful servants. Accordingly, I possess a sure, sweet, and easy means of obtaining this peace :—devotion to Mary. If this devotion is true, pure, and solid within my soul, I shall have peace with God through the testimony of a good conscience, and through unswerving fidelity;—peace with my neighbour by patience, meekness, and endurance,—and peace with myself by that interior calm which always accompanies subdued passions. What precious and desirable advantages!

Colloquy with the Blessed Virgin. Let us pay her our homage of respect and gratitude. Let us thank her humbly for all the graces she has procured for us, even at times when we have been most guilty in the sight of God. Let us ask her to obtain for us from her Divine Son that precious gift of peace which He bequeathed to His followers.

Resolutions. To invoke Mary in all my temptations, in order to overcome them and to obtain peace of mind. To be careful to maintain peace with others.

Offering of the Resolutions, page 3.

Spiritual Bouquet. O Mary! obtain for me that peace which Jesus left to His disciples.

Prayer. Holy Virgin, august Queen of Peace, obtain for me from thy Divine Son that peace which He left as an inheritance to His disciples; the world can neither know it nor give it; it dwells alone in pure souls sanctified by grace. May I ever preserve this peace with my superiors by my respect and submission; with my equals by my meekness; with my inferiors by my patience and kindness. Bestow it also on my family, on my friends, and on all mankind. Obtain for me to live here below in peace and innocence, that so I may deserve to enjoy one day eternal peace in Heaven. Amen.

Examen of the Meditation, page 4.

THIRTY-FIFTH MEDITATION.

For the Feast of Our Lady of Mount Carmel.

"She shall clothe him with a robe of glory" (Eccli. xv. 5).

Preparatory Prayer, page 1.

1st Prelude. Image to yourself Mary giving the Holy Scapular herself to St. Simon Stock, as a token of alliance and a pledge of her protection.

2nd Prelude. O Mary! obtain for me, that in meditating on the great favour thou hast granted to thy servants in making known to them the Devotion of the Holy Scapular, my heart may become penetrated with love, gratitude, and confidence.

1st Point. The Holy Scapular is a symbol of our alliance with Mary.

Mary is the Mother of all Mankind; she adopted us all at the foot of the Cross, and there is no one who does not experience the effects of her tenderness and maternal solicitude. It is, however, true to say that those whom she has invested with the Holy Scapular have a greater share in her affectionate care than any others. This holy Habit, which she herself brought down from Heaven to bestow on those who are devout to her, is, as it were, her special livery; it is a badge, which, in the sight of the Angels, distinguishes those who have the honour to wear it, and causes them to be loved by them as the servants of their Queen. How sweet is this reflection! It is, therefore, true that when I was received into the Association of the Scapular, I solemnly renewed my alliance with Mary; I strengthened the sweet ties which united me to her, I drew down on myself in a special manner her protection, and engaged to serve her with greater fidelity. O Mary! recall to my mind unceasingly thy goodness towards me and my obligations towards thee, that so, acquitting myself lovingly of what I owe thee, I may obtain the favours thou hast promised to those who shall have worthily worn thy blessed Habit.

2nd Point. The graces to be hoped for by those who shall have worthily worn the Holy Scapular.

The Holy Scapular is a pledge of the love and protection of Mary; this is saying that it is an abundant source of all sorts of blessings. The Blessed Virgin has promised that those who shall be wearing this heavenly badge at the hour of death shall not fall under the power of Satan, but that she will preserve them, by a special protection, from the misery of dying in mortal sin. Further still: by a revelation which has been approved by several of the sovereign Pontiffs, she has made known to us that on every Saturday she herself deigns to descend into Purgatory to release from it those who shall have worn the Scapular during their life, and been faithful in fulfilling the obligations it imposes. If to these two favours, which are the greatest, I add the numberless graces attached to this previous devotion; the indulgences bestowed on it by the Church; the share which it gives in the prayers and merits of so many holy Religious of both sexes, and of so many fervent Christians in all states, who wear this holy Habit in union with myself, I shall doubtless conceive an idea of the great abundance of heavenly favours to which a faithful soul may aspire. What gratitude do I not owe to my most holy Mother for having given me a title to such precious advantages.

Colloquy with the Blessed Virgin. Let us offer her humble and lively acts of thanksgiving for the innumerable favours which she has procured for us by means of the Holy Scapular, and for those she still has in store for us. Let us pray to her to penetrate us with esteem for this invaluable devotion, and beg her to help us to gather its fruits more and more abundantly. Let us ask her to make use of us to spread this devotion.

Resolutions. To acquit myself carefully of the pious practices imposed upon me by my aggregation to the Confraternity of the Scapular. To raise my heart to Mary several times in the day to thank her for her benefits.
Offering of the Resolutions, page 3.
Spiritual Bouquet. "O Mary! show thyself my Mother."
Prayer. We fly to thy patronage, etc.
Examen of the Meditation, page 4.

THIRTY-SIXTH MEDITATION.

For the Feast of Our Lady of the Angels.

"With the Lord there is mercy, and with Him there is plentiful redemption" (Ps. cxxix. 7).

Preparatory Prayer, page 1.
1st Prelude. Transport yourself in spirit into the Chapel of the Portiuncula in Assisi, and imagine to yourself the moment in which Mary obtains from her Divine Son the indulgence petitioned for by St. Francis.
2nd Prelude. O Mary, Mother of mercy and clemency! obtain for me the dispositions necessary to participate abundantly in the precious treasure of indulgences.
1st Point. Indulgences are for us a precious means of acquitting ourselves of our debts towards the Divine Justice.

On this day, in which the Church, by the voice of Mary, opens to me the treasure of indulgences, and invites me to profit by them, both for myself and for the souls detained in Purgatory, I ought to reanimate my faith and to excite my fervour; and with this view should ask myself what an indulgence is. As I have learned from my earliest years, an indulgence is a remission of the temporal punishment due to sin; consequently it is a means of paying debts incurred with the Divine Justice, of rendering myself purer in the sight of God, and of placing myself in a condition to enjoy His presence sooner, when death shall have released my soul from its earthly tenement. An indulgence is a powerful help granted to my weakness to compensate, by the superabundant merits of Christ and His saints, for what is wanting to my penance to render it full and perfect, and to restore to me in their entirety the privileges I had acquired through the Sacred Heart of my God. These are the priceless advantages offered me; I shall share therein the more abundantly according to the liveliness of my fervour, the depth of my contrition, the ardour of my love for God, and my firm and entire hope in His goodness. O Mary! place these dispositions, thyself, within my heart.

2nd Point. Indulgences are for us a powerful means of helping the souls in Purgatory.

If the indulgences granted by the Church are a precious advantage offered to the Church Militant, they are also one of the most powerful means of relieving the souls still detained in their place of punishment. I can, then, on any day (if I perform zealously all that depends on me to put to profit the divine mercy), procure for these suffering souls refreshment, freedom, and repose. What could I do more pleasing to my heavenly Mother than to apply to these souls so dear to her heart the price of the Blood of Jesus Christ? What can I conceive at the same time more advantageous to myself than in this way to practise a charity the effects of which are so sure and so excellent? To deliver a soul from Purgatory is to do infinitely more than to set at large a prisoner, or to raise a poor man from the depth of misery, in order to place him in the midst of abundance; or, again, more than to deliver an invalid from the most acute sufferings in order to give him the enjoyment instantly of perfect health. And if the smallest service rendered to another, a glass of cold water simply given in the name of Jesus Christ, will not remain without a recompense, what will not our Blessed Saviour and His holy Mother do for that person who shall have rescued one of the elect from the flames of Purgatory to place it in the possession of eternal bliss?

Colloquy with the Blessed Virgin. Let us return her humble acts of thanksgiving for the signally ample indulgence of the Portiuncula with which she has enriched the Church. Let us beg of her to give us the dispositions which we ought to have in order to share in it fully, and to be able to help powerfully the souls in Purgatory.

Resolutions. To neglect nothing necessary for profiting by this day of grace.

Offering of the Resolutions, page 3.

Spiritual Bouquet. " With the Lord there is mercy, and with Him there is plentiful redemption" (Ps. cxxix. 7).

Prayer. Remember, O most holy Virgin, etc.

Examen of the Meditation, page 4.

THIRTY-SEVENTH MEDITATION.

FOR THE FEAST OF OUR LADY OF THE HOLY ROSARY.

" All generations shall call me blessed " (Luke i. 48).

Preparatory Prayer, page 1.

1st Prelude. Represent to yourself Mary in Heaven seated on a throne of glory; she there accepts graciously all the homage offered to her by the recital of the Rosary: these holy prayers are like so many precious crowns laid by the Angels at her feet.

2nd Prelude. O Mary! deign to revive my piety

towards thee on this day of grace, and give me to understand what great blessings are attached to the fervent recital of the Rosary.

1st Point. What are the sentiments which the Feast of Our Lady of the Rosary should cause to arise within me?

The title of Queen of the Holy Rosary, under which Mary is honoured to-day, recalls to my mind the most touching memories. This pious devotion is, as it were, a memorial of the different mysteries of love, sorrow, and joy, which Jesus fulfilled for mankind, and in which Mary bore so great a share : it enables me to consider by turns this admirable Virgin as the Mother of Jesus Christ, and the instrument through which His earliest favours were conferred in the house of Zachary : it exhibits her to me going to the Temple, there to offer up her Divine Son. It reminds me afterwards of the sorrowful Passion of my Saviour, which was entirely reproduced in His Mother's heart; then it sets before me the glorious mysteries of the Resurrection and the Ascension of Jesus, the Descent of the Holy Ghost, and lastly, the glorious triumph of Mary herself. The first of these mysteries are placed before my eyes to excite me to confidence and love ; the last have for their object to awaken my hopes and renew afresh my ardour in the practice of virtue ; they are like the summary and abridgment of all that can act powerfully upon my heart, in order to strengthen in it more lastingly the dominion of Jesus and Mary. Am I, when saying the Rosary, penetrated with the sentiments which so many mysteries of love ought to awaken within me?

2nd Point. Of the graces of which the recital of the Rosary may become for me the source.

The recital of the holy Rosary, so calculated to excite within me the sentiments of gratitude and love which I owe to Jesus and Mary, offers me, at the same time, a powerful means of salvation and of sanctification. How many victories have been gained, how many perils avoided, how many graces obtained through the aid of this salutary devotion! These are so many examples which invite me, in my turn, to profit by it, in order to overthrow the enemies of my salvation, to draw down on myself the protection of Mary, and to cause those virtues to flourish within me which are so dear to her. The Rosary is called the Crown of Mary: this metaphorical expression gives me to understand that it is as agreeable to her as a crown of sweet-smelling roses would be to us. With what care ought I not then to offer her this homage which pleases her so greatly! I often recite the Rosary; week by week the different mysteries which compose it are repeated several times to arouse my attention. What blessings and favours may I not draw down upon my soul by means of this excellent prayer, if I always recite it with attention and piety!

Colloquy with the Blessed Virgin. Let us offer her our homage of veneration, love, and gratitude. Let us ask her pardon for the negligence and coldness with which we have sometimes recited the holy Rosary. Let us ask her to excite us to piety and fervour, that so we may derive from this holy form of prayer all the fruits attached to it.

Resolutions. Always to recite the Rosary with great attention and piety.

Offering of the Resolutions, page 3.

Spiritual Bouquet. "O Mary! show thyself my Mother."

Prayer. Remember, O most holy Virgin, etc.

Examen of the Meditation, page 4.

THIRTY-EIGHTH MEDITATION.

For the Feast of Our Lady of Victory.

"Who is she that cometh up from the desert, beautiful as the morning rising, fair as the moon, bright as the sun, terrible as an army in battle array?" (Cant. vi. 3-9).

Preparatory Prayer, page 1.

1st Prelude. Represent to yourself Mary seated in Heaven on an elevated throne; imagine, as far as you can, the power and majesty of this Queen of the universe, and behold her covering with her mantle all those who pray to her with confidence.

2nd Prelude. Most holy and powerful Mother of God, inspire me with filial confidence in thy maternal goodness, and vouchsafe to listen to me, and to help me when I call on thee for aid.

1st Point. Mary offers me her help that I may be victorious over the devil, and over myself.

The Church sets before me, for my meditation to-day, a very consoling truth, and one well calculated to encourage me in the combats in which I must incessantly be engaged with my spiritual enemies. Mary offers me her help and her protection; she presents herself to me under the title of Our Lady of Victories, in order to give me to understand that nothing can resist her power, and that we are certain of the victory if we call on her for help. Among the protectors we sometimes look for among men, some interest themselves in our necessities, and manifest good-will towards us; but, their power not being equal to their desires, they can only offer us a barren compassion, or, at the most, some words of encouragement. Others, on the contrary, could do a great deal for us, but their heart is closed to our miseries, and our dangers do not come home to them. This is not the case with Mary, the Mother of our Saviour. She shares His sentiments of love and mercy for us, and, being the depository of His power, she loves to make use of it to come to our aid. Why, then, should I allow myself to give way to trouble and discouragement when I find myself a prey to temptation? The Queen of Heaven does combat for me; she is terrible as an army ranged in battle array; a single glance of hers suffices to overthrow all the powers of darkness, and to give me a complete victory over them. Surely, then, I should fear nothing under such a safeguard.

2nd Point. Mary offers me her help in order to overcome the world.

The world, that enemy of Jesus Christ, which is in league with Satan to contrive our ruin, surrounds me on all sides with its snares and temptations: at one time it seeks to drag me away by the seducing love of its pomps and pleasures; at other times it tries to intimidate me by its railleries and sarcasms. Then, again, it seeks to corrupt me by its perverse maxims, and to ensnare me by its contagious example. Left to my own weakness, I could not resist so many dangers, but Mary offers me her powerful help. She seems to say to me, in the words of her Divine Son: "Have confidence, I have overcome the world". She has indeed overcome it, and will aid me to overcome it, if I will but carry out her teaching, and imitate her example. Mary triumphed over the vanities of the world by her love of being hidden and forgotten; she raised herself above its judgments by seeking the favour of God alone. Constant assiduous meditation on the Word of God put her on her guard against its perverse maxims; she fled from its contagion by confining herself entirely within the circle of her duties. Such precautions, doubtless, were not necessary for the preservation of her innocence, but they are needed for my instruction; they were also necessary for the glory of Mary, who was to crush, not only the hellish serpent, but also the world it has envenomed, and which shares in Satan's power. O Mary, my Mother! how could thy child wear the fetters of this world, which thou hast broken and cast away? No, far be from me its shameful slavery; reign alone in my heart with Jesus, thy adorable Son; cause me to triumph over the corruption of the world, over its vanities and its follies, by enlightening my eyes with the vivid light of faith, and by making me relish the pure delights of virtue.

Colloquy with the most Holy Mary. Let us pay her our homage of respect, veneration, and love. Let us beg of her to help and support us in our temptations, and cause us to triumph over our enemies, both visible and invisible.

Resolutions. To have recourse to Mary in all my temptations and dangers.

Offering of the Resolutions, page 3.

Spiritual Bouquet. "O Mary, come to my assistance! Mother of Mercy, make haste to help me!"

Prayer. We fly to thy patronage, etc.

Examen of the Meditation, page 4.

SECOND PART.

MEDITATIONS FOR THE FEASTS OF THE SAINTS.

FIRST MEDITATION.

(For New Year's Day.)

"I must work the works of Him that sent Me, whilst it is day: the night cometh when no man can work" (John ix. 4).

Preparatory Prayer, page 1.
1st Prelude. Represent to yourself our Divine Lord inviting you lovingly to employ well the New Year.
2nd Prelude. Sacred Heart of Jesus, grant me grace to redeem all the time I have lost since I first came into the world, by redoubled fervour and love during the present year.
1st Point. How greatly it concerns me to make a good use of time.
Another year has passed. . . . How many graces it has bestowed upon me! Holy Sacraments, instructions, pious books, good inspirations, interior lights, secret whisperings to the ear of the soul, have been lavished on me by my Jesus during the twelve months just ended ! . . . How have I profited by them? . . . Am I much more advanced in the virtues needed for my state now than I was this time last year? . . . Have I suffered much and laboured much for God during so many past days, which were given me only to be employed for His glory? . . . My life is pass-

ing rapidly away; the moments that I lose will never be mine again; I know not if I shall live to see the end of this year, the beginning of which my good God has granted me; I have only the present moment in which to love and serve Him. Oh! how nearly it concerns me, then, to employ carefully the short moments which hasten away so rapidly! Above all, it behoves me to understand thoroughly that no time is well employed except that in which the will of God is accomplished with a pure and upright intention; that it is not the number or outward show of our actions which constitutes their merit, but the interior spirit, the love and goodwill which accompanies them!

2nd Point. It is by uniting myself to Jesus, and by imitating His example, that I shall make a good use of my time.

From the very first day of the year holy Church places before my eyes the great and admirable Model, Whose imitation ought to be my study at all times. Jesus is presented to me shedding the first drops of His precious Blood for me, and inviting me to return Him love for love, by uniting myself to His sufferings. A great lesson is given to me in this mystery of love and sorrow: it teaches me that, in order to employ my time well, to animate my actions by those supernatural motives which can alone render them meritorious, to acquire those solid virtues of which I stand in need, to procure the glory of God and to attain Heaven, I must arm myself with a holy severity against myself, and by a spiritual circumcision cut off all the irregular desires of my heart. To-day Jesus takes the sweet name of Saviour, and already fulfils the office which that word expresses; it is in order to invite me to place my confidence in Him, to ask of Him the graces I need to raise me above my own weaknesses, and to cause this New Year to be for me a year of victory, of merits, and of virtue. O my Saviour! grant that I may enter faithfully into all Thy designs, that I may correspond with Thy love, put to profit Thy graces, and employ for Thy glory and Thy service every day and every moment Providence may still deign to grant me.

Colloquy with the Sacred Heart of Jesus. Let us adore Him in the mystery of the Circumcision, in which He is already humbling Himself and suffering for us. . . . Let us thank Him for the time He is giving us in order to work out our sanctification, and let us ask Him for grace to employ it well. Above all, let us beg of Him to inspire us with sufficient courage to practise that spiritual circumcision, the painful correctives of which ought to be renewed daily within us.

Resolutions. To watch carefully over myself, and repress all my bad inclinations. To animate each of my actions by a motive capable of rendering it meritorious.

Offering of the Resolutions, page 3.

Spiritual Bouquet. "While we have time let us do good."

Prayer. Soul of Christ, sanctify me, etc.

Examen of the Meditation, page 4.

MEDITATION FOR THE FEAST OF ST. GENEVIEVE.

(3RD JANUARY.)

"The kingdom of Heaven is like unto a householder who went out early in the morning to hire labourers into his vineyard" (Matt. xx. 1).

Preparatory Prayer, page 1.

1st Prelude. Represent to yourself St. Genevieve at the age of seven years, consecrating herself entirely to God in the presence of two Bishops.

2nd Prelude. Amiable Saint, who having given thyself to God from thy earliest years, never relaxed the fervour of thy first consecration, obtain for me fidelity like unto thine.

1st Point. St. Genevieve gave herself to the service of God from her most tender years.

St. Genevieve was one of those privileged souls who seem to have been chosen by God from their mother's womb, and prevented with His choicest blessings: but if the Almighty showed Himself so eager to possess her young heart, Genevieve, on her side, responded to His loving solicitations by unhesitating compliance. Attentive and docile to the first allurements of grace, she had prepared her soul for the designs of her God; consequently, at the age of seven years, she was judged worthy to become the Spouse of Jesus Christ. What comparison is there between my life and that of this young virgin? Has my love for my Lord been in advance of my years, and my fidelity in His service forestalled the years of my passions? . . . Oh, how just it is that now at least I should make good lost time by redoubled fervour and zeal! The traveller who has stopped on his way and notices that his time is running on, quickens his steps that he may reach the end of his journey before the night comes; so in like manner I must hasten on in the ways of perfection. Happy shall I be if by constant and generous efforts I can repair my past negligence, and redeem the valuable time that I have lost!

2nd Point. St. Genevieve persevered until death in the service of God.

Genevieve never relented in the fervour of her first consecration; assiduous in prayer, generous in embracing lovingly all the practices of Christian mortification, punctually faithful in fulfilling the very least of her duties, constant in the midst of the trials she had to undergo, she advanced from virtue to virtue unto the end of her career. Here again what reflections present themselves to my mind, all calculated to cover me with confusion! What inconstancy and fickleness have I not exhibited in my conduct! One day recollected and fervent, the next cowardly and careless, I do nothing but pass from a good resolution to some want of observance, and from sorrow for my faults to the commission of fresh sins. And why is my conduct so different from that of the Saints? Why is all my life spent in raising up the edifice of my sanctification and then pulling it down? It is because I do not know, as the Saints knew, how to build it up on solid foundations, and how to labour constantly after it is built to make it perfect. Humility, confidence in God, the spirit of prayer and recollection, and courage in overcoming myself, are solid virtues, without which it is impossible to conquer nature and set up within us the reign of grace; as long as I do not with all my heart apply myself to acquire these solid virtues my fervour will be short-lived and my resolutions vain! Sacred Heart of my Jesus, have pity on me, help me; fix the inconstancy of my heart by the strength of my love, and render it able to practise those solid virtues which alone can unite me to Thee for ever.

Colloquy with St. Genevieve. Let us congratulate her on the special graces with which she was prevented from her earliest years, and on her fidelity in corresponding with them. Let us beg of her to interest herself on our behalf with the Sacred Heart of Jesus, in order that we may obtain from His goodness the pardon of our numberless infidelities, and the graces which we need to be henceforth constant and generous in His service.

Resolutions. Often during the day to renew my intention of belonging entirely to God, and of performing all my actions for His glory.

Offering of the Resolutions, page 3.

Spiritual Bouquet. "He who puts his hand to the plough and looks back, is not fit for the kingdom of Heaven."

Prayer. Receive, O Lord, etc., page 18.

Examen of the Meditation, page 4.

MEDITATION FOR THE FEAST OF ST. PETER'S CHAIR.

"Thou art Peter, and upon this rock I will build My Church, and the gates of hell shall not prevail against it" (Matt. xvi. 18).

Preparatory Prayer, page 1.

1st Prelude. Imagine to yourself our Lord surrounded by His disciples and addressing St. Peter in the above words.

2nd Prelude. O Holy Apostle, obtain for me the grace of an inviolable attachment to the supreme head of the Church, together with an ardent zeal for the interests of our Spiritual Mother.

1st Point. Our motives for attachment to the Chair of St. Peter.

"Thou art Peter, and upon this rock I will build My Church, and the gates of hell shall not prevail against it." By these words our adorable Lord promised St. Peter, and all those who were to succeed him in the charge of the Supreme Headship of the Church, an infallibility against which the gates of hell, namely error and impiety, should never prevail. For nearly nineteen centuries the Church, upheld by this divine promise, resists the persecutions of all kinds that are waged against her; in like manner will she resist even to the end of the world; always will she come out victorious from the assaults which the powers of hell will incessantly stir up against her, and will lead safely to salvation those who shall remain attached to her faith, and prove themselves docile and obedient to her laws and counsels. What a happiness and security for me to be the child of this holy Church! Ah! I ought to thank our Lord all the days of my life for having caused me to be born in her bosom; I ought to be penetrated with all the sentiments of gratitude, love, and devotedness with which her numberless benefits should inspire me.

2nd Point. I ought to be alive to the interests of the Church, and show myself eager to enter into her views and to second her efforts.

The Church of Jesus Christ is my Mother; I ought in consequence to honour her, to love her, to rejoice in her triumphs, and grieve with her over the heresies, scandals, and persecutions which beset her; I ought to be afflicted at the loss of her children, who are my brethren in the faith. And, indeed, how could I deserve the precious title of disciple of Jesus Christ if I were insensible to the glory of my Saviour and to the interests of His Church? But I ought not to content myself with passing feelings and sterile affections; I ought to devote myself, with my whole heart, to procure the conversion of sinners and the salvation of souls. I ought, by the course of a life worthy of the holiness found in the Catholic Church, to defend the honour of religion against the calumnies of its enemies, or, at least, be a comfort to the Church in their insults and their outrages by my fervour and fidelity.

Colloquy with Jesus Christ. Let us thank Him for having founded His Church to be the guardian and interpreter of truth to the end of time. Let us pray for the conversion of infidels, heretics, and all in sin, recommending to Him all the intentions which can advance His glory and that of His Church.

Resolutions. To acquit myself faithfully of all my obligations, with a view to obtain the conversion of sinners and the salvation of souls.

Offering of the Resolutions, page 3.

Spiritual Bouquet. " All for the greater glory of God."

Prayer. Pater Noster, etc.

Examen of the Meditation, page 4.

MEDITATION FOR THE FEAST OF ST. AGNES.

(21st January.)

"My soul is strengthened because it is founded on Christ Jesus."

Preparatory Prayer, page 1.

1st Prelude. Represent to yourself St. Agnes before the tyrant; behold the holy firmness with which she confesses her faith, and the supernatural strength with which she seems to be upheld.

2nd Prelude. Grant me grace, O Lord, to increase more and more in interior virtues after the example of St. Agnes, and give me to experience the effects of her powerful intercession.

1st Point. I ought to imitate the virtues of St. Agnes.

The courage of St. Agnes in braving, at so tender an age, the rage of the persecutors; her unshaken confidence in the protection of Jesus Christ; and the miraculous assistance which her Divine Redeemer granted her in her combats, prove strongly that the love of virginity had not remained sterile within her, but that she had accustomed herself to the practice of those Christian and solid virtues which form the true Spouse of Jesus Christ. Do I know how to imitate, according to my state and position, the admirable example this Saint has given me? Does my adorable Saviour behold in me a sincere humility founded on the knowledge of my own miseries and the desire to imitate His humiliations; a lively faith that, raising me above all human consideration, teaches me to act for the sake of God alone, and fills me with a holy intrepidity when there is question of His service and His glory. Have I acquired the holy habit of animating all my actions with this interior spirit and union with the Sacred Heart of Jesus, which alone can give them value? If these virtues are not to be found within me, if at least I have not a sincere will to acquire them, it is in vain that I flatter myself that I am prepared to meet the trials which perhaps are on the point of assaulting me; some temptation of no great strength may cause me to fall into the greatest infidelities. Oh! how much it behoves me to have recourse to the Sacred Heart of my Divine Lord, and to apply myself seriously, with the help of His grace, to advance in those solid virtues which can alone enable me to persevere to the end in His love!

2nd Point. I ought to implore the protection of St. Agnes.

St. Agnes, who was so cautious during her lifetime to preserve the purity of her heart, and to persevere in the love which she had vowed to Jesus Christ, delights in protecting, from her throne in heaven, souls devoted to our Divine Saviour, and obtains for them the help necessary in order to be faithful to Him. With what confidence ought I not, then, to implore to-day the protection of this amiable Saint! Prostrate before the throne of Jesus Christ, she offers Him at this very moment my supplications and requests. What a favourable time for obtaining strength to overcome myself, and for corresponding with the graces of God by a lasting fervour. It is not for myself alone that St. Agnes offers me her powerful suffrages. I can interest her tender charity for all those who are dear to me: with what fervour ought I not to solicit for others and for myself that precious purity of heart without which it is impossible to please the Sacred Heart of Jesus!

Colloquy with St. Agnes. Let us congratulate her in her generous constancy, and on the glorious recompense it merited for her. Let us pray to her to interest herself for us with Jesus Christ, and to obtain for us from His goodness all the special helps of which we stand in need in order to acquire the solid virtues He desires us to possess.

Resolutions. To apply myself to the practice of the spirit of prayer and recollection, performing all my actions in union with the Sacred Heart of Jesus.

Offering of the Resolutions, page 3.

Spiritual Bouquet. "My soul is strengthened, because it is founded on Christ Jesus."

Prayer. Soul of Christ, etc.

Examen of the Meditation, page 4.

MEDITATION FOR THE FEAST OF THE CONVERSION OF ST. PAUL.

(25TH JANUARY.)

"Lord, what wouldst Thou have me to do?" (Acts ix. 6).

Preparatory Prayer, page 1.

1st Prelude. Figure to yourself St. Paul on the road to Damascus, thrown off his horse, and exclaiming while trembling with fear: "Lord, what wouldst Thou have me to do?"

2nd Prelude. Grant me, O Lord, through the intercession of St. Paul, the grace to glorify Thee by a sincere conversion and an ardent zeal.

1st Point. The grace of conversion granted to St. Paul, and his fidelity in corresponding with it.

Paul, changed in an instant from a persecutor into an Apostle, manifests to us the power of grace. Why does this same grace effect so little within me? It is because my will, at times rebellious against the inspirations of grace, at times too cowardly to make the painful efforts asked of me, never ceases to oppose a thousand obstacles to its happy results. As soon as Paul had heard these words, "I am Jesus Whom thou persecutest," he exclaimed, "Lord, what wilt Thou have me to do?" and his docility, bitter repentance, ardent zeal, and fidelity under every trial, amply repaired his past offences. But how often have I not heard the voice of God without profiting by the reproaches and warnings it addressed to me! How many infidelities and culpable delays, how much inconstancy and ingratitude, have I not to reproach myself with? Yet I am not to despair; God calls me again to-day. He offers me powerful graces of conversion, which may change me into a new creature. Shall I not at length make use of these efficacious means of belonging entirely to Him? Experience has pointed out to me the obstacles I ought to overcome, in order to render my conversion full and entire. What measures must I take, what resolutions ought I to form?

2nd Point. The power of prayer and of sacrifice offered to God for the salvation of souls.

St. Augustine attributes to the prayers of St. Stephen this wonderful conversion, which was to procure so much glory to God and usefulness to the Church. The humble supplications of a soul which belongs entirely to Jesus are all-powerful with Him. I can, therefore, if I serve Him faithfully, and if I pray to Him with that lively faith, ardent zeal and true charity, which He looks for in His true disciples, obtain striking conversions and graces of sanctification, useful not alone to the persons whom I shall have recommended to Him, but also to very many others who shall be attracted through their means to His love and service. Oh! how necessary it is for me to renew constantly within my soul the spirit of fervour, and to penetrate myself thoroughly with the thought that the salvation of a great number of souls may depend on my fidelity; that I may do very much for the glory of God by the practice of interior virtue, by an entire sacrifice of myself, and by humble and fervent prayer! St. Stephen had served the Church assiduously during his life, but in offering his death for the salvation of his murderers, he won St. Paul, who served the Church still more usefully. Who knows but that the Sacred

Heart of Jesus may have attached to my prayers and sacrifices the conversion of many chosen souls destined to procure Him very great glory?

Colloquy with our Lord. Let us thank Him for having given to all ages so great an example of the power of His grace in the person of St. Paul. Let us offer Him the merits of this great Apostle, begging Him to grant us, through the intercession of this Saint, the same powerful graces of conversion, and above all, to inspire us with ardent zeal, which may lead us to do all we can for the good of souls.

Resolutions. To overcome myself in whatever costs me most, with a view of being useful to the glory of God and the salvation of souls.

Offering of the Resolutions, page 3.

Spiritual Bouquet. "Lord, what wilt Thou have me to do?"

Prayer. Receive, O Lord, etc.

Examen of the Meditation, page 4.

MEDITATION FOR THE FEAST OF ST. FRANCIS DE SALES.

(29TH JANUARY.)

"Wisdom reacheth from end to end mightily, and ordereth all things sweetly" (Wisdom viii. 1).

Preparatory Prayer, page 1.

1st Prelude. Represent to yourself St. Francis of Sales preaching to the heretics, or else addressing lessons of meekness and self-denial to his spiritual daughters.

2nd Prelude. Great Saint, who, by generous courage in overcoming thyself, didst acquire a meekness which gave thee so great a power over souls to gain them to God, obtain for me the grace to imitate thee, that so I also may gain souls for Jesus.

1st Point. The meekness of St. Francis of Sales.

St. Francis of Sales was born with a lively and impetuous character; but, by studying the meekness of the Sacred Heart of Jesus, he succeeded so perfectly in establishing that virtue on the ruins of his predominant passion, that it seemed to be natural to him. Do I know, after the example of this great Saint, how to substitute for my own inclinations those of my Divine Saviour, which every Christian ought to imitate? The meekness of St. Francis of Sales was the powerful weapon with which he victoriously overcame the prejudices of heretics and the obduracy of sinners. If this precious virtue were to shine forth equally in my conduct, how much good should I not be able to do for the glory of God and the salvation of souls! With what zeal ought I not to ask for it from the Sacred Heart of Jesus, its divine Source! With what confidence should I not have recourse to the gentle St. Francis in order to obtain it more surely, since he has left me so bright an example of trust in God!

2nd Point. The holy energy of St. Francis of Sales.

If this great Saint, on whose example I am now meditating, was distinguished for his unalterable meekness, he was not the less remarkable for his courage and holy generosity of soul: he raised himself by this means above himself, and succeeded in subduing nature, and in mastering his natural inclinations; this it was which enabled him to resist the pressing solicitations of his family, when they all tried to detain him in the world; and, later on, to make him give up the undertakings, so full of risk, in which his charity and zeal had engaged him; in short, this it was which made him ever equal to himself, and never untrue to himself, no matter what obstacles, contradictions, or injustices presented themselves to try his patience. If this courage, this supernatural strength, were found in my soul, should I be seen constantly breaking my good resolutions, yielding to inconstancy in my conduct, giving way under the smallest difficulties, and gratifying my inclinations in all things? Oh! how necessary it is for me to ask the Holy Ghost for His divine aid—to lean on our Blessed Lord, and to labour seriously to triumph over my own weakness! Jesus Christ has said that "the kingdom of Heaven suffereth violence, and the violent only bear it away". I ought, in consequence, to engrave within my heart, and to take for the rule of my conduct, these words of the Holy Spirit —" Wisdom reacheth from end to end mightily, and ordereth all things sweetly" (Wisd. viii. 1).

Colloquy with the Sacred Heart of Jesus. Let us adore him as the Source of meekness and of all the virtues. Let us offer Him the merits of St. Francis of Sales, begging of Him, through the intercession of this great Saint, to grant us the spirit of meekness and generosity; so that, labouring to overcome ourselves, and surmounting all obstacles, we may work efficaciously in gaining souls for His glory.

Resolutions. To practise meekness and forbearance towards others. To combat courageously my predominant fault.

Offering of the Resolutions, page 3.

Spiritual Bouquet. "Jesus, meek and humble of heart, make my heart like unto Thine." "I can do all things in Him that strengtheneth me."

Prayer. Soul of Christ, etc.

Examen of the Meditation, page 4.

MEDITATION FOR THE FEAST OF THE MARTYRS OF JAPAN.

(5TH FEBRUARY.)

"Give and it shall be given unto you" (Luke vi. 38).

Preparatory Prayer, page 1.

1st Prelude. Represent to yourself the holy Martyrs

of Japan, some fastened to crosses, waiting to be pierced through with a lance; others tied to stakes for the purpose of being burnt alive; and see the Angels of God holding over their heads glorious palms and brilliant crowns.

2nd Prelude. Grant me grace, O Lord, to understand with what liberality Thou dost recompense those generous souls who sacrifice themselves for Thy glory.

1st Point. The generosity of the martyrs towards God condemns my cowardice in His service.

In all ages the Church has offered to God faithful children of hers, who have preferred to lose their life in the midst of the most cruel tortures rather than commit sin. Three centuries have scarcely elapsed since the glorious triumph of these holy Martyrs, proposed to-day to our veneration and homage. God Almighty wishes to teach me, by their example, that the power of His grace has not grown less; that now, as in the early ages of the Church, He knows how to raise up those who are faithful to Him, despite their own weakness, and render them like unto the first heroes of the faith. What effects does this victorious grace work within me? What sacrifices, what labours has it not enabled me to embrace in the service of my Divine Lord? He does not ask of me to die in torments, but He orders me to quit myself, and to follow Him in the holy paths leading to Calvary. With what courage and fidelity do I practise this necessary daily immolation?

2nd Point. The strength and spiritual joy with which God has ever filled the souls of His Martyrs, teach me that He always rewards a hundred-fold those who make sacrifices for His sake.

If the divine strength which sustained the Martyrs of the primitive Church is still the same to-day, and if the spiritual delights with which our Lord filled these champions of the faith have lost nothing of their sweetness and charms, the Martyrs of Japan offer me a new proof of this truth: " How sweet it is," said one of them, "to suffer for Jesus Christ! I cannot find words strong enough to express all that I feel. I begin to be a disciple of Jesus Christ, because I am suffering for love of Him." How great an enemy I am, therefore, to myself, when, for want of labouring to overcome myself, I deprive myself of heavenly consolations, of the lights and the helps that God never fails to grant to courageous and fervent souls! Can the vain satisfactions of nature, which I seek at the cost of my duty, ever be compared to those pure joys of divine love which are, as it were, the foretastes of heavenly joy? Adorable Heart of Jesus, support my weakness; help and strengthen me that so I may refuse nothing to the inward drawing of Thy grace.

Colloquy with our Lord. Let us adore Him as the author of grace. Let us offer Him the merits of the Martyrs of Japan, begging Him, through their intercession, to give us strength to overcome ourselves for His love.

Resolutions. To overcome myself generously in whatsoever costs me the most.

Offering of the Resolutions, page 3.

Spiritual Bouquet. Jesus, the Strength of Martyrs, have mercy on me!

Prayer. Soul of Christ, etc.

Examen of the Meditation, page 4.

MEDITATION FOR THE FEAST OF ST. MATTHIAS.
(24TH FEBRUARY.)

"Walk worthy of the vocation in which you are called" (Ephes. iv. 1).

Preparatory Prayer, page 1.

1st Prelude. Be present in spirit in the Upper Room, and see the Apostles and disciples proceeding to the election of St. Matthias.

2nd Prelude. Grant me grace, O God, to fulfil worthily my sublime vocation of being a member of the Church.

1st Point. St. Matthias is substituted for Judas.

Judas, chosen by God to be an Apostle, is lost through his crimes: St. Matthias is chosen in his place. This conduct of Providence teaches me that God, by a just judgment, withdraws His gifts from the ungrateful who abuse them, and transfers the gifts to others more faithful. I ought, consequently, to tremble on account of the graces I have received; the more numerous and signal they are, the more I ought to fear losing them; my vigilance ought to be unceasing, and my generosity ought never to relax: for the smallest faults, if neglected, may lead by degrees to very great falls. The first faults which avarice caused Judas to commit were inconsiderable, but they prepared the way for him to fall into greater sins, and he ended by betraying and selling his Divine Master. With what saving fear ought not such an example to penetrate me, whose frailty is so great, and who every day have such sad experience of my own weakness and dangerous inclinations.

2nd Point. We ought to prepare ourselves with great fidelity for the designs of Providence, as His ways are hidden from us.

God does not owe His graces to any one, and the distribution He makes of them depends absolutely on His sovereign will. Yet, according to the ordinary course of His adorable Providence, His choicest favours are the portion of souls careful to please Him, and to put to profit His gifts! One hundred and twenty disciples are assembled in the Upper Room: two only are proposed to fill up the place of the apostate Apostle, and our Lord Himself marked out, by casting lots, the one He had made choice of. All souls are not called to the same degree of perfection: the designs of God are different with reference to each individual; but these designs are concealed from us, and humble faithfulness often prepares some one who knows it not for the most sublime and important functions. I ought then, for the glory of God and my own salvation, not to fix any limits to my fervour and fidelity. How do I know whether God may not have attached to the fervour of my prayers, the power of my words, or to the edification I am bound to give, the conversion and salvation of a great number of souls?

Colloquy with our Lord. Let us thank Him with heartfelt gratitude for our vocation to the true faith. Let us implore Him, through the intercession of St. Matthias, to grant us the grace to be ever fervent in His service, and zealous for His glory, that so we may place no obstacle to the accomplishment of His designs over us.

Resolutions. To avoid carefully the smallest faults. To fulfil with exactness the very least of my duties.

Offering of the Resolutions, page 3.

Spiritual Bouquet. "He that neglects small faults shall fall by little and little."

Prayer. Soul of Christ, etc.

Examen of the Meditation, page 4.

FIRST MEDITATION FOR THE FEAST OF ST. JOSEPH.

(19TH MARCH.)

"He shall be like a tree which is planted near the running waters, which shall bring forth its fruits in due season" (Ps. i. 3).

Preparatory Prayer, page 1.

1st Prelude. Represent to yourself St. Joseph engaged in prayer or at work, and contemplate God considering with delight from the highest heavens this just man whose heart is so perfectly pure.

2nd Prelude. Great St. Joseph, who hast ever been so docile to the guidance of the Holy Spirit and to all the inspirations of grace, obtain for me that being faithful, as thou ever wert to God, I may accomplish all His designs over me.

1st Point. The greatness of God's Providence over St. Joseph.

Our good God, Who never places any human being on the earth without some special design, had destined St. Joseph for the most sublime and important functions. He was to be the Spouse of Mary, the guardian of her purity, her consoler and her aid under the difficult circumstances through which this holy Virgin had to pass; further, he was destined to conceal from men and from the devil the knowledge of the great mystery of the Incarnation of the Word; to watch over the infancy of the Son of God; and to minister to Him as a Father. Such charges demanded great virtues: St. Joseph well knew how to practise them, and ever showed himself worthy of the choice Heaven had made of him. Have I, since my entrance into the world, corresponded like St. Joseph with the graces which my God has lavished on me? Since my reason has been more fully developed, and the light of grace has become stronger, enabling me to know my duties better, have I at least been faithful to repair the time lost, and to fulfil the will of God as it has been manifested to me? . . . What ought I to think of myself; but, above all, what resolutions ought I to make for the future?

2nd Point. The perfect fidelity of St. Joseph in fulfilling the designs of God over him.

St. Joseph was ignorant of the sublime dignity to which grace was one day to raise him; he was far from suspecting the singular favours which God destined for him; but docile to all the inspirations of grace, he had, from the first, habituated himself to the practice of every virtue, and when God's appointed time came it found him ready for the accomplishment of His designs. My fidelity has not been attended with the promptitude the constancy and perfection of that of this great Saint; and this ought to be for me the subject of bitter grief; but now I still can and ought to prepare myself for the designs of God. I do not know for what employments He may destine me, or what interests He wishes to confide to me. I do not know with what persons or in what offices I can glorify Him the most. But these things He knows, and if I am docile to His interior guidance, He will dispose of me Himself for the accomplishment of His holy will. How necessary it is for me to do with entire fidelity all that grace shall inspire me to do, and to labour earnestly to acquire every Christian virtue!

Colloquy with St. Joseph. Let us congratulate him on the greatness of God's designs over him, and on his fidelity in corresponding with them. Let us ask him to obtain for us the pardon of our negligence in the service of God, and the grace to accomplish in future His adorable will in all things.

Resolutions. To follow faithfully all the inspirations of grace. To be punctual in the fulfilment of the smallest duties.

Offering of the Resolutions, page 3.

Spiritual Bouquet. "St. Joseph, who wast so docile to the guidance of the Holy Spirit, and to all the inspirations of grace, pray for me!"

Prayer. I beseech thee, O glorious St. Joseph, by the Heart of a Father which God gave thee for His Son, and by the Heart of a Son which Jesus had for thee, to take a special interest in the sanctification of my soul. Be thou my guide, my father, and my model in the spiritual life and in the way of perfection, that so, walking in thy footsteps, I may attain the happiness of the blessed, through the same Jesus Christ our Lord. Amen.

Examen of the Meditation, page 4.

SECOND MEDITATION.

(FOR THE SAME DAY.)

" The just man liveth by faith " (Heb. x. 38).

Preparatory Prayer, page 1.

1st Prelude. Imagine to yourself the house at Nazareth where St. Joseph rejoiced habitually in the presence of Jesus and Mary.

2nd Prelude. Great Saint, whose life was full of merit before God, obtain for me the grace to render all my actions meritorious, by a spirit of lively faith and of ardent love.

1st Point. St. Joseph is the perfect model of the interior life.

St. Joseph offers me the model of those interior and solid virtues which are the groundwork of all true perfection. Penetrated with the most lively faith and the most ardent charity, he proposed in his actions only the most holy and exalted intentions, carefully and constantly studying the law of God, in order to conform himself to it ever more and more. Continually attentive to the interior inspirations of the Holy Ghost, in order to follow them with perfect fidelity, he made the will of God his daily bread. Filled with contempt for himself, and entirely dead to the inclinations of corrupt nature, he proposed to himself holy and pure motives; in everything he acquitted himself of his least obligations with such loving care and ardent zeal, that all his actions were of a value and merit before God, infinitely surpassing anything I can conceive. I ought to serve God in the same manner, if I wish to acquire a true interior spirit, that spirit of faith and of love, of mortification, of humility, of fidelity and of zeal, which is the basis of all true Christianity, and which should be the soul of all my actions.

2nd Point. It was in the Sacred Hearts of Jesus

and Mary that St. Joseph had imbibed all the virtues which he practised with such perfection. In order to acquire the interior spirit of which St. Joseph is the perfect model, I ought, after his example, to seek it in the Sacred Hearts of Jesus and Mary. It was in these heavenly books that he studied the grand science of the spiritual life; it was from them that he learned to despise himself, to love God, and to be moved only by the interests of His glory; it was in their school he trained himself to the spirit of recollection and prayer; that he acquired the habit of such close union with God that no exterior occupation was able to distract his mind. Above all, it was from them he learnt the practice of that pure love, and of that complete simplicity of intention which looks towards God alone, and rejects all thought of self-interest : all merely natural motive, and all double intention. It is from these same sources that I ought to seek my own sanctification. Are not the Sacred Hearts of my Saviour and of His most Blessed Mother the inexhaustible treasures of light, of strength, and of sanctity? O great St. Joseph! the friend, protector, and faithful guide of those who tend to perfection, obtain for me from these Sacred Hearts those motives of interior grace, those pure lights and powerful helps which are needed to lead me to the perfection to which I am called.

Colloquy with Jesus, Mary, and Joseph. Let us ask of them the grace to form ourselves after their examples to all interior and solid virtues.

Resolutions. To practise purity of intention, recollection, and fidelity to grace.

Offering of the Resolutions, page 3.

Spiritual Bouquet. "Jesus, Mary, and Joseph, make my heart like unto your hearts."

Prayer. I beseech thee, O glorious Saint, etc.

Examen of the Meditation, page 4.

THIRD MEDITATION.

(FOR THE SAME DAY.)

" Precious in the sight of God is the death of His Saints " (Ps. cxv. 15).

Preparatory Prayer, page 1.

1st Prelude. Represent to yourself St. Joseph on his deathbed ; Jesus and Mary are on either side of him ; the Angels are waiting for his soul to bear it to the place of rest.

2nd Prelude. Great Saint, who didst have the happiness to live with Jesus and Mary, and to die in their arms, deign to watch over me during my earthly pilgrimage, and to assist me in that awful hour which is to decide my eternal lot.

1st Point. The virtues which St. Joseph practised at the hour of death.

The moment is at length arrived when our Lord is going to withdraw from this world the wise and faithful servant to whom he had confided such dear and precious interests. St. Joseph is about to quit the world ; his strength, gradually wasted by sickness, is about to leave him altogether. With love and confidence he sees his last hour approach, but more than one sacrifice demands at this hour all the generosity of his great soul. St. Joseph has known Jesus, he has tasted the sweetness of His holy love, and now is to be separated from Him by death. Heaven, which could not be opened until after the Passion of our Divine Redeemer, will be closed against St. Joseph, and for several years this holy Patriarch, whose love is so ardent and longing so vehement, must go and await Him in Limbo. He is not ignorant of this, but his perfect submission to the will of God makes him accept willingly this severe trial ; he is about to die, as he has lived, like a faithful servant, who regards not his own interests whenever there is question of the will of his Master. O my holy protector! obtain for me the grace to obey God with the same generosity and disinterestedness with which thou didst obey Him.

2nd Point. How holy and peaceful was the death of St. Joseph.

God, Who never allows Himself to be outdone by His creatures in generosity, favoured St. Joseph at the moment of his death with graces the more precious and abundant in proportion to the submission and love manifested towards Him by this great Saint. St. Joseph, full of confidence, and enjoying the most profound peace, died the death of the just, in the arms of Jesus and Mary. What a happy passing away! If I desire my death to be equally precious and tranquil, if I wish my Divine Saviour and His holy Mother to be present at my last moments, I must, after the example of St. Joseph, place no bounds to my generosity towards God, I must apply myself earnestly to self-detachment, and must unite myself closely to the Sacred Heart of Jesus by a conformity of sentiments, affections, and will. If during my life this holy union is the constant object of my efforts, God will grant me at the moment of my death the grace to give back my soul to Him, as St. Joseph did, with submission, love, confidence, and merit.

Colloquy with St. Joseph. Let us congratulate him on his happy passage. Let us implore of him to obtain for us the grace of a holy death, assisted in that awful moment by Jesus and Mary, that so we may give back our soul to God with all the dispositions which we shall need to render that last sacrifice most perfect and most meritorious.

Resolutions. To animate all my actions with great purity of intention, and to perform them in union with the Sacred Heart of Jesus, in order to prepare myself for a holy death.

Offering of the Resolutions, page 3.

Spiritual Bouquet. "Jesus, Mary, and Joseph, help me, now and at the hour of my death."
Prayer. I beseech thee, O glorious Saint, etc.
Examen of the Meditation, page 4.

MEDITATION FOR THE FEAST OF THE PATRONAGE OF ST. JOSEPH.

(Third Sunday after Easter.)

"Go to Joseph" (Gen. xli. 55).

Preparatory Prayer, page 1.

1st Prelude. Imagine to yourself St. Joseph in Heaven, surrounded with glory, and looking down kindly on those who are praying to him.

2nd Prelude. Great Saint, who art all-powerful with the Hearts of Jesus and Mary, obtain for me all the help I need to become pleasing to them, that I may deserve to contemplate them one day in Heaven.

1st Point. St. Joseph is all-powerful with God.

The power which St. Joseph now enjoys in glory is proportionate to the eminence of the virtues which he practised while he was on earth, and to the intimacy of his communications with the Son of God during his life. How could Jesus refuse anything to a Saint who for thirty years cared for Him as a father, and felt towards Him the tenderness of one? to a Saint who watched so assiduously over His infancy, and who practised in its perfection every virtue most dear to Him? How could Mary—that powerful Queen of Heaven and Mother of Mercy, in whose hands the Author of grace placed all His treasures—how could Mary refuse to share her power with him to whom her lot was so long united, and who on every occasion lavished on her with such pure affection all the consolations and helps which she needed? Yes, it cannot be doubted, the suffrages of St. Joseph have an irresistible power in heaven, and those who trust themselves to his protection are always certain to be benefited.

2nd Point. St. Joseph is full of kindness towards all those who invoke him.

If the power of St. Joseph is calculated to inspire me with a holy respect, his tender charity for those who address themselves to him ought to penetrate my soul with the sweetest confidence. His heart, so perfectly in harmony with the Hearts of Jesus and Mary, takes the most lively interest in the wants of all mankind, but above all in those who have recourse to him and implore his help. He loves to obtain the most precious graces for them, to initiate them into the secrets of the interior life, to form them to the great art of prayer, to become their director in the acquisition of all virtues. His zeal for the glory of God makes him desire ardently that every one should serve Him fervently, and when he finds some one full of good-will, who desires earnestly to be delivered from sinfulness and enriched with the treasures of grace, words cannot describe with what eagerness he becomes a father and protector of that person. I am certain of the help of this great Saint, who is so powerful and so good, if I ask him for it with faith; more certain still I am that if I obtain his paternal aid, the means of sanctification and the most signal favours of the Sacred Heart of Jesus will be granted me in profusion. What can I do better than to place myself to-day under his special protection, and abandon myself entirely to his guidance?

Colloquy with St. Joseph. Let us prostrate ourselves in spirit at his feet and pay him profound homage of respect, love, and confidence. Let us implore him to take particular care of our spiritual interests, and place ourselves in his hands that he may lead us himself to Jesus and to Mary.

Resolutions. To have recourse to St. Joseph in all my difficulties and temptations. To practise in his honour the spirit of recollection and of prayer.

Offering of the Resolutions, page 3.
Spiritual Bouquet. "St. Joseph, the guide, friend, and protector of souls who aspire to perfection, pray for me!"
Prayer. I beseech thee, O glorious Saint, etc.
Examen of the Meditation, page 4.

MEDITATION FOR THE FEAST OF ST. BENEDICT.

(21st March.)

"Behold, we have left all things and have followed Thee; what therefore shall we have?" (Matt. xix. 27).

Preparatory Prayer, page 1.
1st Prelude. Represent to yourself St. Benedict, standing before our Divine Lord, having round him the immense multitude of religious who had embraced his rule, and all intent upon the vision of God.
2nd Prelude. O glorious Saint, so admirable in thy own example, and so great a channel of sanctification to a multitude of souls, intercede for me that thy spirit may animate the practice of my life, so that my whole being may exist only to love God.
1st Point. " A man of venerable life, blessed by grace and by name."
Thus it was that Pope St. Gregory the Great styled St. Benedict. This illustrious patriarch of monks was throughout his whole life a pattern of innocence. He was blessed with the goods of this world, yet more blessed in hearing and following the inspirations of the Holy Ghost from his earliest years. In his childhood he despised the world and left it, to live with God his Creator. And God blessed him still more. He chose him to be the father of many nations of religious, and inspired him to write a rule full of heavenly wisdom and divine simplicity. He made him a source of

blessing to the world. Is the example of such a Saint nothing to me? I am taught that innocence is blessedness and the love of God is peace. Let me at once turn away from sin and detach my heart from the love of the world. How often, too, are even my innocent acts commenced and carried out with mere human eagerness! I must learn to await, as St. Benedict did, the voice of the Holy Spirit, and to purify my intention. But I must strive first to deserve the guidance of that Holy Spirit by adhering, like St. Benedict, to the commandments of God. This will make me blessed in the name of Christian, and blessed in God's loving grace.

2nd Point. " To him that looks upon the Creator every creature is very little."

So writes St. Gregory, commenting upon a wondrous vision which God accorded to St. Benedict, in which that chosen soul saw the whole world as in one ray of light. Such a vision is not for me, but I ought to learn the lesson which it teaches me. God is ever calling me to Him by His graces, but I am too often held back by my false view of creatures. Because I look upon them overmuch and go close to them by my desires, they seem great, and they hide God from me. The difficulties which I find in doing good affright me because my self-love magnifies them and shuts out the brightness of God's light, in which I might see how really trivial they are. How I ought to pray to God against the evil of my human conceit and sloth, and resolve to strive to live day by day in God's presence! This was the continual practice and teaching of St. Benedict, and fidelity to that teaching will obtain for me the solid reward of seeing all things in the light of God's interests. Let me sincerely put God first; then will the things of the world no longer be what they have too often seemed to be, but they will appear as they really are, nothing apart from God's holy will.

Colloquy with St. Benedict. Let us turn to St.

Benedict and beg him to intercede for us and obtain for us to imitate somewhat his simple generosity towards God, that the words of his holy rule may be fulfilled in us, "that as we continue in a well-ordered life with faith, we may run, with a generous heart and with unspeakable sweetness of love, in the way of God's commandments".

Resolutions. Sincerely to offer to God each morning every action of the day, and to practise more faithfully the frequent remembrance of the presence of God.

Offering of the Resolutions, page 3.

Spiritual Bouquet. "In all things may God be glorified." (Words from the Rule of St. Benedict.)

Prayer. Raise up, O Lord, in Thy Church the spirit wherewith St. Benedict the abbot was animated; that, filled with the same, we may study to love what he loved and to practise what he taught.

Examen of the Meditation, page 4.

MEDITATION FOR THE FEAST OF ST. MARK, EVANGELIST.

(25TH APRIL.)

"You shall lament and weep, and the world shall rejoice, but your sorrow shall be changed into joy" (John xvi. 20).

Preparatory Prayer, page 1.

1st Prelude. Represent to yourself St. Mark writing the Holy Gospel.

2nd Prelude. O great Saint, who wast chosen by our Lord to write and to announce His Gospel, obtain for me the grace to carry out in all my actions the sacred maxims of this most holy book.

1st Point. What are the motives which induce me to read and meditate on the Holy Gospel?

The feast of St. Mark naturally draws my thoughts to the Holy Gospel which he had the honour to write and to preach. The Gospel is the testament of Jesus Christ; it teaches me what the spiritual riches are to which my Divine Lord has given me the right to aspire, and on what conditions I may acquire them. Nothing is more fitted than the perusal of this sacred book to awaken my hopes, to raise my heart to my true country, to console me in my trials, and to animate me incessantly to the practice of virtue. The Gospel is like a letter written by my Divine Saviour's own hand, to make known to me His love; to instruct me in His will; to preserve for me the history of His labours and of His sufferings; and to place constantly before my eyes His divine example. How careful I ought to be to read and meditate on it frequently! Above all, with what fervour ought I not to apply myself to exemplify its holy maxims in my conduct!

2nd Point. What are the fruits which the reading and meditating on the Gospel ought to produce within me?

The reading of the Holy Gospel produces the happiest effects in souls well disposed: it frees them little by little from the delusions of the world, inspires them with a relish for spiritual things, and penetrates them with the Spirit of Jesus Christ. Such are the fruits which I ought to strive to gather from this precious study, I who have been prevented by the Sacred Heart of Jesus with so many graces, and have been chosen by preference from amongst so many others to know and imitate Him in a special manner. What, then, is this spirit of the Gospel, with which all our actions ought to be animated? It is a spirit of abnegation and of sacrifice: "If any one will come after Me," says Jesus Christ, "let him deny himself, take up his cross, and follow Me". It is a spirit of humility: "When you shall have done all that has been commanded you," says our Divine Lord again, "still say that you are unprofitable servants". It is a spirit of holy confidence and of noble intrepidity: "Fear not, little flock," our Lord says again; and adds elsewhere: "Have confidence, I have overcome the world". Lastly, it is a spirit of love : on one occasion alone Jesus returns five times to the precept of charity towards others. He recommends it as His special commandment, and points it out as the distinctive mark which should characterise His disciples. Universal mortification, profound humility, tender and sincere charity, are, then, the solid virtues which I ought to gather from the perusal of the Holy Gospel, if I desire to share in the magnificent promises which it contains.

Colloquy with St. Mark. Let us render him our homage of veneration. Let us ask him to obtain for us, from the Sacred Heart of Jesus, the true spirit of the Gospel, and all those virtues which should adorn the souls of His fervent followers.

Resolutions. To recall to my mind frequently during the day that God will judge me by the maxims of the Gospel.

Offering of the Resolutions, page 3.

Spiritual Bouquet. "My disciples are not of this world, as I also am not of this world."

Prayer. Soul of Christ, etc.

Examen of the Meditation, page 4.

MEDITATION FOR THE FEASTS OF SS. PHILIP AND JAMES.

(1st May.)

"Jesus went forth into Galilee, and He findeth Philip, and He saith to him, 'Follow Me'" (John i. 43).

Preparatory Prayer, page 1.

1st Prelude. Transport yourself in spirit to the place where Jesus called Philip to follow Him, or else to the marriage feast in Cana, where James and the other disciples were witnesses of Christ's first miracle, and began to believe in Him with a more firm and assured faith.

2nd Prelude. Holy Apostles, who both signalised yourselves by a great love for Jesus and by the practice of virtues so pleasing to Him, obtain for me also the grace to practise virtue for the glory of His Sacred Heart.

1st Point. The zeal of St. Philip to advance perseveringly in the knowledge and love of God.

St. Philip was engaged in the married state, but the obligations of that state, which he faithfully fulfilled, did not hinder him, according to the remark of St. Chrysostom, from meditating assiduously on the Law and the Prophets. He had by this means prepared himself to recognise the Messias in the person of Jesus Christ; consequently, he did not hesitate, after so precious a discovery, to leave all in order to attach himself to Him. Oh! what lights and graces does not constant fidelity in seeking our Lord prepare for some important crisis, and how careful I ought to be to make persevering progress in the knowledge of God and in His holy law! This zeal of St. Philip to instruct himself concerning the great work of salvation increased more and more on following the Son of God. As a consequence of this good disposition, on the night of the Last Supper when Jesus promised His disciples to give them a clear knowledge of His heavenly Father, St. Philip exclaimed, in a transport of holy impatience: " Lord, show us the Father, and that is sufficient ". Now he beholds, in the abode of the elect, that thrice holy Father, Whom he served so faithfully on earth; the ardent love he had for his God, the desire of heavenly things which consumed him during life, are now fully satisfied; and my Divine Saviour, in urging me to walk in the footsteps of this holy Apostle, repeats to me interiorly the living truth, verified in the person of St. Philip: " Blessed are they that hunger and thirst after justice, for they shall be filled ".

2nd Point. The purity of St. James and his love for Jesus.

If the example of St. Philip ought to lead me to the love of our Lord, and to the desire of heavenly things, that of St. James does not teach me lessons of less importance. Spotless purity; constant mortification; an exact observance of the law, which merited for him the appellation of the *just man;* but above all, an inviolable fidelity to the faith of Jesus Christ, and an ardent zeal for His glory, were virtues which could not fail to merit for him the love of his Divine Master; and such are the means I ought to employ in order to become a worthy disciple of the Sacred Heart. A life so holy was crowned by a glorious martyrdom: St. James, after having preached Jesus Christ, had the happiness of giving testimony of Him at the price of his blood. So precious a means of glorifying our Divine Lord is not offered me; but if I am perfectly faithful to the graces with which He never ceases to enrich me, I shall still glorify His Sacred Heart in a very excellent manner. His love, destroying my bad inclinations and self-will, causes me to suffer that interior death of which the Apostle speaks when he says: "You are dead, and your life is hid with Jesus Christ in God".

Colloquy with SS. Philip and James. Let us congratulate them on the choice our Lord made of them, and on their fidelity to the grace of their vocation. Let us pray them to obtain for us from the Sacred Heart of Jesus all the helps of which we shall stand in need in order to accomplish faithfully the designs of God upon us.

Resolutions. To renounce myself in all things, in order that the reign of divine love may be established within me.

Offering of the Resolutions, page 3.

Spiritual Bouquet. " Blessed are they that hunger and thirst after justice, for they shall be filled."

Prayer. Receive, O Lord, etc., page 18.

Examen of the Meditation, page 4.

MEDITATION FOR THE FEAST OF THE FINDING OF THE CROSS.

(3RD MAY.)

" With Thee is the principality in the day of Thy strength " (Ps. cix. 3).

Preparatory Prayer, page 1.

1st Prelude. Imagine to yourself the Cross of Jesus Christ in Heaven, resplendent with glory, and behold the Angels and Saints prostrate before it.

2nd Prelude. Adorable Conqueror, Who by the power of Thy Cross didst bring the entire world under Thy loving rule, reign for ever in my heart, and grant that I may place all my glory in despising the vain judgments of the world.

1st Point. The Cross of Jesus Christ has triumphed over the false wisdom of the world, the power of tyrants, and the dominion of human passions.

How sweet it is, and how consoling, for a true Christian to meditate on the triumphs of the Cross! The whole universe was plunged in darkness, human passions triumphed everywhere, and the demon received divine honours. Twelve poor fishermen proclaim the word of salvation in the midst of these misguided nations: they glory in possessing no other science than that of Jesus crucified. It is the Cross that they present to those who wish to return to God, as the token of reconciliation between heaven and earth. In order to fasten themselves to it, these peoples, brought up in the superstitions of paganism, must submit and humble their spirit to the yoke of faith; they must renounce the prejudices of their birth; must sacrifice their cherished passions; and must expose themselves to the rage of their persecutors. No matter, nothing stops them: the Cross has penetrated their hearts with its secret virtue; they fall down before it and desire no other glory but its ignominy; no other riches than its poverty; no other joys than its rigours. Who can fail to recognise by such wonders the effect of that promise of Jesus Christ: "When I shall be lifted up from the earth I will draw all hearts after Me"? O my Saviour, what joy for my heart to recall to my mind those triumphs which have been so glorious for Thee! Oh! deign to renew them; grant that sinners, and the impious who blaspheme Thee and know Thee not, may experience the power of Thy Divine Cross! Give me also to experience this power, and may my ardour to attach myself to it in company with Thee equal, if possible, that of the first heroes of religion.

2nd Point. The Cross is an inexhaustible source of strength for those who attach themselves to it.

The early triumphal days of the Church are, in part, past and gone; the loving mother of the faithful has no longer the consolation she had formerly, of counting so many Saints amongst her children. Yet the virtue of the Cross has not diminished, and in every age those who have embraced it with courage have experienced the effects of its power. It is the Cross which has sanctified the Anchorets in the desert, the Virgins in the cloisters, the ministers of the Gospel in the midst of their Apostolic labours, and all the Saints in the different positions in which Providence had placed them. I also must cling to the Cross, if I wish to become a Saint. I must cling to it lovingly, since my Divine Saviour chose it for His portion, and presents it to me as a pledge of His love. I must cling to it with courage, since Jesus Himself is my strength and will never abandon me, so long as I shall confide in Him. I must adhere to it in peace and consolation, since its apparent rigours change into joys for those who love Jesus, and become for them a certain pledge of eternal happiness.

Colloquy with our Lord. Let us render Him our homage of adoration and love. Let us thank Him for having saved and converted the world by the power of His Cross. Let us ask Him to fill us with strength and courage, that so, adhering to this holy Cross, we may acquire perfect conformity to and close union with His Sacred Heart.

Resolutions. To sacrifice all the inclinations of nature in order to unite myself to Jesus crucified.

Offering of the Resolutions, page 3.

Spiritual Bouquet. "When I shall be lifted up from the earth I will draw all things to Myself." Lord, draw me as Thou hast promised!

Prayer. Soul of Christ, etc.

Examen of the Meditation, page 4.

MEDITATION FOR THE FEAST OF THE APPARITION OF ST. MICHAEL.

(8TH MAY.)

"At that time shall Michael rise up, the great prince, who standeth for the children of Thy people" (Dan. xii. 1).

Preparatory Prayer, page 1.

1st Prelude. Picture to yourself St. Michael in Heaven crowned with glory and standing continually before the throne of God ready to execute His orders.

2nd Prelude. Holy Archangel, who art the protector of the Church and the guardian of all the faithful, vouchsafe to inspire me with a firm confidence in thee, so that aided by thee I may overcome the enemies of my salvation.

1st Point. St. Michael is the protector of the whole Church.

St. Michael, the prince of God's armies, has not ceased, since the beginning of the world, to protect in a special manner the true adorers of the Divine Majesty. He it was, according to ancient belief, who led the Jewish people into the promised land, who brought them the law on the part of God, and who will even now work so many other prodigies in their favour. The Church attributes in great measure to the assistance of this powerful protector, the countless victories which she has gained over her different enemies. To him, then, I ought to address my prayers, when, grieved at the prolonged afflictions of our holy Mother the Church, and saddened at the ravages hell ceases not to make among her children, I entreat our Lord to put a stop to them. St. Michael, full of zeal for the reign of Jesus Christ and for the salvation of souls, whom our Divine Redeemer has ransomed with His Blood, desires nothing more than to be the bearer of such supplications before God. In consequence, nothing that I can do to-day will honour him better or please him more, than to recommend to his tender charity the interests of the Church, together with the wants of sinners and my own necessities.

2nd Point. St. Michael is the protector of each one of the faithful.

St. Michael is not only the defender of the whole Church; he also offers his protection to each faithful soul. He is looking at me at the present moment with kindness, and is ready to listen to my supplications. Oh! how much I need his aid, and how earnestly I ought to ask him for it! I am surrounded by enemies whose number, malice, and cunning would leave me no resource, if the Almighty had not placed limits to their power against me, and had not given me His holy Angels, and above all the glorious St. Michael, as a pillar of strength whom they dread and who unmasks their hellish projects. With what gratitude, love, and unbounded confidence ought I not to have recourse to such powerful protection! How careful ought I not to be to ensure such help, not only during the course of my life, but above all at the hour of death! It is more than ever in this last combat that I shall need the assistance of the holy Archangel whom I am honouring to-day ; it is then that he will cover me with his protecting shield, will strengthen and sustain my soul, and after rendering it a thousand charitable services, will himself present me before the tribunal of God that I may find grace in His eyes. What motives are not these for tender love and lively confidence!

Colloquy with St. Michael. Let us pay him our homage of love, veneration, and gratitude. Let us beg of him to defend us against the attacks of the wicked spirits, to discover to us their snares, and to help us to escape them. Let us recommend to him in a special manner the hour of our death and the last hour of all those who are dear to us.

Resolutions. To invoke St. Michael with great confidence, above all in time of temptation. To recommend to him the wants of the Church.

Offering of the Resolutions, page 3.

Spiritual Bouquet. St. Michael, zealous protector of the children of God, pray for me now and at the hour of my death.

Prayer. Glorious St. Michael, prince of the heavenly hosts and protector of the Universal Church, defend me against my enemies, visible and invisible, and never permit me to fall under their cruel tyranny. Amen.

Examen of the Meditation, page 4.

MEDITATION FOR THE FEAST OF ST. BARNABAS.

(11TH JUNE.)

"If thou wilt be perfect, go sell what thou hast and give to the poor, then come and follow Me" (Matt. xix. 21).

Preparatory Prayer, page 1.

1st Prelude. Represent to yourself the vast countries into which St. Barnabas carried the light of the Gospel.

CONTEMPLATIONS AND MEDITATIONS. 135

2nd Prelude. Holy Apostle of the Gentiles, who, by thy entire detachment from the things of this world, didst deserve to become an instrument of the divine mercy, obtain for me the grace to despise the false goods of this world, and to labour zealously for the salvation of others.

1st Point. Detachment from all things created, prepared St. Barnabas to accomplish the designs of God.

St. Barnabas was possessed of great wealth, but, illuminated by a supernatural light, he understood that the treasure of evangelical poverty was to be preferred before all things, and following the counsel of Jesus Christ, he dispossessed himself of all his goods in favour of the poor. It cannot be doubted but that this spirit of detachment contributed powerfully to draw down on him the abundant graces which made him a great Saint. Probably also many souls that he would not have gained for Heaven had he been no more than an ordinary preacher, were bought at the price paid by his disinterestedness and generosity towards God. How important it is then for me not to attach my heart to false goods, when to sacrifice them ensures so many claims on the Sacred Heart of our Blessed Lord! If His grace does not demand of me the actual sacrifice of my property, such as it is, I ought at least to detach my heart from all that belongs to me, using all as if I used it not, and I ought to be ever ready to give all back to Him from Whom I have received all. This disposition alone can draw on me His divine blessing, and render me fit to accomplish the works in which His adorable Providence may wish to employ me.

2nd Point. Fidelity to grace and zeal for the salvation of souls rendered St. Barnabas fit to accomplish all the designs God had upon him.

Docile from childhood to the inspirations of grace, and constantly faithful to the practice of every virtue as soon as the Holy Spirit enlightened him about it, St. Barnabas was chosen by God to carry the knowledge of the Gospel to the heathens, and he acquitted himself of this sublime task with all the zeal and care of a faithful servant. It is in imitating him, as far as shall be possible to my weakness, in corresponding with all the interior inspirations of grace, and in conforming myself willingly to every arrangement of Divine Providence, that I shall become, in my turn, an instrument of mercy in the hands of God. Without doubt the good that I can do is very small, or rather, it is absolutely nothing, if compared to the labours of the great Saint whose example is brought before me to-day; yet faith teaches me that prayer, good example, good advice given in due season, together with a hundred other means I have at my disposal, may procure the salvation of many souls. What a subject of reflection to encourage me!

Colloquy with St. Barnabas. Let us pay him our homage of veneration and congratulate him on the virtues which he practised and on the glory in which he now rejoices. Let us beg of him to obtain for us complete detachment from all that savours of sin, entire fidelity to the inspirations of the Holy Spirit, and ardent zeal for the salvation of souls.

Resolutions. To put to profit any opportunities that shall be offered me to-day of practising detachment and zeal for souls.

Offering of the Resolutions, page 3.

Spiritual Bouquet. "Our Father Who art in Heaven . . . Thy kingdom come. . . ."

Prayer. Pater Noster, etc.

Examen of the Meditation, page 4.

MEDITATION FOR THE FEAST OF ST. FRANCIS REGIS.

(16TH JUNE.)

"The zeal of Thy house hath eaten me up" (Ps. lxviii. 10).

Preparatory Prayer, page 1.

1st Prelude. Represent to yourself St. Francis Regis at the foot of the altar, where he loved to pour forth his soul in the presence of Jesus Christ; or in the midst of the poor, announcing to them the Word of God.

2nd Prelude. Great Saint, who didst join to the most tender love for Jesus the most ardent zeal for the salvation of souls redeemed by His Blood, obtain for me the grace to imitate thee in the practice of these two virtues.

1st Point. The love of St. Francis Regis for Jesus Christ.

The fervour of divine love, as the holy Bishop of Geneva has remarked, is to the other virtues what perfume is to flowers, and what brilliancy is to precious stones. All the Saints understood this well, and hence arose their constant efforts to reanimate this sacred fire continually within them. This much to be desired fervour always distinguished the Saint whose feast the Church celebrates to-day. It was from his love for Jesus Christ that all his other virtues derived their strength and beauty; his labours had for their only end to procure the glory of our Divine Redeemer, and it was at the feet of Christ that he went to gain new strength to work in His service. How delightful were the communications with which our Blessed Lord honoured him! How short the nights appeared that he spent at the foot of the Tabernacle, where dwelt the Beloved of his heart! Ah! if my soul, like his, was perfectly pure and detached from self, I should also experience that there is no true joy but in the love of Jesus Christ. Then only should I appreciate as fully as they deserve those graces by which He has so often invited me to conform myself to Him and unite myself closely to His loving Heart.

2nd Point. The zeal of St. Francis Regis for the salvation of souls.

It is impossible for a heart which loves Jesus Christ not to take a lively interest in the salvation of souls redeemed by His death : in consequence, the most pure and ardent zeal was the distinctive characteristic of St. Francis Regis. Those who have written his life say that nothing was capable of discouraging him when there was question of snatching a soul from hell; labours, dangers, prolonged fatigue, accidents, sicknesses, even persecution itself,—all these he bore courageously, that he might hasten to the help of the sheep gone astray, and bring them back to the fold. I am not destined, in the way this great Saint was, to labour for the salvation of souls, yet this same Jesus, for Whose glory he worked, is also my Saviour, and my only Good. Ah! if my heart cannot be consumed with zeal as his was, ought it not at least to contain some sparks of the same divine fire? And if I cannot aspire to the more important labours of the apostolic ministry, ought I not at least to seize with eagerness the numberless opportunities which offer themselves to make the Sacred Heart of my Divine Saviour known and loved?

Colloquy with the Sacred Heart of Jesus. Let us offer Jesus the virtues of St. Francis Regis, and above all his ardent love. Let us implore Him, through the intercession of this great Saint, to fill us with his spirit of fervour, and give us grace to labour efficaciously for His glory.

Resolutions. To offer up all my prayers and all my actions to the Sacred Heart of Jesus, for His glory and the salvation of souls.

CONTEMPLATIONS AND MEDITATIONS. 139

Offering of the Resolutions, page 3.
Spiritual Bouquet. " I came to cast fire upon the earth, and what do I desire but that it be enkindled ?"
Prayer. Soul of Christ, etc.
Examen of the Meditation, page 4.

MEDITATION FOR THE FEAST OF ST. ALOYSIUS.

(21ST JUNE.)

" Thou hast prevented him with blessings of sweetness: Thou hast set on his head a crown of precious stones " (Ps. xx. 4).

Preparatory Prayer, page 1.
1st Prelude. Represent to yourself St. Aloysius, either at the Court, where he already led the life of an angel ; or in religion, where his virtues shone forth with still greater lustre ; or in Heaven, where he is now enjoying immense glory.
2nd Prelude. Great Saint, obtain for me the grace to honour thee worthily, and through thee to glorify the Lord God, the Author of thy sanctity.
. *1st Point.* St. Aloysius merits my homage on account of the great virtues he practised while on earth.
If it be true, as St. Cyprian says, that a pure soul is a living image of the holiness of God ; if the other Christian virtues, carried to a certain degree of perfection, cause Jesus Christ, in some sort, Himself to live anew in His most faithful imitators, what ought I to think of the amiable Saint the Church honours to-day ? He was so pure, that after his death the title of the Angelical Youth was unanimously given to him. His heart was like a beautiful lily, in which our Lord loved to repose ; never did the least stain tarnish for a single instant the spotless purity of his soul. The other virtues dear to the Sacred Heart did not shine forth less conspicuously in Aloysius. What a holy

hatred of himself! What a spirit of penance and mortification! What profound humility! What perfect obedience! What ardent love for his God! What tender charity! What devotedness to the service of others! In short, what a faithful copy of the adorable Model on Whom all the Saints of Jesus, their Lord and Master, are formed! Surely we are honouring our Divine Lord Himself when we offer our homage to a Saint raised by His grace to so perfect a degree of conformity and union with Him?

2nd Point. St. Aloysius merits my homage on account of the high degree of glory he now enjoys in Heaven.

Even during this mortal life, our Lord shows Himself admirable in His saints; but it is, above all, in Heaven that He displays all the riches of His power and goodness in their regard. In this life, however holy they may become, the frailties of human nature give them ever reason to sigh after a more perfect state; but in the abode of the blessed the gifts of God shine forth in them without shadow or cloud; and it is, above all, in this state of glory that they are perfectly worthy of our veneration. How ardently may I not, then, offer my homage on this day to the young Saint whose feast the Church is celebrating! To honour him, to love him, and invoke him is to enter into the designs of God, Who, in order to animate our piety and confidence, has revealed to us, by the lips of a great Saint, something of the glory with which his merits have been crowned. Yes; I cannot doubt of his credit with Jesus, or of his power over the Sacred Heart. I can no longer doubt of his goodness towards me, who, during his life, was so full of zeal for the salvation of souls! So many times has he listened to the requests made to him, even for temporal favours! What will he not, then, do for one who solicits of him the grace to love God, to despise self, and acquire the virtues which he himself practised!

Colloquy with St. Aloysius. Let us pay him our homage of love and veneration. Let us pray to him earnestly to obtain for us the grace to please God by great purity of heart, by the ardour of our love for Him, and by fidelity in His holy service.

Resolutions. To offer all my prayers and actions to God to-day through St. Aloysius.

Offering of the Resolutions, page 3.

Spiritual Bouquet. "St. Aloysius, endowed with choicest blessings of God, pray for us."

Prayer. O God, Who, to arouse the fervour of our souls, didst propose to us, for a model of innocence and penance, the blessed Confessor Aloysius, who despised the pleasures and grandeur of this world, grant, through Thy goodness, that, having had recourse to his intercession, we may never find our condemnation in his example. Through Christ our Lord. Amen.

Examen of the Meditation, page 4.

SECOND MEDITATION.

(FOR THE SAME DAY.)

"He that loveth cleanness of heart, for the grace of his lips shall have the king for his friend" (Prov. xxii. 11).

Preparatory Prayer, page 1.

1st Prelude. Image to yourself St. Aloysius, only seven years of age, consecrating himself to God at the foot of the altar of the Blessed Virgin Mary.

2nd Prelude. Amiable Saint, whose heart was so pure and pleasing to God, obtain for me the grace to repair my lost innocence by penance and humility.

1st Point. The incomparable purity and innocence of St. Aloysius.

The most admirable privileges, the most signal graces, and the most perfect fidelity were united in St.

Aloysius, and these all gave to his innocence a lustre to which nothing can be compared. Called from his infancy to the knowledge of God, to a contempt for the world, and to the most perfect life, he offered to God, under the auspices of the Queen of Heaven, the sacrifice of his body, his mind, and his heart, that he might keep himself during his whole life in the most spotless purity. Yes! if we can offer nothing more pleasing to God than the first fruits of life, if these first fruits are like the first flowers of spring and the first rays of daylight, which gladden nature and restore to her all her beauty, how pleasing must this first offering of the young Aloysius have been to God! We may judge of this by the chosen favours with which it was rewarded, by that admirable privilege which exempted him from the smallest temptations contrary to purity, so that even the least bad thought never presented itself to his mind. What reflections should not the example of this young Saint present to my soul! I have not served God from my childhood as he had, and even from my earliest years I have abused the favours granted to enable me to preserve my innocence; yet the Divine Goodness has waited for me, and still showers on me the most precious favours. What a subject of gratitude! I have not kept without spot the once stainless robe of my baptism; I have committed sin; yet my soul must become again sufficiently pure to unite itself frequently to the Sacred Heart of Jesus through the Sacrament of His love. What a powerful incentive to excite myself to fervour and to the spirit of penance!

2nd Point. The innocence of St. Aloysius disposed him for the most intimate communications with God.

"My Beloved delights among the lilies," are the words of the sacred Canticle; in fact, it is matter of experience that the purest souls are those of whom the Almighty makes choice by preference for His most familiar communications. But among all innocent souls there are few who have had so large a share as St. Aloysius in the interior lights and inexpressible sweetnesses with which God delights to favour them. From the age in which other children scarcely know how to lisp a few vocal prayers, he possessed the rare gift of mental prayer. Later on, his union with God was so close and so constant, that, obliged by his superiors not to occupy his mind with this holy exercise, he struggled in vain against the spirit of God with which he was filled, and made more efforts to distract his mind from these heavenly communications than others have to make in order to keep their attention fixed upon them. This arose from the beauty and purity of his soul, which was like a magnet to our Lord, and constrained him to fix His dwelling within it. If I possessed the like innocence, I should unite myself to God in prayer as the Saints did, and I should share in the same favours and intimate communications. What can I think of my soul when I behold its sluggishness, its want of recollection, its insensibility towards God; in a word, all its miseries? . . .

Colloquy with St. Aloysius. Let us congratulate him on the happy privileges with which he was favoured. Let us pray to him to interest himself for us with the Queen of Virgins and with her Divine Son, that so, aided by grace, we may make good the innocence we have forfeited, and render ourselves worthy once again of the communications of the Sacred Heart of Jesus.

Resolutions. To practise recollection and watchfulness over myself.

Offering of the Resolutions, page 3.

Spiritual Bouquet. "My Beloved feedeth among the lilies."

Prayer (as before).

Examen of the Meditation, page 4.

THIRD MEDITATION.

(For the same Day.)

"They are not of this world, as I also am not of this world" (John xvii. 14).

Preparatory Prayer, page 1.

1st Prelude. Represent to yourself the humble cell which St. Aloysius, having become a religious, exchanged for the sumptuous palace of his family.

2nd Prelude. Loving Saint, who wast so completely undeceived as to the illusions of the world, obtain for me the grace never to let myself be seduced by the witchery of its trifles, but to attach myself to God alone, Who alone possesses all solid goods.

1st Point. The contempt of St. Aloysius for the pleasures, riches, and honours of this world.

Born in the bosom of affluence and pleasure, St. Aloysius could have enjoyed in peace all the advantages which the world so greatly prizes; but, enlightened from his tender years with a ray of heavenly light, he knew the emptiness, the uselessness and danger of worldly vanities, and evinced more anxiety to rid himself of their showy bondage than the vainest and most ambitious of men would ever have had to attain the utmost height of riches and honours. Why were his thoughts on this point so different from those of the children of the world? It was because he had learnt in the school of Jesus Christ what a Christian ought to think of those false goods which the Son of God Himself so greatly despised; it was because he had meditated and tasted these words of his Saviour and his God: "My disciples are not of this world, as I also am not of this world". Do I know how to value them as he did? O Jesus! my Saviour and only Lord! make the light of Thy grace shine into the very depths of my soul; teach me how to form a just judgment of all things; but above all grant that my heart being truly united to Thee alone, I may hate and despise, for Thy love, all that Thou hast judged worthy of Thy contempt and execration.

2nd Point. The esteem of St. Aloysius for the gifts of grace.

The same divine light which had disabused St. Aloysius of the illusions of the world had caused him to recognise the precious treasures hidden in humiliation, poverty, and suffering; so avaricious was he of the Cross, so desirous of exercising a holy ingenuity in sacrificing himself constantly for the God of his love by the practice of universal mortification. These generous efforts were abundantly recompensed. God, Who never allows Himself to be outdone in liberality by His creatures, poured into his soul such torrents of sweet consolations, pure lights, and familiar communications, that it is not given to any human tongue to describe favours so precious. What persuasive lessons are given me in the example of this amiable Saint! I seek for happiness and desire it; my heart yearns for pleasures in a thousand different ways; but because I do not seek them at their true source, they are false, deceitful, and transitory. Union with my Saviour, the sharing His spirit, and fidelity to grace, can alone ensure me solid joy and lasting happiness. O great St. Aloysius, obtain for me the strength to be sufficiently faithful to experience these happy results.

Colloquy with St. Aloysius. Let us beg of him to become our director in the interior ways of perfection, and ask him to reform our inclinations and affections, and draw us after his example into the steps of Jesus crucified.

Resolutions. To impose on myself some acts of mortification and humility, with a view of obtaining the grace to despise external things, and to attach myself alone to such as are interior.

Offering of the Resolutions, page 3.

Spiritual Bouquet. " I belong to Jesus Christ, not to the world."
Prayer. Soul of Christ, etc.
Examen of the Meditation, page 4.

MEDITATION FOR THE FEAST OF THE NATIVITY OF ST. JOHN THE BAPTIST.

(24TH JUNE.)

" He shall be great before the Lord " (Luke i. 15).

Preparatory Prayer, page 1.

1st Prelude. Represent to yourself the banks of the Jordan, where John the Baptist prepared the Jews to receive the Messias, by preaching to them a baptism of penance.

2nd Prelude. Great Saint, who wast endowed with so many privileges, and wast so faithful in corresponding with divine grace, grant that through thy intercession I may obtain the help I stand in need of to put to profit the many graces I have received.

1st Point. The special graces with which St. John the Baptist was favoured.

The conception, the birth, and whole life of St. John the Baptist were a succession of wonders, a union of all sorts of privileges. His conception was a miracle; he was sanctified in his mother's womb; he was born in the midst of such wonders that every one asked, " Who, think you, shall this child be ? " From his tender years he lived in the desert; solitude and penance are for others a means of expiation to recover the innocence they have lost, but it was for him a preservative with which he shielded his from danger: it was necessary that this fair lily should grow and develop far away from the contagion of the world : it was necessary that this Angel of the earth should learn to commune with his God before speaking with men. Every kind of grace is united in him. He is a prophet and more than a prophet, according to the testimony of Jesus Christ Himself. He is an Apostle: he announces the Messias, and points Him out to the people of Israel. He is a Virgin, or rather he is an Angel clothed with a human body. "It is of him that it is written," Jesus says, "I will send My angel before Thee, who shall prepare Thy way." In short, God destined him to be a martyr, and the first of all the martyrs. How many gifts were united in one man! What a masterpiece of grace! How worthy should not this great Saint be of my veneration, and how eager I ought to be to pay him my homage and to implore his powerful protection!

2nd Point. The virtues practised by St. John the Baptist.

The gifts of God were not sterile in St. John the Baptist; his whole conduct offers us a perfect model of the most excellent virtues. Scarcely had he commenced life than he withdrew from his family home and went to bury himself in the desert, giving himself up to the rigours of the most austere penance. There, in constant communication with God, he gained instruction in the school of the Holy Spirit, and formed himself to the most sublime virtues, to profound humility, angelical purity, ardent love of God, perfect submission to His holy will, burning zeal for His glory, contempt for human respect, noble intrepidity for the defence of the law. At length God's hour strikes: John the Baptist hearkens to the call which summons him, and comes forth to preach the baptism of penance on the banks of the Jordan. Then it was that all the qualities with which his soul was adorned shone forth in his conduct. Such an example teaches me that recollection and interior solitude are necessary to the soul which wishes to acquire solid virtue, and that we ought not to face the world until we have been strengthened with prolonged intimacy with God. In a word, if I wish to be saved and to become useful to others, I must apply myself seriously to the holy exercises of prayer and meditation.

Colloquy with our Lord. Let us adore Jesus as the Author of every grace, and thank Him for those He conferred on St. John the Baptist. Let us offer our Saviour the merits of this great Saint, and beg of Him to grant us also, through the Baptist's intercession, humility, purity of heart, generosity, and zeal like that of His own Sacred Heart.

Resolutions. Often to remember the presence of God. To animate each one of my actions with a supernatural motive.

Offering of the Resolutions, page 3.

Spiritual Bouquet. "I will hearken to what the Lord my God shall say to me, in the depth of my soul."

Prayer. Soul of Christ, etc.

Examen of the Meditation, page 4.

MEDITATION FOR THE FEAST OF ST. PETER.

(29th June.)

"Blessed art thou, Simon, son of John" (Matt. xvi. 17).

Preparatory Prayer, page 1.

1st Prelude. Transport yourself in spirit to the shore of the lake of Tiberias where Jesus risen asked of St. Peter the triple protestation of his love, confided to him the care of the Church, and foretold to him the manner of his death.

2nd Prelude. Holy Apostle, obtain for me the grace to love and imitate Jesus, that so I may become, like thyself, the object of His special love.

1st Point. The graces by which the three Persons of

the adorable Trinity prepared St. Peter for the dignity of being supreme head of the Church.

St. Peter, chosen by God to be the first representative of Jesus Christ on earth, was favoured by the three Divine Persons of the Trinity with the august prerogatives corresponding with that high dignity. The eternal Father chose him by revealing to him the divinity of His Son. "Blessed art thou, Simon, son of John," said our adorable Lord to him, "because flesh and blood hath not revealed it to thee, but My Father Who is in Heaven." God the Son established him Head of His Church and dispenser of its treasures: "Thou art Peter," He said to him, "and upon this rock I will build My Church. And I will give to thee the keys of the kingdom of Heaven. And whatsoever thou shalt bind on earth, it shall be bound also in Heaven; and whatsoever thou shalt loose on earth, it shall be loosed also in Heaven" (Matt. xvi. 17, *seqq.*). The Holy Ghost confirmed him in his title and his office by coming down upon him on Whit-Sunday: it was then that, pouring the abundance of His gifts into St. Peter's soul, He changed him into a new man, and placed him in a condition to accomplish worthily his high destiny. Do not the favours which have been granted to me bear a very striking resemblance to the prerogatives of this illustrious Saint? I also have been chosen by my heavenly Father. He adopted me in Baptism. Jesus has ratified this adoption: He has perfected it, and caused me to rejoice in all the gifts promised me, by giving Himself to me in the Holy Communion; and the Holy Ghost has put the finishing stroke to so many graces by imprinting on my soul the character of a perfect Christian. What motives for love and gratitude!

2nd Point. In establishing St. Peter Head of the Church, Jesus made him like unto Himself.

We can, in some measure, form an estimate of the sanctity of the first Head of the Church of Jesus

Christ, from the conformity he bore to his Divine Master—a conformity not alone consisting in the eminent virtues of the holy Apostle, but still more in the glorious titles bestowed on him by our Lord, and by the different circumstances connected with these. In effect, Jesus Christ is called in the holy Scripture "the corner stone and the foundation on which we are built"; it was His wish that the first of the Apostles should share with Him the name and office these words express: "Thou art Peter," He says to the Apostle, "and upon this rock I will build My Church". Jesus calls Himself the Good Shepherd: He says He received His sheep from the hands of His heavenly Father, and He confides them to St. Peter: "Feed My lambs," He says to him, "feed My sheep". Jesus, God equal to His Father, and sharing with Him the sovereign dominion over all things, delights in saying that He has received all things from Him: "The Father," He says, "loves the Son, and He has given all things into His hands". The treasures and graces of which He is the dispenser, He gives Himself into the hands of St. Peter, saying to him: "I give thee the keys of the kingdom of Heaven". Lastly, the most striking circumstance of all is that Peter has the honour to die in the same way as his Divine Master: he is fastened to the Cross, and breathes his last upon it. How worthy of my homage is this great Saint in whom Jesus took such pleasure in reproducing Himself in so perfect and excellent a manner! With what confidence may I not address myself to him in order that I may likewise obtain this ever to be desired conformity with my Lord!

Colloquy with St. Peter. Let us congratulate him on the splendid prerogatives with which he was favoured, and on the intimate communications which united him to his Divine Master. Let us beg of him to obtain for us the grace to imitate Jesus Christ, and to accomplish all His designs upon us.

CONTEMPLATIONS AND MEDITATIONS. 151

Resolutions. To unite and conform myself to the Divine Heart of Jesus in all my thoughts, words, and actions.
Offering of the Resolutions, page 3.
Spiritual Bouquet. "Lord, Thou knowest all things; Thou knowest that I love Thee."
Prayer. Receive, O Lord, etc., page 18.
Examen of the Meditation, page 4.

MEDITATION FOR THE FEAST OF THE COMMEMORATION OF ST. PAUL.

(30TH JUNE.)

"By the grace of God I am what I am, for His grace in me hath not been made void" (1 Cor. xv. 10).

Preparatory Prayer, page 1.
1st Prelude. Represent to yourself St. Paul in chains.
2nd Prelude. Holy Apostle, who wast endowed with so many graces, and wast so faithful in profiting by them, obtain for me the grace to serve God with a zeal and generosity worthy of His benefits and of His love.
1st Point. God gave St. Paul a share in all His treasures.

There are in God three treasures, wherein are contained all the gifts of nature, of grace, and of glory. The first is a treasure of Power, which belongs to the Father; the second is a treasure of Wisdom, which is attributed to the Son; the third is the treasure of Mercy, which belongs to the Holy Ghost. Now, our Divine Lord, wishing to pour out upon St. Paul a rich effusion of all graces, caused him to participate in these three ineffable treasures: in the treasure of mercy through his conversion, which changed him from a persecutor into an apostle; in that of wisdom, by the divine illuminations which, above all others, he received when he was ravished to the third Heaven, for it was there he learned secrets which it is not given to mortal man to explain; thirdly, he shared in the treasure of the divine power, through the choice God made of him to work the conversion of the Gentiles, and to ensure the success of his preaching by a multitude of prodigies. Holy Apostle, of what liberality hast thou not been the object! I implore of thee to intercede for me with Jesus Christ; beg of Him to open to me the treasure of His power, that I may be enabled to overcome all the obstacles which hinder me from doing good; and also the treasure of His wisdom, to regulate my conduct according to the maxims of the Gospel. In a word, ask Him to open to me His Sacred Heart, that inexhaustible source of grace, of strength, and of light!

2nd Point. St. Paul corresponded faithfully with all the graces of God.

St. Paul, gifted with so many graces, used them faithfully for the salvation of souls and for his own perfection. He profited advantageously by the treasure of mercy, by leaving all to follow Jesus Christ. Upon the first reproach made to him by his Divine Master, he disengaged himself from the love of flesh and blood; did away with all attachment to the world; discharged himself of the burden of his sins; renounced all the pleasures of the senses; despised human respect; in fine, quitted himself to belong to Jesus Christ alone, and to live only for His glory. In like manner he made a holy use of the two other treasures which were communicated to him, by preaching to the Gentiles, and practising with as much wisdom as strength the evangelical maxims which he taught. I ought, after the example of this great Saint, to put to profit the grace of God; I ought to glorify His gifts and His mercy by an entire self-renovation; His wisdom by unreserved abandonment into His hands, His power by complete fidelity to grace, and by great courage in accomplishing all the designs of His love.

Colloquy with the Sacred Heart of Jesus. Let us return Him thanks for the signal favours He has bestowed on St. Paul. Let us offer Him the merits of this great Apostle, begging Him, through the Saint's intercession, to make us also partakers of His treasures, and to aid us to make a faithful use of them.

Resolutions. To follow faithfully all the inspirations of grace.

Offering of the Resolutions, page 3.

Spiritual Bouquet. "Grant, O Lord, that I may be able to say with Thy holy Apostle, ' It is not I who live, but Christ Jesus Who lives in me '."

Prayer. Soul of Christ, etc.

Examen of the Meditation, page 4.

MEDITATION FOR THE FEAST OF ST. VINCENT OF PAUL.

(19TH JULY.)

" He that loveth his neighbour hath fulfilled the law "(Rom. xiii. 8).

Preparatory Prayer, page 1.

1st Prelude. Represent to yourself St. Vincent of Paul gathering together all the poor little abandoned children he met with, or else see him exhorting and instructing the poor in hamlets and villages.

2nd Prelude. Great Saint, who didst ever distinguish thyself by the most tender charity and unfeigned humility, obtain for me the grace to practise, after thy example, these two precious virtues.

1st Point. The works by which St. Vincent of Paul signalised his charity for others.

It may be said of St. Vincent of Paul that he was dear both to God and man, and that, following the example of our Divine Lord, he passed through life doing good to all. How many were the miseries he relieved; how many tears he wiped away; how many misfortunes he soothed, both in his life and after his death! How much good he effected through the useful establishments he founded, whether for the help of the poor and the sick, or for sheltering orphans, or for the instruction of youth, or, in fine, to procure through numberless missions, the conversion of sinners and the sanctification of the just! Such were the unquestionable proofs which he gave of his charity for others. Charity cannot be genuine in a heart without producing external proofs of its existence by its works. What token have I given, up to the present time, of possessing this virtue, without which it is impossible to please the Sacred Heart of my Divine Saviour? Have I not lost many opportunities of being useful to others? Do I at least acquit myself zealously of the good works which circumstances render in some sort indispensable for me? How many reproaches have I not to make to myself, and how great is my need to implore the assistance of the great Saint whom the Church honours this day, that I may obtain through him this very necessary virtue!

2nd Point. The interior virtues which accompanied the glorious works of St. Vincent of Paul.

If the great Saint, on whose example I am now meditating, was to be admired for the multiplicity of good works to which he gave himself up for the good of others, he was not less admirable for the interior virtues which were the soul of all his actions. He was full of tenderness for the miserable, only because he beheld in them Jesus Christ Himself. The vivacity of his faith made him penetrate the exterior, which under the form of bodies extenuated by misery, concealed souls redeemed at the price of the Blood of Jesus Christ, and the help which he offered them had for its chief end to raise their souls to Heaven, and snatch them from the abyss of despair and sin. To the most lively faith he joined the most profound humility ; he believed himself indebted to others for the results of his industrious charity ; yet the poor had always the first place in his heart, and the largest share in the effects of his zeal. In truth his will was always so closely united to that of his God, that the most annoying contradictions were not capable of troubling the peace of his soul. This was because the glory and the service of God were the only objects he sought ; he was indifferent as to whether God was glorified by his success or by his personal sufferings. Oh ! what great good Jesus might work through my means, if the virtues of His faithful servant were perfectly copied in my soul.

Colloquy with St. Vincent of Paul. Let us pay him our homage of veneration, and congratulate him on the good which God has been pleased to work through his tender charity for others. Let us beg of him to obtain for us the grace to walk in his footsteps by the practice of this excellent and necessary virtue.

Resolutions. To practise meekness towards others, and to be ready and willing to serve them on every occasion.

Offering of the Resolutions, page 3.

Spiritual Bouquet. " This is My commandment, that you love one another, as I have loved you."

Prayer. Soul of Christ, etc.

Examen of the Meditation, page 4.

MEDITATION FOR THE FEAST OF ST. MARY MAGDALEN.

(22ND JULY.)

" Many sins are forgiven her, because she hath loved much " (Luke vii. 47).

Preparatory Prayer, page 1.

1st Prelude. Represent to yourself St. Mary Magdalen, in the house of the Pharisee where she obtained the forgiveness of her sins ; or in that of Lazarus her brother, at the feet of Jesus, listening to His sacred Word : or on Mount Calvary, or at the Sepulchre, where she gave her adorable Lord such ardent and generous proofs of her love.

2nd Prelude. Holy lover of the Sacred Heart of Jesus, obtain for me the grace to know, love, serve, and imitate this adorable Heart as thou didst.

1st Point. St. Mary Magdalen knew the Sacred Heart of Jesus.

In devotion to the Sacred Heart of Jesus there are five characteristics and five, as it were, degrees through which we may attain to the greatest perfection it offers us. The first degree consists in knowing thoroughly this Sacred Heart, the Source of grace and Throne of mercy ; the second is to love it with a tender and generous love ; the third is to be penetrated and nourished with its sentiments and affections ; the fourth is to suffer for Jesus and with Him ; the fifth, and last, is to devote oneself to His glory, and in order to labour in this more efficaciously, to copy His divine example. All these characteristics shone forth in St. Mary Magdalen in the most lively and striking manner. This illustrious penitent well knew the loving Heart of her Saviour ; covered as she was with the stains of her sins, even notorious in Jerusalem on account of her disorderly conduct, it would seem that she ought to fear to appear before Him Whose looks are so penetrating and so pure ; but no! touched with an interior grace, she has understood that Jesus is the good Shepherd seeking His wandering sheep ; the charitable Physician of souls Who has not come to those who are well, but to such as are sick ; she hastens therefore to throw herself at His feet ; she washes them with her tears, wipes them with her hair, and pours perfumes on them, and then hears from the lips of her Divine

Master these consoling words : " Many sins are forgiven her, because she hath loved much ". Oh ! how sweet it is to know Jesus ! how sweet to love Him and confide in Him ! This is the shortest means of obtaining pardon for sin and partaking of the most precious favours.

2nd Point. St. Mary Magdalen loved, served, and imitated the Sacred Heart of Jesus Christ.

The intimate knowledge of the goodness of the Sacred Heart of Jesus, and a loving confidence accompanied by bitter sorrow, had commenced the conversion of Magdalen ; thus there had shone forth in her the two first characteristics of devotion to the Sacred Heart. The three others were not less brilliantly remarkable in the remainder of her life. Jesus deigns to honour with His presence the house where she lived with Martha and Lazarus ; she places herself at His feet, and there receives with avidity His sacred words; nourishes herself with them, becomes penetrated with them, engraves them in her heart in order to imprint upon it the sentiments also and affections of the Heart of her Divine Master. Soon our adorable Saviour is to be immolated for the salvation of the world. Magdalen follows Him to the mountain of His sacrifice. She suffers there with Him ; all the torments He endures are sorrowfully repeated within her heart. After the resurrection of Jesus Christ she manifests the generosity of her love by the promptitude of her obedience, when He ordered her to leave Him in order to bear from Him to His disciples the happy news of His triumph. Finally, when Jesus had quitted this earth, Mary Magdalen buried herself in a deep cavern, there to pass the remainder of her days in love and sorrow; thus imitating Jesus, Whose entire life was but one long tissue of love and sufferings. When shall I imitate Him as she did ? When shall I understand practically that suffering is the most efficacious means of conforming myself to Him and uniting myself to Him ?

Colloquy with St. Mary Magdalen. Let us pay our homage of respect, love and confidence, as to the first adorer of the Sacred Heart of Jesus. Let us beg of her to make our heart like hers, by inspiring us with a tender confidence in, and true love for, Jesus Christ.

Resolutions. To apply myself with renewed assiduity to the holy exercise of meditation, in order to draw from it the knowledge and love of the Sacred Heart of Jesus. To unite all my sufferings to the Cross of my Divine Lord.

Offering of the Resolutions, page 3.

Spiritual Bouquet. " Mary hath chosen the better part, which shall not be taken from her."

Prayer. Open to me Thy Sacred Heart, O Jesus! Show me Its charms, unite me to It for ever; grant that every breath I draw, even every beat of my heart during sleep, may be so many testimonies of my love, saying to Thee unceasingly : " Yes, Lord, I am all Thine ; accept of the little good I do ; grant me grace to repair all the evil : that so I may bless Thee during this life, and praise Thee for all eternity in the next ". Amen.

Examen of the Meditation, page 4.

MEDITATION FOR THE FEAST OF ST. JAMES THE GREAT.

(25TH JULY.)

" Can you drink the chalice that I shall drink ? " (Matt. xx. 22).

Preparatory Prayer, page 1.

1st Prelude. Figure to yourself St. James near to his Divine Lord, with St. Peter and St. John, either on Mount Thabor, where he was a witness of Christ's glory, or in the garden of Olives, where he shared in His sadness.

2nd Prelude. Holy Apostle, who wast prepared by great trials for special favours, obtain for me the grace to put to equal profit both consolations and sufferings, and to make of both the one and the other so many means to unite myself more closely to Jesus Christ.

1st Point. The example of St. James teaches me with what wisdom Jesus prepares His elect for the trials they are one day to undergo.

Jesus had chosen Peter, James, and John to be witnesses of His glory on Mount Thabor. It was these same three Apostles that He led to the garden of Olives, there to reveal to them the mortal anguish with which His soul was oppressed. His profound wisdom had prepared them by the most striking proofs of His Divinity, to sustain the sight of His humiliations and apparent weakness. It is thus He has always acted towards those souls who belong to Him; when He intends to submit them to great trials, He strengthens their faith and their love beforehand, by special graces, that so they may not fall under temptation, but on the contrary, draw from it very precious advantages. This conduct of our Lord teaches me another truth also; namely, that the consolations with which He sometimes favours His elect are to be followed by painful trials; and that in such happy moments the faithful soul should think of preparing for the combat. O Jesus! teach me to understand in a practical manner these great principles of the spiritual life, and that uniting myself to Thee in joy as well as in sorrow, I may defy all creatures to separate me from Thy holy love.

2nd Point. The example of St. James teaches me with what care the faithful soul ought to profit by all that can advance us in the love of Jesus.

The signal favours which St. James received on Mount Thabor, and the important lessons which he must have learnt in the garden of Olives, did not remain sterile within him. Filled with a tender love for his Divine Master, a faithful imitator of the virtues dearest to Him, the Saint devoted his life with zeal to the preaching of the Gospel, and sealed his faith with his blood. Whatever may be the paths along which it may please our Lord to conduct me, I ought incessantly to recall to my mind that all that comes from His hand tends to my sanctification, and to enable me to accomplish His holy designs. The more faithful I shall be in putting to profit the graces He grants me and the trials He arranges for me, the more I shall procure His glory and enrich myself with merits, whatever success my good works may have otherwise. St. James had not, like the other Apostles, the consolation of seeing his preaching crowned with abundant success; but he did not the less obtain the recompense promised to the ministers of the Gospel. It is thus God acts towards His servants; He does not judge of their works by the fruit they produce, but by the interior motives which animate them; and the more ardent their love is, the richer and more precious is the crown which He prepares for them.

Colloquy with St. James. Let us congratulate him on the special predilection with which Jesus honoured him, and on his zeal for the glory of his Divine Master. Let us beg of him to obtain for us from the divine bounty the grace to profit by everything in order to attach ourselves inviolably to Him, and to devote ourselves to His glory and service.

Resolutions. To receive from the hand of God consolations and trials with equal acts of thanksgiving.

Offering of the Resolutions, page 3.

Spiritual Bouquet. "I will bless the Lord at all times. His praise shall be ever in my mouth."

Prayer. Receive, O Lord, etc., page 18.

Examen of the Meditation, page 4.

MEDITATION FOR THE FEAST OF ST. ANNE, THE MOTHER OF THE BLESSED VIRGIN.

(26TH JULY.)

"And there shall come forth a rod out of the root of Jesse, and a flower shall rise up out of his root" (Isaias xi. 1).

Preparatory Prayer, page 1.

1st Prelude. Figure to yourself, as far as it may be possible, the glory of St. Anne in Heaven, and see how kindly she listens to and grants the requests which are addressed to her on earth.

2nd Prelude. Blessed Mother of the Mother of God, grant that meditating on thy example I may be animated to the practice of solid virtues.

1st Point. How glorious it was to St. Anne to be made choice of by God to give birth to Mary!

If the principal glory of Mary and the most illustrious of her prerogatives was to have been the Mother of God, may it not be said that she who gave birth to Mary merits also our special homages of respect and veneration? "There shall come forth from the root of Jesse," one of the Prophets had foretold, "a shoot, and a flower shall spring up from its stem." This holy offshoot, this mysterious flower, is Jesus Christ Himself, the eternal Son of God, Who was to be born in time of a mortal Mother. Mary is the virginal stem which has brought Him forth; but this shoot has itself sprung from a fertile root, and who does not behold in this root the expressive figure of the great Saint whom the Church honours on this day? Yes, St. Anne was chosen by God to give birth to Mary. She proved herself worthy of this high dignity by her eminent virtues; and thus the glory of the daughter will shed its rays for ever on the happy Mother. Mary will for ever give a share to St. Anne of her elevation and of her power. How sweet it ought to be to me on this day to render to this illustrious Saint my profound homage of veneration, and to claim her protecting guardianship, and go through her to Mary, that so Mary, in her turn, may lead me to Jesus.

2nd Point. How advantageous it was to St. Anne to make to God the sacrifice of her Child.

The glory of St. Anne was to have Mary for her daughter; her merit was to consecrate her generously to the Lord, and to deprive herself, for His glory, of this precious treasure, almost as soon as she had received it from His goodness. What lessons of generosity and gratitude are contained for me in the example of this great Saint! She had clearly understood, and I ought likewise to understand, that all belongs to God, and that a heart truly enamoured of Him ought to solicit His gifts with a view only to render them subservient to His glory; and that the accomplishment of His holy will and of His good pleasure ought to be preferred to all sorts of advantages and enjoyments. But we can never lose anything by giving all to this good Master; never will He let Himself be outdone by His creatures in liberality and love. St. Anne had sweet experience of this. She consecrated to God the fruit of benediction He had granted to her prayers, and by this generous act she merited that the Child she had borne within her should become the Mother of the Messias. How little do I know my dearest interests when I hesitate to make to God with generosity the sacrifices asked of me by His grace!

Colloquy with St. Anne. Let us congratulate her on the singular grace God bestowed on her by choosing her to become the mother of the Queen of Heaven. Let us pray to her to obtain for us the graces we need to serve our Lord with a full and generous heart.

Resolutions. To refuse nothing to grace. To perform all my actions from a motive of love.

Offering of the Resolutions, page 3.

Spiritual Bouquet. "Give, and it shall be given unto you."

Prayer. O God, Who didst confer grace upon St. Anne so that she became worthy to be the mother of her who brought forth Thy only begotten Son; mercifully grant that we may be assisted by the intercession with Thee of her whose solemnity we celebrate: through Jesus Christ our Lord. Amen.
Examen of the Meditation, page 4.

MEDITATION FOR THE FEAST OF ST. IGNATIUS OF LOYOLA.

(31st July.)

"Create a clean heart in me, O God, and renew a right spirit within me" (Ps. iv. 12).

Preparatory Prayer, page 1.

1st Prelude. Represent to yourself St. Ignatius, either in the Castle of Loyola, reading the lives of the Saints, and feeling himself touched with a strong and powerful grace; or in the grotto of Manresa, exercising upon himself the rigours of the most austere penance.

2nd Prelude. Great Saint, who wast so faithful to the interior inspirations which urged thee to be converted, obtain for me the grace to begin at length to serve God with persevering fervour.

1st Point. The causes which led to the conversion of St. Ignatius.

It was in reading the life of Jesus Christ and the lives of the Saints that St. Ignatius, moved with an interior grace, understood the vanity of the things of this world, and began to form a design of leading a penitent life. Why does not the perusal of the same lives work the like effects in me? It is because I do not read them with the same dispositions as this great Saint did. As soon as Ignatius felt the first emotions of grace, he reflected deeply; compared what the Holy

Spirit, on the one side, caused him to experience within himself, leading him on to make great sacrifices, and yet keeping him in profound peace; and on the other side, what the spirit of the world and of nature, which, under the form of deceitful pleasures and frivolous enjoyments, brought him, namely, nothing but trouble and agitation of mind; then, balancing both in the scales of the sanctuary, he resolved, once for all, to break the ties which still held him captive, in order to follow the inspirations of grace. It was reflection, firmness of soul, and generosity of heart, which engaged him in the noble career in which he walked with such gigantic steps. . . . Alas! When shall I know how to reflect and to overcome myself as he did?

2nd Point. By what works St. Ignatius proved himself to be truly converted.

I often form good purposes and holy resolutions; but, because I am deficient in generosity and constancy, all my projects of amendment and perfection disappear, to give place to my habitual tepidity. It was not so with this great Saint, on whose example I am now meditating. His first step was a total renunciation of all that he had ever loved and esteemed on earth; then studying afterwards how he might immolate himself entirely to our Lord as a perfect holocaust of penance, he declared a deadly war against his tastes and inclinations. To overcome the passion he once had for the esteem of others and for honours, he affected a rustic and repulsive exterior, in order to draw down on himself more surely humiliations and contempt. Who could recount the severities he exercised on himself; his rigorous self-imposed fasts, his prolonged prayers, his industry in rendering the most abject and fatiguing services to the sick poor in the hospitals? God does not demand the same works of me; but how calculated to put to shame my cowardice is the fervour which inspired St. Ignatius to practise them!

Colloquy with St. Ignatius. Let us offer him our

homage of veneration. Let us beg of him to obtain for us the grace to overcome our tepidity, and begin to serve God at length with entire generosity.

Resolutions. To overcome myself courageously in that which will cost me the most.

Offering of the Resolutions, page 3.

Spiritual Bouquet. "Happy is the man whose sins are forgiven, and whose faults are blotted out."

Prayer. Receive, O Lord, etc., page 18.

Examen of the Meditation, page 4.

SECOND MEDITATION.

(FOR THE SAME DAY.)

"The zeal of Thy house hath eaten me up" (Ps. lxviii. 10).

Preparatory Prayer, page 1.

1st Prelude. Imagine to yourself St. Ignatius gathering around him little children and the poor in order to teach them the law of God.

2nd Prelude. Great Saint, whose generosity and zeal knew no bounds, obtain for me the grace to rise above myself, in order to serve the Almighty with entire devotedness.

1st Point. The zeal of St. Ignatius for the glory of God.

The Spirit of God works great things in a short time in a soul when He finds no obstacles to His action; thus the heart of St. Ignatius was quickly and entirely changed; his motives became ever more perfect and his love ever more pure; zeal for the divine glory was daily enkindled within him, and everything, even his own eternal salvation, seemed little compared with that greatest of interests, the principal end of the mysteries accomplished by the Son of God. Like to an eagle whose youth has just been renewed, and which rises with rapid flight to the loftiest summits, this great Saint entered into the designs of God which had been made known to him by the interior light which guided him. How many obstacles it would seem might have stopped him, or at least limited the results of the holy earnestness which animated him! Arrived at the age of thirty-six, without ever having studied deeply, enfeebled also by his fasts and other austerities, could he promise himself great success in the apostolic labours to which his courageous spirit excited him? Thus would human prudence and craven cowardice have reasoned; but the great soul of St. Ignatius was deaf to such thoughts; a grand idea had taken possession of his mind: "I can do all things in Him that strengtheneth me": a sublime device was engraven in his heart; "All for the greater glory of God". Armed with faith, hope, and love, he went forth to the combat against the enemies of the Lord, and soon the powers of hell felt the effects of his valour. Oh! who will give to me to follow this great example, at least at a distance? Who will give to me to arm myself for the service of the Lord with that noble intrepidity which no obstacle can disconcert, because it is founded on the divine aid and refuses nothing to the inspirations of grace?

2nd Point. In what ways I may imitate the zeal of St. Ignatius.

The spirit of zeal which distinguished St. Ignatius ought to be mirrored within me. I cannot love our Lord without interesting myself in His glory. I cannot have for others that true charity which the Gospel recommends, unless I labour according to the best of my power to procure for them the only goods which are true and solid—the love of God and eternal salvation. I ought, then, to occupy myself earnestly in extending the reign of Jesus Christ, by leading sinners back to Him, by strengthening the just in His holy love, and by endeavouring to make Him known, loved, served, and glorified, if possible, by all creatures. How many means are within my reach of working for this end! A kind word, timely advice, a service rendered with that amiability which gains confidence, and disposes those who suffer to speak freely about their eternal interests, may become powerful means in my hands to overthrow the empire of Satan. There are others likely to prove still more successful; these are the example of solid and enlightened piety; the prayers of a soul inflamed with zeal; the daily sacrifices of a generous heart, which does not know how to refuse anything to God. By such means I may walk in the footsteps of St. Ignatius, prove my love to Jesus, open Heaven to many who, perhaps, had I not helped them, would never have reached it. What motives for encouragement!

Colloquy with our Lord. Let us offer Him the exalted virtues and abundant merits of St. Ignatius. Let us beg of Jesus to give us some conformity to this great Saint, by disengaging us from all self-love, and filling us with pure zeal and great generosity.

Resolutions. To devote myself to the service of God with all my heart. To seize zealously every opportunity of leading others to the practice of virtue.

Offering of the Resolutions, page 3.

Spiritual Bouquet. "All for the greater glory of God."

Prayer. Receive, O Lord, etc., page 18.

Examen of the Meditation, page 4.

THIRD MEDITATION.

(For the same Day.)

"He that shall do and teach" (all the commandments of God) "he shall be called great in the kingdom of Heaven" (Matt. v. 19).

Preparatory Prayer, page 1.

1st Prelude. Figure to yourself St. Ignatius addressing one of those pathetic exhortations to his religious which inflamed them with zeal for the salvation of souls.

2nd Prelude. Illustrious Saint, who didst bring about such great things for God, obtain for me the grace to occupy myself, according to my ability, in making Him known, loved, and served.

1st Point. The success which crowned the zeal of St. Ignatius during his life.

"If the grain of wheat dieth not after being thrown into the ground," says Jesus Christ, "itself remaineth alone; but if it die, it bringeth forth fruit a hundredfold." This promise, the sense of which is allegorical, and which marks the detachment from self with which we ought to give ourselves up to works of zeal, if we would succeed in them, was carried out by St. Ignatius to its fullest extent: he was dead to himself and to created things. This great Saint, indifferent alike to praise or blame, looking upon the riches of this world as worthless dust, reckoning as nothing his body, his health, or even his life, could say with St. Paul, "It is not I that live, but Jesus Christ that liveth within me". Thus with what happy success was not his zeal crowned! Without speaking of the innumerable conversions of which he was the instrument, of the many monasteries he reformed, of the number of sinners reclaimed, and of obstinate criminals gained over to virtue by the united force of his prayers and exhortations, what good did he not effect by the institution of the Society of Jesus alone! All the infidels instructed and baptised by St. Francis Xavier, all the souls guided to Heaven by the labours, anxieties, and holy industry of the other members of the infant society, owed their salvation to him as to the first author of the means of conversion which had been offered to them. Oh! what power ought not such a great example to exercise over me! How calculated it is to make me feel forcibly the necessity of renouncing myself and overcoming my imperfect inclinations if I desire, in my relations with others, to procure the glory of God and the salvation of souls.

2nd Point. The success of the zeal of St. Ignatius still continues after his death.

Our Blessed Saviour, instructing His Apostles on the sublimity of the designs He had upon them, said to them: "I have established you that you may bring forth fruit, and that your fruit may remain". The great Saint, on whose life I am now meditating, was also chosen by our Lord to work a lasting good in the Church. From the highest Heaven, where he now reigns with Jesus Christ, he has seen, and still beholds, the fruits of his labours being perpetuated from age to age; his spirit diffusing itself in his spiritual children; and the society which he has founded, providing pious institutions for youth, learned teachers for the people of the science of the Saints, evangelical labourers for the Church, worthy of her confidence; saints and martyrs for Heaven. The innocence of an Aloysius Gonzaga and of a Stanislaus Kostka, the sublime detachment of a St. Francis Borgia, the zealous labours of a St. Francis Regis, the humble virtues of an Alphonsus Rodriguez are, as it were, so many precious stones in his crown, to enhance the splendour of his triumph. How worthy of my homage is this Saint, so elevated in glory! How greatly does this generous Father of so many Apostles and Saints merit my confidence! If during life he was so full of ardour to gain souls to God, can he now reject my prayers, when I invoke him not only to obtain my own sanctification, but still more that I may be made useful for that glory of God which was the sole end of all his labours?

Colloquy with St. Ignatius. Let us pay him our homage of respect and veneration. Let us thank him humbly for the special graces which we owe to his zeal and to his prayers. Let us beg of him to obtain for us a truly Christian spirit, a spirit of entire devotedness, of pure zeal, of ardent, enlightened, and universal charity.

Resolutions. To seize every opportunity of labouring for the glory of God and for the salvation of souls. To offer up my prayers and actions for the same end.

Offering of the Resolutions, page 3.

Spiritual Bouquet. "All for the honour and glory of God."

Prayer. O God, Who for the increase of the glory of Thy holy Name wast pleased by the blessed Ignatius to strengthen Thy Church militant with a new aid, grant that being assisted by his prayers during our warfare on earth, we may so imitate his virtues as to be happily crowned with him in Heaven, through Christ our Lord. Amen.

Examen of the Meditation, page 4.

MEDITATION FOR THE FEAST OF ST. DOMINIC.

(4TH AUGUST.)

" Pray without ceasing " (1 Thess. v. 17).

Preparatory Prayer, page 1.

1st Prelude. Represent to yourself St. Dominic, after a hard day's toil for the salvation of souls, passing the night before the altar in prayer.

CONTEMPLATIONS AND MEDITATIONS. 171

2nd Prelude. Illustrious Saint, who didst so perfectly unite the contemplative and active life, obtain for us the grace while we labour for others never to neglect our own salvation.

1st Point. The contemplative life of St. Dominic.

Prayer, silence, and spiritual reading are the chief characteristics of the contemplative life. The prayer of St. Dominic was continual. He used to pass the night before the altar, kneeling, lying prostrate or standing with his arms stretched out in the form of a cross. There was neither place nor time in which he did not pray, but especially during the silent hours when others rested. Sometimes standing before a crucifix he would genuflect a hundred times with ardent petitions. At other times he used to prostrate himself flat on the ground (St. Mark xiv. 35), praying with intense fervour, repeating verses of the Psalms, and weeping abundantly. " My soul hath cleaved to the earth ; quicken Thou me according to Thy word " (Ps. cxviii. 25). On his journeys, made on foot, he prayed incessantly and often sang hymns and Psalms, and frequently walked behind his companions that he might commune more freely with God. His love of silence was so great that those who knew him best declared that he never spoke save to God or of God. He always carried with him the book of the Gospels and constantly read it after kissing it with reverence. If I cannot spend the whole night in prayer, how careful should I be to rise in time to make my mental prayer. How earnest ought I to be in the practice of aspirations to God wherever I may be. Am I a lover of mental prayer and spiritual reading? If I love Jesus Christ, I shall love to converse with Him, and to read about Him.

2nd Point. With his contemplative life of prayer and penance St. Dominic combined heroic labour for souls.

St. Dominic was an apostle. Though loving the

repose of prayer, he never spared himself but laboured unceasingly for souls. "Endeavour in every way to save souls, and as many as possible," was one of his favourite maxims. Two intense desires filled his soul, a thirst for the salvation of others and for the crown of martyrdom, both springing from his ardent love of God. According to tradition, our Lady revealed to him the devotion of the Rosary, by which he impressed on men's minds the life, death, and glory of our Lord. He founded and propagated the order of Preaching Friars, which he animated with his spirit and left to carry on his work. Having fought the good fight and saved a multitude of souls, he finished his course in his fifty-first year in 1221. The fire of charity if really kindled in my heart must make me burn with zeal to save the souls of men. How do I show this zeal? Do I deny myself anything in order to help foreign missions and the propagation of the Faith? Do I instruct the ignorant? Do I try to convert sinners by word and example? Do I pray for the living and the dead?

Colloquy with St. Dominic. Thank him for the institution of the Rosary and the order of Preachers. Ask him to obtain for us the spirit of prayer and zeal for souls. Pray for his order.

Resolutions. To do something to-day at least by prayer for the salvation of souls.

Offering of the Resolutions, page 3.

Spiritual Bouquet. "I came to cast fire on the earth, and what will I but that it be enkindled?" (Luke xii. 49).

Prayer. O God, Who hast deigned to enlighten Thy Church by the merits and teaching of St. Dominic, Thy Confessor, grant that by his intercession we may not lack temporal help, and may ever advance in spiritual goods, through Jesus Christ Thy Son. Amen.

Examen of the Meditation, page 4.

MEDITATION FOR THE FEAST OF ST. PHILOMENA.

(11TH AUGUST.)

"To him that overcometh, I will give to eat of the tree of life" (Apoc. ii. 7).

Preparatory Prayer, page 1.

1st Prelude. Figure to yourself St. Philomena in Heaven depositing a palm branch and a lily at the foot of the throne of Jesus Christ, the emblems of her twofold victory, and praying to Him for those who address themselves to her with confidence.

2nd Prelude. Glorious Virgin and Martyr, so tenderly loved by my Divine Saviour, obtain for me the grace to imitate thy perfect purity of heart, and the greatness of thy courage and constancy in His love.

1st Point. The virtues practised by St. Philomena ought to excite a holy emulation within me.

What touching examples are offered to a truly faithful soul by the young Virgin whose memory the Church honours on this day! As soon as she was able to know the amiability of Jesus and to taste the sweetness of His love, she consecrated her heart as well as her entire being to Him. How pure was the heart of this Saint, who, from her most tender years, preferred to face the fury of the most cruel of tyrants rather than accept his hand and his crown at the expense of the fidelity which she had vowed to her Heavenly Spouse! How generous that heart which could not be moved by the tears of a father who loved her dearly; nor by the multiplicity of the torments which the fury of the tyrant invented one after the other to weary out her constancy! Oh! how strong was the love of Jesus Christ in her holy soul! But how weak it is in mine! The smallest difficulties terrify me, the least obstacles discourage me, and I allow myself to be overcome by the most trifling temptations. Yet I aspire, with St. Philomena, to the eternal happiness of Heaven; like her, I can rely on the help of divine grace; why, then, not be generous as she was? Is it not at length time that, blushing for my cowardice, I should become animated with a holy courage to overthrow my enemies, and procure the glory of my Divine Master?

2nd Point. The power of St. Philomena with God ought to excite my confidence.

If the example of the Saints is a powerful incentive to excite us to the practice of virtues, their help is also an efficacious means to acquire them. Consumed with the love of God, they interest themselves earnestly about the divine glory and about our salvation; they love to intercede for us with God; but above all they occupy themselves with special affection to obtain for us the virtues they themselves have practised. What, then, can I do to-day more glorious for God or more salutary for myself than to address myself to St. Philomena, in order to obtain great purity of heart and entire generosity in the service of my good Master? If this amiable Saint has listened so favourably to so many prayers, soliciting from her temporal only and transitory favours, how much more will she not interest herself in favour of holy desires inspired by faith which have no other end in view but to render me more pleasing to our Lord! Yes, I cannot doubt it. St. Philomena is attentive to my prayers; my own want of fervour and confidence can alone hinder me from being heard; for she desires indefinitely more to obtain for me the graces I solicit than I do to receive them. O holy and youthful Maiden! if in addressing thee my heart has not sufficient confidence and fervour, obtain for me as a first favour these holy dispositions, and then listen to all my requests.

Colloquy with St. Philomena. Let us congratulate her on the abundant graces with which she was gifted, and on her perfect fidelity in corresponding with them. Let us offer her merits to our Lord. Let us pray to her to interest herself for us with our Divine Saviour, and to obtain for us from His goodness, a purity of heart and a generous and constant wish to love Him, which may enable us to accomplish willingly all the sacrifices He may please to ask of us.

Resolutions. To be generous in sacrificing all inclinations, repugnances, and self-will, to the accomplishment of God's good pleasure.

Offering of the Resolutions, page 3.

Spiritual Bouquet. " If any one will come after Me, let him deny himself." " Blessed are the clean of heart, for they shall see God."

Prayer. Receive, O Lord, etc., page 18.

Examen of the Meditation, page 4.

MEDITATION FOR THE FEAST OF ST. JANE FRANCES DE CHANTAL.

(21st August.)

" Let your light so shine before men that they may see your good works and glorify your Father Who is in Heaven " (Matt. v. 16).

Preparatory Prayer, page 1.

1st Prelude. Represent to yourself St. Jane Frances praying in her oratory, or instructing her children, or visiting the cabins of the poor in order to carry them relief.

2nd Prelude. Great Saint, who didst know so well how to unite the duties of thy state with those imposed by Christian piety, obtain for me the grace to practise, after thy example, those gentle and loving virtues which give glory to Jesus and gain souls to Him.

1st Point. The virtues of St. Jane Frances were solid and interior.

The Saint honoured by the Church to-day is an accomplished model for all states of life; but I ought principally to consider her in the midst of the world, since her example there concerns me more directly. St. Jane Frances had built on a firm rock the edifice of her perfection; her conduct was not the result of a passing fervour, or of that seeking after sensible devotion, which but too often has so great a share in the piety of many who make profession of serving our Lord. A firm and enlightened faith, a sincere desire to please and give glory to God, a constant attention to carry out, in her life, the maxims of the Gospel, were the soul of all her actions. From these arose that profound contempt for the world and its vanities, and that prudence which caused order, peace, and concord to reign in her house; above all, from these arose that assiduous care to bring up her children in the love and fear of God, to watch over their innocence, and to inspire them, from their earliest years, with the love of religion and of all the virtues it inspires. It was by such exercises as these that she knew how to sanctify herself in the position in which Providence had placed her; teaching me, by her example, that sanctity is attainable by every one, and that our own personal defects are the only obstacles which we have to overcome in order to possess it.

2nd Point. The piety of St. Jane Frances was sweet and condescending as regards others.

The true spirit of religion is a spirit of peace, concord, and holy joy, which renders the servants of God gentle and amiable in their communications with others. Our Saint understood this; she was far removed in her bearing from that reserve and austerity which a mistaken devotion sometimes inspires; she knew, after the example of the great Apostle, how to make herself "all to all," that she "might gain souls to Jesus Christ". The principal exercise of her mortification consisted in bending her will and inclinations to those of others in all that was not opposed to the law of God. The duties towards her family, and towards society, which she had to fulfil, offered her opportunities for practising at one time patience and forbearance, at another charity and meekness; now forgetfulness of self and of her own interests; now zeal for the salvation of souls: in a word, every Christian virtue.

The exalted motives with which she animated all her actions gave them a high value in the sight of God, and the interior spirit by which she was animated made her temper so equal, and her intercourse with others so amiable, that she caused virtue to be loved and esteemed wherever she appeared. It is by such an example as this that I ought to regulate my conduct, if I desire to work for the glory of Jesus Christ, in accordance with the numberless graces bestowed on me by my Divine Lord.

Colloquy with St. Jane Frances. Let us pray to her to obtain for us from the Sacred Heart of Jesus those solid and interior virtues which may enable us to live in the midst of the world without sharing its corruption; and also those amiable and gentle virtues necessary to procure the glory of God and the salvation of souls.

Resolutions. To perform all my actions for God. To practise meekness towards others.

Offering of the Resolutions, page 3.

Spiritual Bouquet. "Our Father, hallowed be Thy Name."

Prayer. Soul of Christ, etc.

Examen of the Meditation, page 4.

MEDITATION FOR THE FEAST OF ST. LOUIS, KING.

(25TH AUGUST.)

"He shall judge the poor of the people . . . and shall continue with the sun . . . throughout all generations" (Ps. lxxi. 4, 5).

Preparatory Prayer, page 1.

1st Prelude. Represent to yourself St. Louis serving the sick in the hospitals, or humbling himself before our Lord in his private oratory.

2nd Prelude. Holy King, who didst unite such profound humility to so much greatness, obtain for me the grace to despise myself, that so I may find grace before God.

1st Point. Greatness was without danger for St. Louis, because he was truly humble.

" He that is the greatest amongst you shall be your servant" (Matt. xxiii. 11), said our ever Blessed Lord. These words teach us that sincere humility is the only road to glory, and that a true disciple of Jesus Christ ought to fear honours, cherish obscurity, and keep himself humbly wrapped up in the sentiment of his own unworthiness.

St. Louis understood this well; thus, in consequence, the high rank in which he had been placed by Providence, and which had been for so many others the occasion of grievous falls, presented no danger to him, but even served to procure his sanctification. Such an example ought to teach me that, in the designs of God, everything concurs to the good of the elect; and that apparent obstacles become means leading to good, when used with fidelity; and that, with the help of God's grace, the virtues which He demands of His servants can always be practised. St. Louis knew on occasions how to show a holy firmness and a truly royal dignity; he knew how, using his authority, to put down scandals and abuses, and how to repress firmly impiety and injustice: but this noble courage did not prevent humility from reigning in his heart; he humbled himself in the presence of God, exercised his royal prerogatives only through submission to the orders of Providence, and, when left the liberty to follow his own inclinations, was to be found among the poor, serving them with the greatest affection. It was thus that he merited a crown infinitely more precious than the one he had received from his ancestors ; and it is in imitating these holy dispositions that I myself shall share in the promise of our Lord : " He that humbleth himself shall be exalted ".

2nd Point. St. Louis sanctified himself, while commanding others, because he knew how to obey God.

The study of the law of God had constituted the delight of this holy monarch from his earliest years; he preferred the title of a Christian to that of King of France ; and, docile to the lessons of his virtuous mother, he ever accustomed himself to look upon sin as a far greater evil than death. Thus, justice, prudence, and all other virtues seated themselves on the throne with him, and caused religion to reign in the land, and holiness to reign in his heart ; he governed his people, but it was the Holy Spirit Who presided in his councils ; it was zeal for the glory of God, and for the happiness of his subjects, which guided his decisions ; he only reigned himself in order to extend the reign of our Lord ; he only took pleasure in being raised above others because in his high position his example had more weight in leading them to observe the law of God. The conduct of this great Saint teaches me that ardent zeal for the observance of the divine law is the distinctive character of the true disciples of Jesus ; it teaches me, above all, that in order to employ myself successfully in causing that law to be observed by others, I ought first to practise myself what I recommend to them.

Colloquy with St. Louis. Let us pay him our homage of veneration and respect. Let us implore his protection on behalf of France. Let us implore his help for ourselves, that after his example we may practise humility and zeal for the glory of God.

Resolutions. To practise humility in my intercourse with others.

Offering of the Resolutions, page 3.

Spiritual Bouquet. "He that humbleth himself shall be exalted."
Prayer. Pater Noster, etc.
Examen of the Meditation, page 4.

MEDITATION FOR THE FEAST OF ST. AUGUSTINE.

(28th August.)

"Thou shalt love the Lord thy God with thy whole heart, and with thy whole soul, and with thy whole mind, and with thy whole strength" (Mark xii. 30).

Preparatory Prayer, page 1.

1st Prelude. Represent to yourself St. Augustine at the moment when, yielding to the divine grace which inspired him, he resolved to return to God.

2nd Prelude. Illustrious Saint, who didst repair the disorders of thy life by the most pure and ardent love, obtain for me the grace to love much, that thus many sins may be forgiven me.

1st Point. The extent of the divine mercy manifested in the conversion of St. Augustine.

The conversion of St. Augustine was a masterpiece of God's grace, and on no other occasion has the divine mercy shone more brightly: it would seem, indeed, that our Lord wished, through the example of this great Saint, to offer to repentant sinners in all ages a model of the most perfect penance, and a motive for the most unshaken confidence. St. Augustine had sinned grievously : pride, heresy, and the most shameful vices had stained his early years; for a long time he had even resisted the interior grace which urged him to return to God. But at length he opened his heart to the Holy Spirit; he burst asunder the ties of iniquity which held him captive; he deplored with bitterness all his past wanderings. Then the treasures of the divine mercy were poured out on him abundantly: deep compunction, abundant tears, powerful aids to avoid sin, signal victories over his passions, were all granted to him. The difficulties in the way of virtue, which had alarmed him for so long, were smoothed away for him: nothing any longer alarmed his courage; he found the purest delights in the efforts which formerly seemed impossible to his weakness. Oh! how good is the Lord to those who return to Him! How liberal He is to those generous souls who abandon themselves without opposition to the inspirations of His grace! How much longer shall I make use of reserve in my fidelity towards the Almighty? How long shall I force Him, by my cowardice and resistance to grace, to put limits to His liberality in my regard?

2nd Point. The riches of divine love shown in the sanctification of St. Augustine.

As soon as the spirit of grace had taken possession of the soul of St. Augustine, the most wonderful miracles were worked within it; but above all, a charity so perfect was communicated to him that the heart of this great Saint became forthwith a burning furnace of the purest and intensest love. Who could tell the joys which this divine love caused him to enjoy? Who could describe the transports with which this love inspired him, and the sublime virtues of which it became the source? It suffices to open the writings of this incomparable doctor to feel that his pen was guided by his heart, and that his heart had fathomed the depth of all the mysteries of love accomplished by our Lord in favour of His creatures. Oh! if my heart, like that of this great Saint, would but disengage itself from self-love and affection to all created things, I also should have a share in heavenly communications, and should know by experience the height and breadth and depth of the love of Jesus for us. . . . Adorable Heart, all my hope is in Thee; grant me those pure and powerful graces which can alone raise me above myself and render me worthy of Thy favours.

Colloquy with the Sacred Heart of Jesus. Let us thank Him for the abundance of the graces He has bestowed on St. Augustine. Let us offer Him the merits of this holy doctor. Let us beg, through his intercession, for the grace of a perfect conversion and an ardent love of the Divine Majesty.

Resolutions. To overcome myself generously in all that costs me dearest. To perform all my actions through love.

Offering of the Resolutions, page 3.

Spiritual Bouquet. "O my God, give me Thy love."

Prayer. Receive, O Lord, etc., page 18.

Examen of the Meditation, page 4.

MEDITATION FOR THE FEAST OF THE EXALTATION OF THE CROSS.
(14TH SEPTEMBER.)

"The Lord hath reigned, He is clothed with beauty: the Lord is clothed with strength, and hath girded Himself" (Ps. xcii. 1).

Preparatory Prayer, page 1.

1st Prelude. Figure Heaven to yourself, where the Cross, shining with glory, will eternally receive the homage of Angels and of men.

2nd Prelude. Grant me grace, O Lord, to place all my hopes in Thy holy Cross, and to allow myself to be fastened upon it all the days of my life.

1st Point. Jesus has saved me by the Cross.

The sight of the Cross of my Saviour ought to inspire me with sentiments of lively gratitude, ardent love, and unbounded confidence. By dying on that sacred tree, He snatched me from hell. His Blood, with which it is empurpled, is the pledge of the divine mercy for me, and the source of all the graces that come to me. Whatever may have been my past sins and vices, and my present miseries, if I embrace the Cross of my Saviour with a penitent and humble heart, I am certain to recover all my claims upon the Sacred Heart of my God, and to gain the victory over all the enemies of my soul. O saving Cross, O tree of life! the flowers and fruits which thou dost bear are sovereign remedies, powerful to heal all my wounds; from thy branches are suspended the spoils of hell: for thou art the victorious weapon with which my Saviour has overthrown the powers of darkness. How, then, shall I not be filled with courage and confidence on beholding thee?

2nd Point. It is by attaching myself to the Cross that I shall apply to myself the merits of my Saviour.

My adorable Lord has merited Heaven for me by His sufferings and death; but if I am to attain Heaven, I must produce some resemblance between my own life and the example Jesus has given me. "If any one will come after Me," said our most Blessed Saviour, "let him deny himself and take up his cross and follow Me." It is consequently only by crucifying all my unruly inclinations, and in dying to all that is not God, that I shall render myself worthy of His favours. A few external religious acts will not suffice to apply to me the fruits of redemption; a constant spirit of sacrifice, and great courage in resisting my passions, can alone make me victorious over the enemies that attack me, and alone enable me to triumph with Jesus. What a joy for me when He shall appear in His glory, if His Cross have always been the object of my love, and if I have allowed myself to be fastened to it according to the designs of His Providence! Then this saving sign, far from inspiring me with terror, will fill me with the sweetest confidence. Grant, O Lord, that being profoundly penetrated with these thoughts, I may be raised above my own weakness, and die to myself as Thou didst die for me.

Colloquy with the Divine Heart of Jesus. Let us thank Jesus for having saved us by His Cross. Let us beg of Him to plant this tree of life within our soul, and to grant us the grace ever to regard it as our most precious treasure.

Resolutions. To practise a spirit of mortification in all things, with a view to apply to myself the merits of Christ my Saviour.

Offering of the Resolutions, page 3.

Spiritual Bouquet. " Cross of Christ, be my only possession."

Prayer. Soul of Christ, etc.

Examen of the Meditation, page 4.

MEDITATION FOR THE FEAST OF ST. MATTHEW, APOSTLE AND EVANGELIST.

(21st September.)

" And when Jesus passed on, He saw a man sitting in the custom-house, named Matthew, and He saith to him : ' Follow Me '. And he arose up and followed Him " (Matt. ix. 9).

Preparatory Prayer, page 1.

1st Prelude. Represent to yourself Jesus calling St. Matthew, and the Apostle rising up immediately and following Christ.

2nd Prelude. Holy Apostle, obtain for me the grace to imitate thy fidelity to the voice of Jesus, and thy zeal in making Him known to others.

1st Point. The fidelity of St. Matthew to the call of our Lord.

" Jesus saw a man sitting in the custom-house, named Matthew, and He saith to him : ' Follow Me '. And he arose up and followed Him " (Matt. ix. 9).

This passage of the holy Gospel presents me with ample material for reflection; it teaches me that frequently the grace of conversion and a renewal of fervour is offered to us suddenly, and if we allow the passing moment to escape in which it is offered to us, we run the risk of losing it, without any hope of its return. How many times have I not in this way neglected the graces offered me by Jesus in His mercy! What would have been my fate had He retired from me, as I deserved, on account of my stubborn resistance? O Sacred Heart of Jesus, Thou hast never been willing to do this; Thy perseverance in loading me with benefits has preserved me from dying in sin; but it remains for me to acquire very many virtues, for which I still need special grace. Grant, then, that, being attentive to all Thy inspirations, and generous in following them without delay, I may merit ever to tread in Thy footsteps the path of Christian perfection.

2nd Point. The perseverance of St. Matthew in the service of Jesus Christ.

It is something to correspond faithfully with a first grace, and to set oneself to follow Jesus Christ courageously; but this is not everything: perseverance alone can crown the happy beginning, and complete the sanctification of the soul. In this respect, likewise, St. Matthew serves me as a model; when once he had devoted himself to Jesus Christ, he never more left Him: he was an Apostle, an Evangelist, and a Martyr of our Blessed Saviour. I ought, like him, to repay, by the most devoted fidelity and zeal, the signal graces which have been lavished on me. I ought to become an apostle of my Divine Lord by my ardour in making Him known and loved; to be full of zeal to spread the maxims of the Gospel by exactitude in reproducing them in my whole mode of life; to be a martyr of divine love, by sacrificing my inclinations and repugnances, on all occasions, in order to do the good pleasure of my Divine Saviour. O Sacred Heart of Jesus, I can do nothing without Thy help; help me to walk with courage in the holy career Thou hast opened out for me; grant that I may happily reach my goal, for Thy glory and my own salvation.

Colloquy with St. Matthew. Let us pay him our homage of respect and veneration. Let us congratulate him on his fidelity to grace, and on his constancy in serving God. Let us pray to him to obtain for us the strength we need to imitate him, and to labour for the glory of our Blessed Lord.

Resolutions. To follow faithfully all the inspirations of grace.

Offering of the Resolutions, page 3.

Spiritual Bouquet. "Lord, what wouldst Thou have me to do?"

Prayer. Receive, O Lord, etc., page 18.

Examen of the Meditation, page 4.

MEDITATION FOR THE FEAST OF ST. MICHAEL AND OF ALL THE HOLY ANGELS.

(29TH SEPTEMBER.)

"And there was a great battle in Heaven, Michael and his Angels fought with the dragon" (Apoc. xii. 7).

Preparatory Prayer, page 1.

1st Prelude. Imagine you see in Heaven the triumphant legions of holy Angels offering their prayers to God for you, and inviting you to come and share their happiness.

2nd Prelude. Glorious St. Michael, and all you blessed Spirits who contemplate the glory of the Lord, obtain for me the grace to imitate your fidelity, that so I may one day share your reward.

1st Point. The holy Angels are our Protectors.

The Church to-day presents to my veneration those

pure Spirits who have never offended God—holy and innocent creatures, who, by well-tried fidelity, have merited to enjoy for ever the glory of Heaven. How worthy of my veneration are these blessed Spirits in whom God has been pleased to trace His own infinite perfections, and who glorify Him exceedingly by their continual praises! But my homage would be imperfect if I were to limit myself to reverencing them, without at the same time opening my heart to the love and confidence I owe them. God has given them to us as our Protectors: they have a tender love for us; they look on us as their friends and companions, and earnestly desire our salvation; they are our intercessors with the Divine Majesty; they obtain for us the pardon of our sins and the grace to escape the dangers by which we are surrounded. O my God! how good Thou art to have established such a communication between us and the princes of Thy court! Who am I, especially, that Thy Angels should interest themselves about me and shield me with their protection? I thank Thee for this favour with all my heart, and beg of Thee to make me worthy of their care by causing me to imitate the virtues of which they give me so perfect an example.

2nd Point. The holy Angels are our Protectors against the powers of darkness.

"The Lord hath given thee His angels to watch over thee," says the Holy Scripture, "and they shall bear thee up lest thou dash thy foot against a stone." These blessed Spirits take a loving care in preserving us from the dangers which menace our health or our life; but above all things they desire the salvation of our souls. Spiritual dangers are those they dread the most for us, and they apply themselves especially to enable us to avoid them. Constantly attentive to the snares and ambushes laid for us by our invisible enemies, they strive to preserve us from them: at one time they enlighten us interiorly on the danger which threatens us; at other times they inspire us with a salutary horror of the seductions employed against us; then, again, they obtain by their prayers that we be not exposed to too great trials; or, if we have fallen, they hinder the devil from taking advantage of our falls by helping us to rise again immediately. Oh! if at this moment all the services that have ever been rendered me by these generous Protectors were revealed to me, with what sentiments of gratitude would not my heart be penetrated! No, I can never form a just idea of their anxious zeal and charitable offices here below; only in eternity shall I be able to understand the extent to which I am indebted to them.

Colloquy with the holy Angels. Let us pay them our homage of reverence, gratitude, and love. Let us thank them for the charitable care they have lavished upon us ever since our birth. Let us pray to them to obtain for us a complete victory over the enemies of our soul, and beg them to enable us to reach Heaven, notwithstanding the many dangers by which we are surrounded.

Resolutions. Often to call to mind the presence of God, and to perform all my actions to please Him. To invoke the holy Angels in my trials and difficulties.

Offering of the Resolutions, page 3.

Spiritual Bouquet. The Angels of God are my guardians and protectors.

Prayer. Angel of God, to whose care Divine Providence has committed me, enlighten me, protect me against my enemies, and guide me in the way of salvation.

Examen of the Meditation, page 4.

MEDITATION FOR THE FEAST OF THE GUARDIAN ANGELS.

(2ND OCTOBER.)

"He hath given His Angels charge over thee, and they shall bear thee up lest thou dash thy foot against a stone" (Ps. xc. 11).

Preparatory Prayer, page 1.

1st Prelude. Imagine that you see a number of Angels on the earth eager to render all kinds of good offices to mankind. Behold in particular the Angel God has given you to be your guardian, and recollect yourself in his presence.

2nd Prelude. O my good Angel! obtain for me the grace to understand how tender and continual is thy care for me, and enable me to correspond with thy goodness by my gratitude and love.

1st Point. What the office is of the guardian Angels in our regard.

"He hath given His Angels charge over thee." Let us consider how precious and honourable are the relations established by our good God between us and His Angels. These heavenly Spirits, who constantly behold His face, have received from Him the command to protect and watch over us, and guide us in the way of salvation; each one of us has for a protector and guide a prince of the heavenly court. What a subject for confidence and joy! What is man, O Lord, to merit such a favour? Is a creature made from the dust of the earth worthy that so sublime a Spirit should watch over him and preserve him from all danger? Can a sinful soul deserve to have for a friend an Angel whose looks are so pure and who has never offended Thee? These blessed Spirits love us with an incomprehensible tenderness; they shield us from the dangers which threaten our soul or body; they defend us against the attacks of the wicked spirits, present our prayers to God, instruct us interiorly, and are, in all places and circumstances, the ministers of the divine bounty in our regard. O my holy Angel! What gratitude do I not owe thee for so much charitable care! And yet, alas! what ingratitude I have to reproach myself with towards thee! My holy Protector, pardon my coldness, my indifference, and the culpable resistance by which I have so often grieved thee. I wish at length to correspond with thy goodness and show myself worthy of the care thou hast deigned to take of me.

2nd Point. What our duties are towards our guardian Angel.

St. Bernard sums up in three words all the duties which we have to fulfil towards our guardian Angels. "We owe them," he says, "respect, devotion, and confidence." Our good Angel follows us everywhere; always we have his most pure eyes for witnesses: with what modesty, what watchfulness over self, what holy purity ought not his holy presence to inspire us! The result of our respect for him ought to be the most perfect watchfulness in all our actions. Our guardian Angel presents us with a perfect model of every virtue: obedience, humility, zeal for the glory of God and the salvation of souls, unreserved devotedness to the holy will of God, unshaken fidelity in accomplishing all it ordains. Our devotion to him should consist above all in imitating his example and practising the virtues which are so dear to him. Our good Angel is a warrior of God Almighty's army who has fought and overthrown our enemies; a zealous protector who is willing to help us to overcome them ourselves. We ought, then, to have recourse to him with entire confidence in all our dangers and temptations. I thank Thee, O my God, for having given me such a guardian. Give me grace to be ever faithful to his salutary inspirations, and courageous in repelling under his guidance the attacks of the spirit of darkness; to the end that, having at the hour of my death gained a last victory over the enemy of all good, I may be presented by my good Angel before Thy sacred tribunal, there to receive from Thee a favourable sentence.

Colloquy with our good Angel Guardian. Let us thank him for the charitable care he has been pleased to take of us ever since our birth. Let us ask his pardon for our infidelities and resistance to his holy inspirations; promising him to be more faithful for the future. Let us beg of him to obtain for us all the graces necessary for us in order to triumph over the enemies of our salvation.

Resolutions. Often to call to mind the presence of my good Angel, and to address myself to him in my many necessities with the most entire confidence.

Offering of the Resolutions, page 3.

Spiritual Bouquet. " The Angel of the Lord is with me."

Prayer. Angel of God, etc.

Examen of the Meditation, page 4.

MEDITATION FOR THE FEAST OF ST. FRANCIS OF ASSISI.

(4TH OCTOBER.)

" I bear in my body the wounds of Jesus crucified."

Preparatory Prayer, page 1.

1st Prelude. Represent to yourself St. Francis of Assisi at the moment in which a Seraph marked him with the sacred stigmata of the Passion of our Lord.

2nd Prelude. Great Saint, who wast so perfect a model of religious poverty and mortification, obtain for me the grace to detach my heart from the things of this world, and help me to overcome entirely all my vicious inclinations.

1st Point. The poverty of St. Francis of Assisi.

St. Francis of Assisi was a perfect model of evangelical poverty; he carried this virtue so far, that finding a house which had been built for himself and his brethren too large and convenient, he caused it to be taken down and rebuilt smaller and poorer. On being asked one day which of all the virtues was most agreeable to God, " Poverty," he replied, " is the way to Heaven, the nurse of humility, and the root of perfection. Its fruits are hidden, but they multiply in numberless ways." Such was the extent to which this great Saint, enlightened from on high, loved and esteemed holy poverty. What ought to be my sentiments on this important matter? Our Lord does not demand of all Christians the sacrifice of the goods which Providence has bestowed on them; but the spirit of Christianity insists that we detach our heart from them, that we regard them as a deposit placed in our hands for the term of our life, and for the use of which we shall have one day to render a rigorous account. Again, faith teaches us that these temporal advantages are often dangerous to salvation; that it is difficult for a rich man to enter the Kingdom of Heaven, however little he may love and esteem his riches; that the poor are blessed, etc. . . . Are these maxims engraven in my mind, and in my heart? Do I know how to conform my conduct to them?

2nd Point. The mortification of St. Francis of Assisi.

Few of the Saints have carried the practice of penance and holy austerity so far as St. Francis of Assisi; it was through his conformity with Jesus crucified that he merited to receive in his body the sacred stigmata of the Passion of our Divine Saviour. Here again my position and the duties of my state forbid me the pious excesses to which the Saints gave themselves up; but the mortification of the body is only the least part of that universal abnegation which has to destroy sin within me. What a vast field opens itself out to my zeal if I will but labour seriously to die to myself! Bearing with defects of others, kindness towards those with whom I live, watchfulness in repressing curiosity, the wanderings of my imagination and the superfluous desires of my heart, in order to acquire the spirit of recollection and prayer, are so many precious means granted to me to subdue and immolate nature, and to carry imprinted, not in my flesh, but in my heart and in all the faculties of my soul, the mortification of Jesus Christ. Am I faithful in making good use of them?

Colloquy with our Lord. Let us offer Him the merits and virtues of His faithful servant, St. Francis of Assisi, and ask Him, through the intercession of this great Saint, for the spirit of detachment, interior mortification, and of all the virtues we ought to practise in our state of life.

Resolutions. To examine, before God, if my heart be not somewhat too much attached to what I possess. To bear with meekness and patience the little contradictions which Divine Providence may send me to-day.

Offering of the Resolutions, page 3.
Spiritual Bouquet. "My God and my all!"
Prayer. Receive, O Lord, etc., page 18.
Examen of the Meditation, page 4.

MEDITATION FOR THE FEAST OF ST. FRANCIS BORGIA.

(10TH OCTOBER.)

"I count all things to be but loss . . . that I may gain Christ" (Phil. iii. 8).

Preparatory Prayer, page 1.
1st Prelude. Figure to yourself St. Francis Borgia at the moment when, beholding the dead body of the

Empress Isabella, he formed the design of quitting the world, and consecrating himself to God.

2nd Prelude. Grant me grace, O Lord, to imitate Thy servant St. Francis Borgia, by despising as he did the glory and pleasures of the earth, in order to seek happiness in loving and serving Thee alone.

1st Point. The contempt of St. Francis Borgia for the honours and pleasures of this world.

Divine Providence had surrounded St. Francis Borgia with all that the world terms pleasure and happiness; but, illuminated with a supernatural light and appreciating all things according to the rules of the spirit of faith, he knew how to be humble in the midst of honours, and mortified in the lap of luxury. More than this, penetrated with contempt for the figure of this world which is passing away, he considered that the precious treasure of religious poverty would not be too dearly purchased at the price of all his possessions, and that the glory of being a servant in the house of God was preferable to ruling over others in the world. Are my judgments concerning the honours and goods of this present life like those of this great Saint? If I possess riches, do I know how to use them as if I used them not, according to the words of the Apostle; that is to say, do I look on them as a deposit which God has confided to me for a time, and do I employ them only according to His holy will? If I am deprived of them, do I know how to love and esteem my position, as being the most precious in the eyes of faith, the most safe for my salvation, and the most conformable to that of my adorable model? The judgments of Jesus Christ and those of the world concerning rank and riches are totally opposed: on which side do I find myself?

2nd Point. The esteem of St. Francis Borgia for the practices of the interior life.

As soon as St. Francis Borgia had broken the ties which had detained him in the world, he applied himself to the practice of religious virtues with an ardour worthy of the generosity of his early sacrifices. Even before quitting the world, he had habituated himself to prayer and the spirit of recollection, both which could not fail to increase in religion : thus, in a short time, he became so perfect in his prayer that it was continual, and the most distracting occupations could not withdraw him from the presence of God, nor interrupt the holy communications which he held with Him. If I were faithful in disengaging my heart from all disorderly affections, and in practising, as well as I might, this holy recollection which the Saints have so greatly esteemed, my God would take a pleasure in communicating Himself to me. He would illuminate me with His light, and would deliver me more and more from the illusions which seduce me. He would strengthen me with His grace, in order to enable me to triumph over the obstacles by which I am surrounded, and would cause me to taste the sweet unction of His love, to console me in my trials and continually refresh the vigour of my soul. Oh! how great an enemy am I not to myself, when I give way to that thoughtlessness which deprives me of so much good! Shall I not at length make efforts to share in those precious and chosen favours with which the Sacred Heart of Jesus blesses interior and faithful souls?

Colloquy with our Lord. Let us offer Him the virtues and merits of St. Francis Borgia. Let us beg of Him through the intercession of this great Saint to grant us the spirit of humility, mortification, recollection, prayer, and union with His Sacred Heart.

Resolutions. To practise recollection frequently during the day, and not to let any opportunity escape me of practising humility.

Offering of the Resolutions, page 3.

Spiritual Bouquet. "The Kingdom of God is within you."

Prayer. Receive, O Lord, etc., page 18.

Examen of the Meditation, page 4.

MEDITATION FOR THE FEAST OF ST. TERESA.

(15TH OCTOBER.)

"Thou shalt love the Lord thy God with thy whole heart, with thy whole mind, with all thy soul, and with all thy strength" (Matt. xxii. 37).

Preparatory Prayer, page 1.

1st Prelude. Represent to yourself St. Teresa in Heaven on a high throne, or else praying in her oratory.

2nd Prelude. O great Saint, obtain for me the grace to imitate thee in thy love for God, in thy fidelity to His grace, in thy zeal for His glory.

1st Point. The interior spirit of St. Teresa.

Let us consider how well calculated the example of St. Teresa is to inspire us with a love and esteem for that interior life and spirit of prayer which ought to be the animating principle of the whole life of a Christian. St. Teresa was always united to God; all her actions, all the movements of her heart, had no other end in view but His glory and the accomplishment of His divine will. How pure were all her motives! Even in the lamentations in which she deplores what she calls the infidelities and wanderings of her life, she cannot prevent herself from owning that her intention was good in all her actions, and that she erred alone from not being sufficiently enlightened. What a spirit of prayer and love for the things of God, in the very avowals in which she deplores her imperfections with so much bitterness! She took pleasure in speaking of God alone, and in hearing Him spoken of: already prayer had become her delight, and she engaged all those who were intimate with her to make trial of its sweetness. What Saint ever carried further the spirit of abnegation and forgetfulness of self? The love of God reigned within her unopposed: consequently the adorable Object of her affections honoured her with His most intimate communications; she found Him everywhere, and even when asleep she was actually occupied in declaring her love for Him. No heart, after that of the Queen of the Saints, was ever more closely united to the adorable Heart of Jesus than was the heart of St. Teresa. What more perfect model, then, can they who desire to give pleasure to our ever Blessed Lord propose to themselves than this seraphic Virgin, whose love was so pure and so perfect, and whose every action, every thought, and every feeling were guided by this love alone, which had become the soul of her soul?

2nd Point. The zeal of St. Teresa.

St. Teresa excelled in all virtue, and we may find abundant food for our soul in her example of detachment, of meekness, of charity, and of love of mortification. But, above all, she excelled in that pure and ardent zeal with which a soul that loves Jesus ought to be penetrated. It was this zeal which inspired her with the thought of reforming the entire Order of Mount Carmel, and of founding a number of convents into which she infused the fervour with which she was herself inspired, in order that God might be glorified by so many holy souls whose prayers and sacrifices would draw down on sinners the graces of conversion and salvation. What great success crowned her labours! Her trials, and the combats she had to undergo, were amply recompensed by the joy which she experienced in seeing the reign of Jesus Christ extended by her agency; and a number of those who up to that time had known and served Him only imperfectly, attached themselves closely to Him and followed Him lovingly in the narrow and difficult paths of religious perfection. Like her I ought to endeavour to infuse into the souls of others the sacred fire which my Divine Lord brought down upon the earth. Undoubtedly I am not destined for such a great work; yet, according to circumstances, I can edify, instruct, exhort, and advise; above all, I can make use of prayer and mortification,—means the efficacy of which is always certain. After the example of St. Teresa, I ought constantly to increase within my soul generosity and zeal, to spare no effort, to shrink from no sacrifice so soon as there shall be question of the glory of God and the salvation of souls.

Colloquy with St. Teresa. Let us congratulate her on the happiness she now enjoys, and on the wonderful success which has crowned her devotedness and fidelity. Let us beg of her to obtain for us from Jesus the grace to imitate her spirit of prayer, her self-contempt, her generosity, her zeal and untiring efforts to make Him known and loved.

Resolutions. To practise recollection and fidelity to grace.

Offering of the Resolutions, page 3.

Spiritual Bouquet. "Seraphic St. Teresa, pray for us who have recourse to thee."

Prayer. Receive, O Lord, etc., page 18.

Examen of the Meditation, page 4.

MEDITATION FOR THE FEAST OF ST. LUKE THE EVANGELIST.

(18TH OCTOBER.)

"You have not chosen Me; but I have chosen you, and have appointed you that you should go, and should bring forth fruit; and your fruit should remain" (John xv. 16).

Preparatory Prayer, page 1.

1st Prelude. Represent to yourself St. Luke writing his Gospel.

2nd Prelude. Great Saint, who wast a Disciple, Evangelist, and Martyr of Jesus Christ, obtain for me the grace to glorify my Divine Lord by conforming my life to the maxims of the Gospel.

1st Point. St. Luke wrote and preached the holy Gospel; I ought to exemplify it in my conduct, and thus preach it by my example.

St. Luke was chosen by our Lord to write the holy Gospel and to preach it to the idolaters; he acquitted himself faithfully of this two-fold task, and thus helped to spread the Kingdom of Jesus Christ. I also am called to do this: as the disciple of Jesus, I ought to occupy myself about His glory and the salvation of souls, whatever may be the duties assigned me by Providence. If I am charged to instruct, I should, by assiduous meditation on the words of life contained in the holy Gospel, qualify myself to teach others to relish them and nourish their souls with them. If the duties of my state have no direct bearing upon the salvation of souls, I ought still to exhort and instruct others by the holiness of my life, and by my constant application to carry out in my conduct the maxims of the Christian religion. This silent preaching is often the most efficacious of all, and God alone knows all the fruits of grace which may be produced by one who is careful to put them in practice. Sacred Heart of Jesus, grant me grace to be interior and faithful; grant that becoming profoundly penetrated with the spirit of the holy Gospel, I may inspire all those with whom Thy Divine Providence may place me, with the love and esteem of that spirit.

2nd Point. St. Luke painted the picture of our Lady; I ought to trace her image within me by practising her virtues.

St. Luke was the first, according to a pious tradition, who painted the likeness of the Blessed Virgin; he drew a portrait of her which is preserved to this day in the eternal City. I ought also to form within me this sacred likeness, not upon canvas, but within my own heart: purity, humility, meekness, and all other Christian virtues, are the colours which I ought to make use of, in order to produce this sacred likeness. This task is for me of indispensable obligation; there is no salvation to be hoped for except for those in whom our Heavenly Father shall find a resemblance with His beloved Son. Now, I cannot be like Jesus without imitating Mary also, since the Heart of the Son and that of the Mother are so like each other and so intimately united; it even seems that the imitation of Mary ought to be, in some sense, easier for me and better suited to my weakness; she is but a pure creature, she is my tender Mother, and her love offers me, in order to aid my weakness, the most precious and abundant aid. With what confidence, then, ought I not to have recourse to her! With what zeal ought I not to study her immaculate Heart that I may conform mine to it, and thus deserve the love of the Sacred Heart of Jesus!

Colloquy with St. Luke. Let us pay him homage of veneration. Let us beg of him to obtain for us the grace to meditate on his holy Gospel with fruit, and to impress its spirit upon the souls of those with whom we may have intercourse. Let us ask him also for the aid of his intercession with the Mother of God, in order to obtain the grace to imitate her, and be pleasing in her sight.

Resolutions. To perform all my actions to-day in union with those of Jesus and Mary.

Offering of the Resolutions, page 3.

Spiritual Bouquet. Jesus and Mary, may my heart be like Yours.

Prayer. Pater Noster.

Examen of the Meditation, page 4.

MEDITATION FOR THE FEAST OF ST. RAPHAEL THE ARCHANGEL.

(24TH OCTOBER.)

" He hath given His Angels charge over thee; they shall bear thee up lest thou dash thy foot against a stone " (Ps. xc. 12).

Preparatory Prayer, page 1.

1st Prelude. Represent to yourself the road to Rages, along which the Archangel Raphael accompanied the young Tobias.

2nd Prelude. God of goodness, Who dost grant us so many helps through Thy heavenly messengers, deign to inspire me with the gratitude, love, respect and confidence with which I ought to be filled for these blessed Spirits.

1st Point. The Archangel Raphael accompanies the young Tobias in his journey, and preserves him from all dangers.

The touching history of the care which the Archangel Raphael took of the young Tobias in his journey is well fitted to awaken within me those sentiments of love, gratitude, tender confidence and holy respect which I ought to have in regard to the Guardian Angel appointed to watch over me by Divine Providence. This blessed Spirit performs for me invisibly what the Angel Raphael did in visible form for the young man he was charged to lead on his way; he keeps me from all danger, defends me against those infernal enemies who would destroy my soul and snatch from me the precious life of grace : he guides me in the sure path of salvation. If I am docile to his voice I shall never go astray ; in fine, he directs me so wisely by his counsels that unless I offer resistance I shall acquire, not temporal goods as did the spouse of the young Sarah, but riches infinitely more precious : the riches of grace and of most intimate union with God Himself. Oh, how great is my happiness to have such a guide ! With what confidence ought not his charity to inspire me! With what docility ought I not to follow his guidance in all things!

2nd Point. The Archangel Raphael restores sight to the father of the young Tobias.

This new blessing reminds me again of all those which my Guardian Angel ceases not to lavish on me. The blindness of the holy patriarch Tobias is the symbol of that which often affects my soul and robs me of light from on high. In fact, how often have not pride, self-love and resistance to grace enveloped my understanding with thick darkness, and deprived me of the knowledge of that which God was asking from me! At such times what has my zealous protector done for me? He has prayed for me, and has applied to my soul a saving remedy, which has restored to me that sacred light of which I had rendered myself unworthy. He has frequently renewed within me this precious cure, he still renews it every day, and if I profited by it as I ought to do, I should walk in the fulness of light and in the paths of perfection. O, faithful and zealous guardian of my soul! I return thee thanks for so much valuable aid; vouchsafe to continue to help me notwithstanding my many infidelities: I wish at length to cease my resistance to that light of my soul which thou dost cause to shine before my eyes, that so I may deserve to be freed from all blindness.

Colloquy with my Guardian Angel. Let us thank him for all the kind offices he never ceases to render us on all occasions. Let us ask his pardon for our ingratitude and resistance, begging him not to cease to help and enlighten us. Let us promise him to be docile to his heavenly inspirations.

Resolutions. To follow faithfully all the interior lights which shall be given me to avoid sin and make progress in virtue.

Offering of the Resolutions, page 3.

Spiritual Bouquet. "Holy Angel, my good Guardian, enlighten me with thy light."
Prayer. Angel of God, etc.
Examen of the Meditation, page 4.

MEDITATION FOR THE FEAST OF SS. SIMON AND JUDE.

(28TH OCTOBER.)

"Go ye and teach all nations, baptising them in the name of the Father and of the Son and of the Holy Ghost ; teaching them to observe all things whatsoever I have commanded you" (Matt. xxiii.).
"He that believeth and is baptised shall be saved; but he that believeth not shall be condemned" (Mark xvi.).

Preparatory Prayer, page 1.

1st Prelude. Imagine to yourself the moment in which Jesus, about to ascend to Heaven, gave the command to His Apostles to preach the Gospel to the whole world.

2nd Prelude. Grant me grace, O my Lord, to gain from this meditation a spirit of lively faith, ardent zeal and great generosity.

1st Point. I owe never-ending acts of thanksgiving to God for having bestowed on me the precious gift of faith.

St. Simon and St. Jude were apostles : they contributed to the establishment of the Church. What gratitude ought not to arise within me every time the feasts come round of these first preachers of the Gospel ! They recall to my mind the priceless gift of faith, given to me by God from my infancy, in preference to so many others who are plunged in the darkness of idolatry, or are led astray by false doctrines. God could see nothing in me to merit such a benefit. He bestowed it on me through His pure mercy, and because He loved me with a special love. Can I, in my turn, remain unmoved with love and gratitude ? But I must not confine myself to sterile acts of thanksgiving; my God expects something more of me; He wishes me to labour to keep alive the faith which He has given me, by conforming my actions to my belief. I believe that no one can serve two masters; that the world is the object of the denunciations of Jesus Christ; that my Divine Saviour will acknowledge before His Father those only who have not been ashamed of Him before men. I must, in consequence, belong entirely to God, and not adopt the practices of the world, nor share in its unlawful pleasures. I must declare myself openly on the side of my Divine Lord by conduct eminently Christian. By acting thus I shall live by faith, and shall share in all the blessings it procures for the truly faithful soul.

2nd Point. The example of the Apostles teaches me how great my zeal should be for the glory of God and the salvation of souls.

The characteristic virtues which distinguished the Apostles teach me important lessons. The zeal which consumed them for the glory of God and the salvation of souls caused them to embrace with courage all labours and sacrifices. Nothing seemed to them beyond their strength; the greatest dangers were not able to stay their activity. All of them sealed with their blood the truths which they preached. I am not called, it is true, as they were, to preach the Gospel; yet I am the child of God, and the interests of such a Father ought not to leave me indifferent. I am a disciple of Jesus, and I ought to esteem myself happy to be able to work for the establishment of the reign of my Divine Lord. This zeal, so very just, ought to inspire me with a holy industry to gain souls for God! What a happiness and merit for me if I am able to snatch souls from hell and lead them to Heaven! What a glory and joy for me if when I myself enter my heavenly country, I shall be able to offer to God these conquests of my prayers and labours! O Holy Apostles! obtain for me the grace to ensure for myself so sweet a triumph, by seizing every opportunity that shall be offered me of leading others to virtue.

Colloquy with the Sacred Heart of Jesus. Let us thank Him for the precious gift of faith which He bestowed on us even before we were capable of desiring it. Let us pray for the grace of zeal for the salvation of souls, and endeavour to procure this zeal by our prayers, our good example, our words, and by every other means in our power.

Resolutions. To offer up all my actions for the salvation of souls.

Offering of the Resolutions, page 3.
Spiritual Bouquet. " Lord, help my unbelief."
Prayer. Pater Noster, etc.
Examen of the Meditation, page 4.

MEDITATION FOR THE FEAST OF BLESSED ALPHONSUS RODRIGUEZ.

(3RD OCTOBER.)

" The just man shall be like a tree which is planted near the running waters, which shall bring forth fruit in due season " (Ps. i. 3).

Preparatory Prayer, page 1.
1st Prelude. Represent to yourself the Blessed Alphonsus in prayer ; everything in him breathes recollection, respect, and fervour.
2nd Prelude. Grant me grace, O Lord, to love Thee perfectly, and to despise myself, following in this the example of Thy holy servant.
1st Point. The love of the Blessed Alphonsus for God.

All the virtues practised by this perfect model of interior life may be reduced to two principal virtues— love of God and hatred of self. The Blessed

Alphonsus was so entirely filled with the love of God that he found his greatest pleasure in prayer. His prayer was continual. No exterior actions could draw his mind from the presence of his Beloved: he knew how to find Him everywhere, and how to behold Him in all things. It was God Whom he obeyed in his superiors: he respected and loved Him in each one of his brethren; and even in the smallest duties of his state he recognised so many orders emanating from the will of God, which he faithfully accomplished through his love of Him. It was this same love which made him hanker after sufferings, so that he shed bitter tears because the weakness caused by advancing old age did not permit him any longer to chastise his body so severely as had been his custom. It was love, also, which inspired him with so tender a devotion towards the Mother of God; he beheld in her the Mother of Jesus, cherished above all other creatures by the adorable Trinity; thence arose that eagerness to be pleasing to her, and that zeal in honouring her which knew no bounds. Does the love of God work like effects in me? Have I that ardent love which makes me take delight in prayer and in the spirit of recollection? that generous love which yearns after the Cross? that filial devotion towards Mary, which in the judgment of the Saints was always inseparable from the perfect love of Jesus? O Blessed Alphonsus! obtain for me the grace to imitate thee, and by my ardent love to glorify that infinitely good God Who has prevented me with so many graces.

2nd Point. The hatred of the Blessed Alphonsus for himself.

The love which consumed this fervent religious filled him with a holy indignation against his own depraved inclinations, whence arose his indefatigable zeal in mortifying his body and his senses; whence, above all, sprang his profound and sincere humility, his love of contempt and abjection, which rendered him as eager for humiliations as the proudest men of this world are for praise and honour. Here, again, what a difference there is between his conduct and mine! Far from relishing and loving humiliations, I recoil from them and shun them; the life of the senses and of nature is full of vigour in me; I scarcely know what it is to carry the Cross; thus the charms of an interior life are unknown to me. I am ignorant of the sweetness flowing from union with God, because I have not yet learnt to forsake myself; I cannot taste of the manna from Heaven, because I am fed from the flesh-pots of Egypt. God of goodness, deign to have mercy on me; grant me grace, through the merits of Thy holy servant, to overcome myself so completely that I may live in future for Thee alone.

Colloquy with our Lord. Let us thank Him for the wonderful favours with which He has been pleased to enrich the soul of the Blessed Alphonsus. Let us offer to Him the merits of His faithful servant, and implore through his intercession the grace to practise those interior and solid virtues which God so earnestly desires to find in those who belong to Him.

Resolutions. To practise recollection, humility, and fidelity to grace.

Offering of the Resolutions, page 3.

Spiritual Bouquet. "Grant, O Lord, that I may know Thee in order to love Thee, and that I may know myself in order to hate myself."

Prayer. Receive, O Lord, etc., page 18.

Examen of the Meditation, page 4.

FIRST MEDITATION FOR THE FEAST OF ALL SAINTS.

(1st November.)

"Blessed are the poor in spirit, for theirs is the kingdom of Heaven. Blessed are the clean of heart, for they shall see God. Blessed are they that suffer persecution for justice' sake, for theirs is the kingdom of Heaven" (Matt. v. 3, 8, 10).

Preparatory Prayer, page 1.

1st Prelude. Imagine that you see Heaven open above you, and all the Saints stretching out their arms to you, and inviting you to come and share their happiness and their glory.

2nd Prelude. O happy Saints of God! obtain for me the grace to tread in your footsteps in the holy path of self-renunciation and Christian perfection.

1st Point. The Gospel of this day marks out for me three principal means of sanctification.

A multitude of Saints of all ages and positions in life have preceded me to the abode of eternal glory. I am called to follow after them; consequently it is of the greatest importance for me to consider attentively the means by which they reached Heaven. The Gospel, appointed to be read on this Festival, places before my eyes the eight principal virtues which I ought to practise if I wish to be happy; but there are three above all, to which the kingdom of Heaven is more directly promised. These three virtues are those which combat immediately the triple concupiscence which we brought with us into the world. Poverty of spirit is the destruction of avarice; purity of heart rejects all sensuality and undue love of the wanton pleasures of this life; while courage to bear up against the persecution of the world and of hell is the remedy for pride. Consequently, there is no other way for me to practise these three virtues, if I wish to overcome nature, make myself like Jesus, and attain eternal happiness.

2nd Point. There are different degrees in the practice of virtue.

What ought I to do in order to fulfil perfectly the three conditions to which Jesus attaches the promise of eternal happiness? " Blessed are the poor in spirit," says our Divine Lord, " for theirs is the kingdom of Heaven." Poverty of spirit has three degrees, of which the first is to detach our affections from the goods of this life; the second is to submit willingly to the guidance of Providence when God permits us to be deprived of gifts of mind and of heart, of our reputation, of the esteem of creatures, or the affection of our friends; the third, and the most perfect, consists in being detached even from goods of a superior order, when they are not necessary for our advancement in virtue. Thus, one who is truly poor easily renounces spiritual sweetnesses and interior consolations when our Lord judges fit to refuse them. Purity of heart has equally three degrees: it consists, first, in being penetrated with horror for mortal sin; secondly, in having an equal horror for all venial faults, and in never committing any deliberately, as they wound the sanctity of God; thirdly and lastly, to conform our affections so perfectly to those of the Sacred Heart of Jesus, as to love only what He loved—the cross, humiliations, and sufferings; and to hate what He detested—the spirit of the world, the satisfactions of nature, and all that is comprised in these three words—*pleasures, honours,* and *riches.* The third beatitude engages the faithful soul to sustain with courage all combats, all contradictions of hell, all painful struggles after virtue; to esteem and love them as the most appropriate means of conforming oneself to the great Model of the predestined, and of treading in the footprints of Jesus as we journey towards the goal of a blessed eternity. Such is the path traced out for me—it is narrow and difficult; but all-powerful aid is offered me through the Sacred Heart of my Divine Lord, for Jesus is a just and good God, Who cannot insist on the end without giving the means.

Colloquy with our Lord. Let us thank Him for the grace He has bestowed upon us by having caused us to be born in the true Faith, and for all the means of sanctification by which we are surrounded. Let us ask Him for the true spirit of Christianity, the grace to attach ourselves with all our heart to the practice of the three great virtues to which He has promised the kingdom of Heaven, and to acquire them, cost what it may.

Resolutions. To watch carefully over myself, to sacrifice all the inclinations of nature, and to follow all the impressions of grace.

Offering of the Resolutions, page 3.

Spiritual Bouquet. "Blessed are the poor in spirit, for they shall possess the land. Blessed are the clean of heart, for they shall see God. Blessed are they that suffer persecution for justice' sake, for theirs is the kingdom of Heaven."

Prayer. Soul of Christ, sanctify me, etc.

Examen of the Meditation, page 4.

SECOND MEDITATION.
(For the same Day.)

"I heard as it were the voice of much people in Heaven saying: Alleluia, salvation and glory and power is to our God" (Apoc. xix. 1).

Preparatory Prayer, page 1.

1st Prelude. Represent to yourself Heaven, where all the Saints are assembled together; they surround the Throne of Jesus, and celebrate His glory, repeating these words: "Thou alone art Holy, Thou alone art Lord, Thou alone most High". Jesus looks down lovingly upon me, discloses to me His Sacred Heart, and addresses me in these words : " I am the Way, the Truth, and the Life ".

2nd Prelude. Heart of Jesus, Source of all holiness, speak to my heart and fill it with a desire to imitate all Thy divine virtues.

1st Point. Jesus is the Saint of Saints and the Author of Grace.

It is from Jesus that all the Saints have derived their sanctity ; He is the model of them all, and it is His grace which has worked in them the prodigies of virtue which have rendered them so worthy of veneration. It is from the Sacred Heart of Jesus that the Apostles have derived their zeal ; the Martyrs their generous spirit of self-sacrifice ; the Confessors their strength ; the Doctors their light ; and the Virgins their purity. From this adorable Heart has flowed into their hearts that powerful grace which has raised them above human weakness, has renewed their youth, has sanctified them and enriched them with all virtues. Jesus was their Saviour and Sanctifier upon earth ; He is now their happiness and their glory in Heaven. They love to praise Him for their eternal glory ; they bless Him with a gratitude, love, and joy corresponding to the knowledge they have of His benefits. On this day they urge me to unite my praises to theirs : I can do nothing which will honour them more, or be more pleasing to them, than to offer to Jesus their merits, their holiness, their happiness, and their glory.

2nd Point. We ought to seek for sanctity in Jesus Christ, and ask it of Him through the intercession of the Saints.

I am a Christian, that is to say, a disciple of Jesus Christ ; I am an adopted child of my Heavenly Father, called upon to walk in the footsteps of the Saints. Consequently, I ought, after their example, to unite myself to Jesus as to the only Author of all sanctity. I ought to seek in His example, in His teaching, and in

His grace, for the light and strength I need to triumph over nature and become a new creature. Such obligations bind me, it is true, to combats and to sacrifices, but what powerful aids are placed at my disposal! All the inhabitants of Heaven interest themselves in my salvation; all offer me their suffrages, and desire to obtain for me from the Saint of Saints the same graces and the same virtues which have enabled them to attain to eternal happiness. With what confidence and holy joy ought not such a thought to inspire me! Whatever my wants may be, I have zealous protectors in Heaven, who are ready to help me. The Martyrs wish to obtain strength for me; the Confessors a generous spirit; the Doctors prudence; the Patriarchs holy longings for salvation; the Virgins unsullied purity; the Anchorets and holy penitents the spirit of mortification; all the Saints, in a word, abundant graces calculated to raise me above myself, and to unite me to Him Who is the Way, the Truth, and the Life. O holy friends of God! I cast myself at your feet with the most entire confidence; obtain for me of your Master and mine that He may vouchsafe to produce in my heart all the virtues of His Sacred Heart, and to associate me one day to your glory and your triumph.

Colloquy with our Lord. Let us adore Him as the Saint of Saints, the Source of every grace, and only Author of all sanctity. Let us offer Him the merits of His elect, and bless Him, in union with them, for the wonders which He has worked in their souls. Let us ask Him, through their intercession, for the grace to imitate them, and to give Him glory in our turn by leading a life conformable to His example and doctrine.

Resolutions. To keep myself united to the Sacred Heart of Jesus, the Source of all sanctity, and to perform all my actions with a view to His greater glory.

Offering of the Resolutions, page 3.

Spiritual Bouquet. " Jesus, crown of all the Saints, have mercy on me."
Prayer. Soul of Christ, etc.
Examen of the Meditation, page 4.

THIRD MEDITATION FOR THE SAME DAY.

APPLICATION OF THE SENSES.

Preparatory Prayer, page 1.
1st Prelude. Recall to your mind what faith teaches us of Heaven—that it is an abode of peace and happiness, where our Lord rewards for ever those who have been faithful to Him.
2nd Prelude. Figure to yourself the interior of Heaven, that happy abode lit up with the glory of God; contemplate the sacred humanity of Jesus Christ; gaze upon Mary, upon the Angels and the Saints.
3rd Prelude. Grant me, O Lord, to earnestly desire and esteem the goods of Heaven, so that these may serve as a spur to my fervour, and as a motive for my fidelity.
1st Point—Sight. Let us view all that is contained in the dwelling of the Saints; God in all His majesty . . . Jesus Christ, in Whom the divine and human natures are united, filling the heavenly Jerusalem with brightness and joy . . . Mary Immaculate, resplendent with glory, exalted above the Angels and the Saints, seated on a throne beside her Divine Son. All the Choirs of the heavenly Spirits shining with sanctity and crowned with glory . . . the venerable assembly of the Patriarchs, Prophets, and Apostles . . . the triumphant hosts of the Martyrs . . . the august assemblage of the Doctors, and the happy choir of the Virgins consecrated to the Lamb without spot. Again, let us behold that countless multitude of all ranks and

all ages, of all nations and all conditions, admitted to the heavenly Jerusalem. What beauty, what grandeur and splendour, what joy in their countenances, what transport in their hearts! . . . Let us further consider the radiant beauty of that holy city; it is illuminated, not by torches or by the light of the stars, but the Lamb of God, Jesus, "is the lamp thereof"; He fills it with divine splendour. " Never shall there be night there," says the holy Scripture; "they shall not need a lamp, for the Lord their God shall enlighten them, and they shall reign for ever and ever."

2nd Point—Hearing. Let us hearken to the canticles of love, praise, and thanksgiving with which the Saints cause their heavenly abode to resound. "Salvation to our God, Who sitteth upon the throne, and to the Lamb," they cry in unison. "Benediction and glory, and wisdom and thanksgiving, honour and power and strength to our God, for ever and ever. Amen! Holy, holy, holy, Lord God of Hosts, Hosanna in the highest! salvation and glory to our God."

3rd Point—Smell. Let us inhale the odour of the Divinity, of the immortality and perfect happiness with which Heaven is filled.

4th Point—Taste. Let us taste of the glory of the blessed . . . the holy transports of their gratitude . . . the ardour of their love . . . and the eternal peace which fills them with delights too great for words.

5th Point—Touch. Let us kiss in spirit that land of the living, which is not a land of earth but of pure gold; those sacred walls, those mystic gates . . . and that Book of Life, in which our names are now all written. . . . Let us kiss the Cross also, that instrument of our salvation which constitutes the glory and the ornament of Heaven; but let us remember, at the same time, that the Cross is the ladder by which we mount to Heaven, and that in order to reign with Jesus Christ we must first share in His sufferings and humiliations.

Colloquy with the Most Blessed Trinity, with Mary, with the Angels and the Saints. Let us adore the three Divine Persons, offering them the merits and the praises of all the Angels and all the Saints. Let us offer to Jesus Christ the sanctity and happiness of His elect, as the fruit of His redemption and the triumph of His grace. Let us pay our homage to Mary as to the Queen of the Heavenly City, begging of her to show herself to be our Mother. Let us invoke in succession all the Choirs of the heavenly Spirits, and the different ranks of the elect, congratulating them on their glory, and asking each for some special grace, in accordance with the distinctive character of each.

Resolutions. To encourage myself with the thought of Heaven, when I am in difficulties in which the practice of virtue demands painful efforts.

Offering of the Resolutions, page 3.

Spiritual Bouquet. " How vile this earth appears when I contemplate Heaven!" (St. Ignatius). " Heaven is my true country!"

Prayer. Pater Noster, etc.

Examen of the Meditation, page 4.

MEDITATION FOR THE COMMEMORATION OF ALL SOULS.

(2ND NOVEMBER.)

" It is a holy and wholesome thought to pray for the dead " (2 Machabees xii. 46).

Preparatory Prayer, page 1.

1st Prelude. Represent to yourself the fiery vaults of that prison of fire wherein the divine justice detains those who are its debtors.

2nd Prelude. Grant me, O Lord, a gift of tender and solid piety for the relief of the souls in Purgatory.

1st Point. The souls in Purgatory ought to excite our pity by the greatness of their sufferings.

All that the holy doctors tell us of the pains suffered in Purgatory is calculated to penetrate us with tender pity for the souls detained there. St. Ambrose and St. John Chrysostom seem to think that all the torments invented for the Martyrs by the fury of the persecutors, and even by demons, do not come near to those endured by some who are in that prison of expiation. Another Father of the Church went so far as to think that the fires enkindled in this prison of the divine justice are the same as those raging in hell, and that there is no difference between the one and the other, except the hope of being one day set free, joined to the love of God dwelling in the souls of the just. This love, in a certain sense, softens the excessive pains of these holy souls; but, on the other hand, it is a new torment to them, since it causes them to feel in an agonising way the privation of that God, separated from Whom they can find neither repose nor happiness. How calculated to excite my compassion is such a state! But suffering is not the only title these poor souls have to my love and help; several among them have been united to me on earth by the ties of relationship or of friendship; all are children of the Church, members of Jesus Christ, destined to see and glorify Him for ever in Heaven. How can I help being moved with what they endure, and how refuse to devote myself with all my heart to their relief?

2nd Point. The souls in Purgatory can do nothing themselves to alleviate their sufferings.

The poor and afflicted who live on earth, if they cannot help themselves, have at least a voice with which to excite pity; and when they cannot speak, the sight alone of their misery suffices to affect us, and engage us to help them; but the poor souls who suffer and moan in the flames of Purgatory have not even this resource: unable to make us hear their plaintive cries, removed far from our sight, they uselessly utter those sighs and lamentations which their sufferings draw from them within the depths of their prison-house; it is in vain they say to us, "Have pity on me, at least you my friends!" We are deaf to their prayers. If they raise their looks towards the God of goodness and Father of the miserable, they behold in God a just Judge, Who reminds them that the time of His mercy is past, and that He exacts of them with rigour the last farthing which they owe Him. They would be without any resource, if the Church, that tender and compassionate Mother, did not interest the faithful in their favour. Oh! what an impression these warnings and solicitations ought to make on me. It is so easy for me to help these suffering souls! A short prayer, an act of virtue suffices to relieve them; an Indulgence gained for them fervently may entirely release them; would it not be unjust, and even cruel of me to acquit myself negligently of this duty of charity during the present time, when the Church reminds me of my duty by putting before my mind so many pressing motives?

Colloquy with God the Father, with our Lord, and with the holy Angels. Let us adore the justice of God in the chastisements which He imposes. Let us implore His mercy in favour of those suffering souls who are so dear to Him although He now chastises them. Let us address ourselves to the Sacred Heart of Jesus, the inexhaustible treasure of satisfaction and merit, begging of our Lord to permit His infinitely precious blood to descend on the fires of Purgatory, and to extinguish their flames. Let us implore the Guardian Angels of these suffering souls to join their supplications with our own, in order to obtain mercy for them.

Resolutions. To offer for the souls in Purgatory all my prayers, labours, struggles, acts of virtue, and even the indifferent actions of this very day, in union with the merits of Jesus.

Offering of the Resolutions, page 3.
Spirtiual Bouquet. "Have pity on me, have pity on me, at least you my friends" (Job xix. 21).
Prayer. Pater Noster, etc.
Examen of the Meditation, page 4.

MEDITATION FOR THE FEAST OF THE HOLY RELICS.

(8TH NOVEMBER.)

"I am the Resurrection and the Life; he that believeth in Me though he be dead shall live" (John xi. 25).

Preparatory Prayer, page 1.
1st Prelude. Represent to yourself the moment in which the Saints will resume their bodies resplendent with glory.
2nd Prelude. Grant, O Lord, that in venerating the relics of the Saints I may remember that I have myself been sanctified by baptism, and that I, like them, am destined to rise again to life eternal.
1st Point. I ought to venerate with faith the relics of the Saints.

The holy relics, which the Church proposes to me this day for my veneration, are truly worthy of respect and honour. They are the precious remains of bodies consecrated by baptism, united to the divine flesh of Jesus, and destined to rise again in glory; these same relics, which are here on earth confided to our care, will one day resume the life they have lost and ascend to Heaven. With what respect then ought I not to be inspired towards these holy relics of the friends of God! God Himself honours them. He attaches a secret virtue to them, which puts the devils to flight, and communicates sentiments of piety and purity to those who venerate them. How many times has He not sanctioned by miracles the worship which the faithful render to them! Consequently I am certain of pleasing Him, of giving Him glory, and of drawing down His graces on myself, by paying the respect and honour to holy relics which is due to them.

2nd Point. I ought to respect myself, and make a holy use of my body, for it is destined, like the bodies of the Saints, to rise again in glory.

The feast of the Holy Relics, in proposing to my veneration the precious remains of the bodies of the Saints, reminds me that I also am a member of the mystical body of Jesus Christ, that my body has been sanctified by baptism, and has become the temple of the adorable Trinity; that the flesh and blood of my Saviour have frequently sanctified and consecrated my members in a manner infinitely more excellent than baptism, and that my body is destined for a happy resurrection. I ought then to honour my body, never to allow it to be to me an occasion of sin, but, on the contrary, to purify it, and sanctify it unceasingly by the practice of Christian mortification; I ought to adorn it with modesty, and to watch carefully over all its senses, in order to preserve myself from the corruption of vice. It is in this way I shall prepare myself for the great day of the resurrection. If the practice of penance is accompanied with what is painful, how calculated is the thought of this happy day to sustain my courage! How sweet it will then be to me to clothe myself with that robe of immortal glory promised to the true disciples of Jesus; to those who shall have applied to themselves, by the mortification of their senses, the merits of His sufferings and the price of His blood.

Colloquy with our Lord. Let us adore Him as the Saint of Saints. Let us thank Him for the many means which He gives us to animate our fervour and enable us to attain Heaven. Let us ask Him, through the intercession of the Saints, for the grace to make a holy use both of soul and body, and thereby to prepare for a happy resurrection.

Resolutions. To venerate with great respect the relics of the Saints. To practise penance and mortification, according to my strength, by the advice of my spiritual guides.
Offering of the Resolutions, page 3.
Spiritual Bouquet. "Jesus, my resurrection and my life, sanctify me."
Prayer. Soul of Christ, etc.
Examen of the Meditation, page 4.

FIRST MEDITATION FOR THE FEAST OF ST. STANISLAUS.

(13TH NOVEMBER.)

" The kingdom of God is within you."

Preparatory Prayer, page 1.
1st Prelude. Represent to yourself St. Stanislaus in prayer.
2nd Prelude. Great Saint, who in so tender an age didst attain the highest perfection, obtain for me the grace to sanctify my least actions, as thou didst, by the spirit of prayer and recollection.
1st Point. The interior spirit of St. Stanislaus.
The young Saint whose feast the Church is now celebrating, presents me with the model of all virtues; but one virtue above all others was in him the very soul of all his other virtues, and this was his spirit of recollection. We sometimes apply ourselves to the practice of virtue; but because we have not an interior spirit the soul becomes weary, and we fail to acquire that perseverance which finishes and perfects the work begun. These isolated acts of virtue are to be compared to well-cut stones, adapted to building purposes, but which, not being properly arranged in order or connected together, cannot form an edifice. In what, then, consists

that interior spirit, which is alone capable of rendering our efforts efficacious and lasting? It may be defined the disposition of a person, who, directing all thoughts and affections towards God, seeks the truth in simplicity, desires it sincerely, and when the truth has been found follows it with courage and generosity. This interior spirit is a pure and persevering intention which gives life and merit to all our actions; it is the spirit of a lively faith which manifests itself in all the details of our conduct; the spirit of a confidence in God which bears up under all trials; and the spirit of a strong love which surmounts every obstacle. Oh! how necessary is this virtue for me, and how earnestly I ought to beg it of God!

2nd Point. What the means were which St. Stanislaus employed in order to acquire this interior spirit.

The Saints were but weak creatures like myself, inclined to evil, and by nature enemies to all restraint. No doubt, St. Stanislaus needed time and effort in order to acquire that spirit of prayer which produced in him such great fruits: he began by keeping a guard over his eyes; repressing his curiosity; watching over his thoughts; praying much; but, above all, by frequently raising his heart to God and desiring constantly to please Him. His soul, thus prepared. received still greater abundance of grace; he co-operated with it, and by degrees attained that exalted sanctity which has placed him on our Altars. His vigilance and fidelity in avoiding the snares of the enemy of our salvation, were not less to be admired than his generosity in overcoming himself. The wicked spirit, who cannot endure that we should apply ourselves to the practice of the spirit of prayer, because he knows how precious are its advantages, probably attacked him many times, by presenting to his mind useless and flattering thoughts, calculated to distract him, or to lead him to be scrupulous and over anxious about his faults, both past and present, in order to draw his attention from the practice of virtue. But this young Saint, so full of simplicity and confidence in God, humbled himself profoundly for the faults he had the light to discover, accused himself of them with sincerity, and then remained in peace. Perhaps also he had to endure those undefinable trials which sometimes cause so much suffering to upright souls; if so, he triumphed over them by humble confidence in God, and by renouncing in general terms all that could displease Him. Such conduct is the model I ought to propose to myself, if I wish to advance in a short time in the practice of every virtue.

Colloquy with St. Stanislaus. Let us pay him our homage of veneration. Let us congratulate him on the abundant graces with which he was so lavishly endowed when on earth, and on the glory in which he now rejoices in Heaven. Let us beg of him to obtain for us from the divine goodness that true interior spirit which should be the soul of all our virtues.

Resolutions. To recollect myself from time to time during the day. To combat my predominant defect, and offer my victories over it to God, in order to obtain the spirit of prayer.

Offering of the Resolutions, page 3.

Spiritual Bouquet. "I will hearken to what the Lord my God shall say to me in the depth of my soul. My God, give me Thy spirit."

Prayer. O God, Who, amongst the other miracles of Thy wisdom, hast bestowed the grace of matured sanctity, even in a tender age, upon St. Stanislaus, grant, we beseech Thee, that redeeming the time by prompt labour, after his example, we may hasten to enter into eternal rest; through Jesus Christ our Lord. Amen.

Examen of the Meditation, page 4.

SECOND MEDITATION.

(For the same Day.)

" Blessed are the clean of heart, for they shall see God."

Preparatory Prayer, page 1.

1st Prelude. Imagine to yourself St. Stanislaus kneeling before the Altar of Mary, and receiving the Infant Jesus from His holy Mother.

2nd Prelude. Cherished Child of the Queen of Virgins, obtain for me the gift of perfect purity, together with a tender and solid piety.

1st Point. The innocence of St. Stanislaus.

The spirit of prayer which animated St. Stanislaus produced the happiest fruits within his soul. Foremost amongst these fruits was that angelic purity which rendered him so dear to the Sacred Hearts of Jesus and Mary. His careful custody of all his senses and his constant union with God preserved in all its freshness this beautiful lily, which was watered abundantly each day by the healing waters of grace. What heavenly favours his innocence drew down upon him! This innocence it was which disposed him for those intimate communications with which our Lord favoured him in prayer, this rendered him so pleasing in the sight of the Divine Majesty. Jesus took such delight in the heart of this youth that He nourished him miraculously with the Divine Eucharist, causing this heavenly bread to be carried to him by Angels, when he was unable to receive it in any other way. This innocence it was which merited for him also the favour of receiving the Infant Jesus from the hands of His most holy Mother, and of enjoying His caresses—sweeter than words can paint. Such favours are not reserved for me, and I should be rash if I were to desire them; but if Jesus does not give Himself to me by the ministry of His Angels, I do not receive Him less truly at

His altars; if He does not favour me with His sensible presence, faith teaches me that He is always with me, ready to pour out abundantly His graces upon me. Purity of heart is not less necessary for me than it was for St. Stanislaus. I ought, in consequence, to use the greatest care in acquiring and preserving it; and above all, I should ask it most earnestly of the Sacred Hearts of Jesus and Mary, and through the intercession of the young Saint who possessed it so perfectly.

2nd Point. The piety of St. Stanislaus.

The tender piety of St. Stanislaus was not less admirable than his perfect purity; and both the one and the other were the effect of that interior spirit which he cultivated so carefully in his soul. Who could tell the delight with which this young Saint applied himself to prayer? It was in prayer that he poured fourth his soul with joy and confidence at the feet of his Heavenly Father; that he listened to the secret inspirations of God and received from Him the most precious favours; it was in prayer also that Mary enriched him with her gifts, discovered to him all the secrets of the spiritual life, and formed him to the perfect love of Jesus. St. Stanislaus came from prayer inflamed with the love of God; and this sacred fire, which he kept constantly alive by recollection and fidelity to grace, became the soul of all his actions. Oh! how pleasing I should be to the Sacred Heart of my Divine Saviour, if I knew how to form myself on this great model! How useful I should be to those who are dear to me! What blessings I should draw down on myself! Amiable Saint, my zealous protector, thou art so powerful before that infinitely good God Whom thou didst love so much on earth, that thou canst obtain for me from His adorable Heart the gift of solid piety that shall render all my prayers efficacious and all my actions meritorious.

Colloquy with Jesus Christ. Let us thank Him for the singular favours He granted to St. Stanislaus. Let us offer Him the merits of this young Saint. Let us ask through his intercession for purity of heart, for the gift of piety, and for every Christian virtue.

Resolutions. To practise recollection and the spirit of mortification.

Offering of the Resolutions, page 3.

Spiritual Bouquet. "He who loves purity shall have the king for his friend."

Prayer. O God, Who amongst the other, etc.

Examen of the Meditation, page 4.

MEDITATION FOR THE FEAST OF THE DEDICATION OF A CHURCH.

"My delight is to be with the children of men."

Preparatory Prayer, page 1.

1st Prelude. Imagine you see Jesus Christ in the splendour of His Majesty within our churches, and diffusing His graces abundantly on all those who draw near to Him.

2nd Prelude. Inspire me, O Lord, with profound respect for the temples Thou dost honour with Thy presence, and make me zealous to adorn my soul with all virtues, since I am myself Thy temple.

1st Point. With what sentiments we ought to present ourselves in the temples of God.

The feast of this day is established to renew the memory of the consecration of our churches, and to thank our Lord for having vouchsafed to dwell amongst us. Gratitude, joy, profound respect for the holy place where our Divine Lord resides as God and as man; a loving confidence in that veiled Majesty Which asks only to scatter abroad His gifts; such are the sentiments which ought on this day to possess my soul. But in the midst of these aspirations of my soul a profound sorrow should be present also : for this God so good, this Saviour so loving, Who has made Himself our companion and our friend, is outraged in His holy temples. His people do not go to them to visit Him. Sinners present themselves before Him without piety or respect; the impious make a sacrilegious diversion of profaning His most sacred mysteries; and while He multiplies His presence in order to render Himself more accessible to the children of men, His ungrateful creatures abuse the prodigies of His love, in order to multiply their offences. Ah! if my heart were alive to the glory of my Divine Master, should it not burst with grief at the remembrance of so many indignities? Ought I not above all to devote myself with ardent zeal to repair the majesty thus outraged, by paying the most profound and loving homage to Jesus in the Blessed Sacrament?

2nd Point. I am myself the temple of God.

In holy Baptism I received a solemn consecration, which made me become the temple of the adorable Trinity; consequently, I ought to-day to examine if God Almighty is honoured and served in His temple as He deserves to be. A temple is a holy place consecrated exclusively to the worship of the true God; it is a place of silence and recollection in which nothing should be heard but the word of God and the humble prayers addressed to Him: a temple is a place in which every day sacrifices are offered to the Divine Majesty. Is my soul habitually recollected and ready to listen to the voice of the Holy Spirit? Do I know how to send up to the throne of Christ those fervent prayers which obtain everything from His Sacred Heart? Am I careful to banish from my mind every wrong thought, every undue affection, every intention foreign to the love of God? Am I faithful, above all, to offer continually on the altar of my heart those sacrifices which He expects from me? Sacred Heart of Jesus, come Thyself and purify the sanctuary Thou hast deigned to make choice of; adorn my soul with every virtue pleasing to Thee; make me attentive to the inspirations of Thy grace, faithful to accomplish Thy holy Will in the smallest things, generous to sacrifice for Thy love my inclinations and passions; in one word, make me worthy to be ever Thy temple, and to offer Thee a place of repose and delight within my heart.

Colloquy with Jesus Christ. Let us thank Him for having deigned to fix His abode on earth, and let us consecrate to Him our heart, as a sanctuary in which He may love to dwell. Let us make reparation to Him for all the outrages which are offered Him in His holy places, asking His pardon for our own irreverences. Let us consecrate anew to Him our heart and entire being, that so we may repair our offences and those of all sinners.

Resolutions. Always to present myself in the house of God with lively faith and profound respect. To watch over my heart that I may preserve its purity, and never place any obstacle to the graces with which Jesus desires to adorn it.

Offering of the Resolutions, page 3.

Spiritual Bouquet. " How lovely are Thy tabernacles, O Lord of Hosts!"

Prayer. Soul of Christ, etc.

Examen of the Meditation, page 4.

MEDITATION FOR THE FEAST OF ST. CECILIA.

(22ND NOVEMBER.)

" In the presence of Thy holy Angels I will sing praises to Thy name."

Preparatory Prayer, page 1.

1st Prelude. Represent to yourself St. Cecilia surrounded by the heavenly spirits, who sing the praises of God with her.

2nd Prelude. Happy Virgin, who, after having sung the praises of Jesus Christ on earth, didst shed thy blood for His sake, and dost now celebrate His glory in Heaven, obtain for me the grace to merit His love as thou didst, by the purity of my heart and by my generosity in His service.

1st Point. The lessons which the virginal purity and the martyrdom of St. Cecilia offer me.

St. Cecilia was a Virgin and a Martyr: both these titles ought to speak powerfully to my heart. She was a Virgin: she knew how to maintain her mind and heart in perfect purity by an exact watchfulness over her senses, her thoughts, and her affections; by constant prayer, by a true spirit of mortification, and, above all, by sincere humility, which prompted God to shield her with His protection in the midst of the dangers by which she was surrounded. Such are the means of which I ought myself to make use, if I wish to please Jesus and merit the communications of His Sacred Heart. St. Cecilia was a Martyr; the sacrifice which she made of her blood and her life also teaches me important lessons; a lively faith, a generous love, and magnanimous courage were the arms with which she fought the grand fight which won for her so glorious a crown. Probably the martyr's palm and crown are not in reserve for me; but there is another sort of martyrdom which should immolate me as it did St. Cecilia to the glory of Jesus Christ: it is the daily sacrifice of my inclinations, of my desires, and of all the emotions of my heart. This sacrifice should last as long as my life, and make of me a victim ever dying and ever living. Consequently I have need, in my turn, to arm myself with faith, generosity and courage. Holy Spouse of my Saviour, obtain for me these precious graces, that so, imitating thy virtues, I also may glorify my Divine Lord, Who has given me so many proofs of ⁖is love.

⁖d Point. The example of St. Cecilia teaches

me to refer everything to the glory and service of God.

St. Cecilia delighted in singing the praises of God, and the historians of her life assure us that the Angels often joined her psalmody, and caused her to enjoy beforehand the delights of the heavenly canticles. God has tried to teach me by the example of this Saint that all the faculties of my soul and body, all my useful or pleasing talents, ought to be employed in His service, and that if profane music weakens the soul and excites the passions, sacred music assists the longings of piety, raises the affections of the heart towards Heaven, and thus becomes the prelude to the eternal melodies, in which all the blessed will celebrate the glory and the benefits of God. O great Saint, obtain for me of the God of goodness the grace to employ in His service, as faithfully as thou didst, all the gifts of nature and of grace with which He has endowed me, that so, after having praised Him and blessed Him on earth, I may with thee celebrate eternally in Heaven His love, His mercy, and His generosity towards those who serve Him.

Colloquy with Jesus Christ. Let us offer Him the virtues and merits of St. Cecilia, and thank Him for the graces He has lavished on her. Let us ask Him, through the intercession of this holy Virgin, for purity of heart, the spirit of generosity, and every other virtue which He desires to find in His true disciples.

Resolutions. To practise recollection, fidelity to grace, and generosity in overcoming myself.

Offering of the Resolutions, page 3.

Spiritual Bouquet. "Behold me ready to do Thy will, O my God!"

Prayer. Receive, O Lord, etc., page 18.

Examen of the Meditation, page 4.

MEDITATION FOR THE FEAST OF ST. CATHERINE.
(25TH NOVEMBER.)

"God chooses the weak to confound the strong."

Preparatory Prayer, page 1.

1st Prelude. Represent to yourself St. Catherine in the presence of an assembly of philosophers, who listen to her with astonishment and respect.

2nd Prelude. Prudent Virgin, who, in consequence of the purity of thy heart and the liveliness of thy faith, didst gain such glorious triumphs, obtain for me the grace to imitate thee, and to procure as thou didst thyself the glory of my adorable Lord.

1st Point. St. Catherine triumphed over the depraved inclinations of nature by the purity of her heart.

The words of St. Paul, "God chooses the weak to confound the strong," were fully accomplished in the young Virgin whose memory the Church celebrates to-day. From her tender infancy St. Catherine, ravished with the attractive charms of the fairest of virtues, understood that her heart was created to belong to Jesus Christ alone, and that no other Spouse should ever share in her affections; hence she consecrated herself to Him by a vow of virginity, and from that time all her study, all her care and fervour led her to ponder and meditate upon the law of God, and to strengthen herself day by day in the practice of the solid virtues which immolate nature and raise souls above their own weakness, by causing the power of Him Who upholds them to shine forth. If I wish to triumph over the many bad inclinations which weigh down my soul and hinder it from taking its flight towards God, I ought, after the example of St. Catherine, to love purity of heart, and to cultivate it carefully. The Spirit of ngth, the Sanctifier of our souls, communicates

Himself only to the pure of heart. Jesus, our Strength and the Author of life, has His delight alone among the lilies; in consequence, by a holy purity of heart and of conscience, I must dispose myself for the divine communications, and render myself worthy of those powerful graces which alone can enable me to triumph over myself and gain a complete victory over all natural inclinations.

2nd Point. St. Catherine triumphed by her faith over the errors of pagan philosophy, as well as over the fury of her persecutors.

The heart of St. Catherine, honoured by the most intimate communications of the Spirit of God, because it was eminently a pure heart, had drawn from the deep study and continual meditation of the holy Scriptures the science which forms Saints, and the courage which makes Martyrs. Full of zeal, and desiring the triumph of God's cause, she presented herself before the tyrant Maximinian, reproached him fearlessly with his injustice towards the Christians, and spoke to him with so much energy of the divinity of their religion, that the tyrant, ashamed and bewildered, knew not what to answer her. He assembled his learned doctors and opposed them to Catherine, but she convinced and converted them all. Maximinian, enraged, caused a wheel armed with sharp teeth to be prepared for the young Martyr. The faith of Catherine was rewarded with a striking miracle: the instrument of torture broke in pieces in her sight, and the crowd by which she was surrounded cried out that the God protecting her was the true God. She was thrown into a dungeon, there to be starved to death, but her faith supported her; her soul was nourished with the divine word, and the strength of her body was miraculously preserved. At length, the fury of the tyrant not being disarmed by these multiplied prodigies, he condemned her to be beheaded. She offered her life joyfully, and thus consummated her sacrifice. This holy Martyr is especially offered to me as a model; the Church has given her to me for a patroness and protectress; consequently, I ought to imitate her faith, her generosity, and her courage. It is not against the fury of tyrants that I am destined to struggle, but against the seductions of the world. This kind of combat, far more perilous, calls for a heroism and constancy which faith alone can give. O great Saint! obtain for me these indispensable virtues; grant that I may imitate thy triumph on earth, that so I may one day partake of thy glory in Heaven.

Colloquy with St. Catherine. Let us congratulate her on her fidelity in corresponding with the grace of God, by meditating on His law and consecrating all her affections to Him. Let us beg of her to obtain for us the grace to imitate her and to triumph over the enemies of our salvation as she did.

Resolutions. Courageously to brave human respect, the inclinations of nature, and the seductions of the world.

Offering of the Resolutions, page 3.

Spiritual Bouquet. "I can do all things in Him that strengtheneth me."

Prayer. Soul of Christ, etc.

Examen of the Meditation, page 4.

MEDITATION FOR THE FEAST OF ST. ANDREW.

(30th November.)

"They who belong to Jesus Christ have crucified their flesh with its vices and concupiscences."

Preparatory Prayer, page 1.

1st Prelude. Represent to yourself St. Andrew,

when, perceiving the Cross which was prepared, he exclaimed: "All hail to thee, O precious Cross!"

2nd Prelude. Obtain for me, O holy Apostle, the grace to esteem and love the Cross of my Divine Saviour, and to submit to be fastened upon it, according to His good pleasure.

1st Point. The Cross is precious in the eyes of the true disciples of Jesus.

Esteem and love for the Cross are the subjects of meditation which naturally present themselves on the feast of a Saint whose whole desire was a yearning to be crucified with his Divine Lord. St. Andrew had well understood and accepted the maxim, so opposed to nature, that in order to be happy we must never be without suffering. I must strive to imitate him in this, since Jesus desires that I should unite myself to His sentiments, His affections, and His will. What, then, are the considerations that should make me love suffering? They are very many. By suffering I can satisfy for my sins, repair the injury they have done to God, and acquire that purity of conscience which Jesus wishes to find in His true disciples. By suffering I accomplish the will of my Heavenly Father, I conform myself to my Divine Model, I unite myself intimately to His Sacred Heart, and I destroy in myself the reign of concupiscence, and substitute for it that of His holy love. By suffering I can draw down on those dear to me numberless and powerful graces, and obtain for sinners the means of conversion; for suffering is the means through which Jesus Christ saved the world, and it is by suffering that His followers must carry on His work. Oh! how precious, then, ought not the Cross to be to me, and how eager I ought to be to accept it, from whatever side it may come to me!

2nd Point. The Cross appears amiable to the true followers of Jesus.

The Cross is not only worthy of esteem for the many

precious advantages which it procures for faithful souls, it is even yet more sweet to those enamoured with the love of Jesus. As it is the bed of suffering on which our Divine Lord breathed His last sigh, and as by reddening it with His Blood He has given us the strongest and most touching proof of His love for us, His true friends long, in their turn, to be fastened to it, in order that they may love their Divine Lord with the same love with which He has loved them, and so give back to Him suffering for suffering, life for life. It was this sentiment which inspired St. Andrew, when he beheld the Cross on which he was to die, with those words which so well described his soul: "All hail to thee, O precious Cross, which has been consecrated by the body of my Lord, and adorned with His sacred members as with precious jewels; I draw near to thee in lively transports of joy! O saving Cross, which has been made beauteous by the members of my Lord, ardently have I loved thee, long have I desired and sought thee, now at length my wishes are accomplished; receive me into thy arms, by taking me from the world and presenting me to my God. May He Who made use of thee to redeem me now receive me from thy arms!" These sentiments have been those of all the Saints—are they mine? Am I desirous to unite myself to the Cross of my adorable Spouse? Do I at least know how to receive willingly, and support patiently, the trifling sufferings and petty contradictions by which His love wishes to produce in me some resemblance to Himself?

Colloquy with Jesus Crucified. Let us offer Him the love and merits of St. Andrew, and those of all the Saints who have loved and embraced the Cross. Let us humble ourselves to find our dispositions so different from those of these great Saints. Let us beg our Divine Lord to give us a relish for suffering, joy under trials, and that strong and generous love which is nourished by labours and sufferings alone.

Resolutions. To accept willingly all the trials, contradictions, and annoyances our Lord may please to send me this very day. To impose on myself some mortification, above all interior mortification.
Offering of the Resolutions, page 3.
Spiritual Bouquet. " Sacred Heart of Jesus, immolated for me upon the Cross, grant that I may love Thee as Thou hast loved me."
Prayer. Receive, O Lord, etc., page 18.
Examen of the Meditation, page 4.

MEDITATION FOR THE FEAST OF ST. FRANCIS XAVIER.

(3RD DECEMBER.)

" What doth it profit a man if he gain the whole world and lose his own soul?"

Preparatory Prayer, page 1.
1st Prelude. Represent to yourself St. Francis Xavier traversing the Indies, a crucifix in his hand, announcing the Gospel to the infidels. Or behold him stretched on the ground in a poor hut on the sea-shore, ready to breathe his last sigh.
2nd Prelude. Great Saint, who didst labour so zealously for thy own salvation and for the salvation of thy neighbour, obtain for me the grace to be deeply penetrated with that maxim which made so great an impression on thyself: "What doth it profit a man if he gain the whole world and suffer the loss of his own soul?"
1st Point. The necessity of salvation.
"What doth it profit a man if he gain the whole world and lose his own soul?" These words of eternal life opened the eyes of St. Francis Xavier, and disabused him of the illusions of the world. Born with an ele-

vated mind, an extraordinary capacity and great facility for the study of the sciences, he had opened his heart to ambition, and was rejoicing in the brilliant prospect of the future ; but from the moment the light of Heaven revealed to him the vanity of his projects, and he heard in the depths of his soul the powerful words: "What doth it profit a man to gain the whole world and lose his own soul?" he straightway became changed into another man ; he understood that the glory of this world is nothing but a little vapour ; its goods nothing more than things that we hold in trust for a time, and which we must leave at death ; and that the glory and treasures of eternity can alone satisfy a heart infinite in its desires and insatiable in its demands. Then the holy folly of the Cross seemed the only thing worthy to be sought after, and all his yearnings were for humiliations, labours, sufferings, and sacrifices. How calculated is such an example to instruct and stimulate me! Why should I not recognise the nothingness of this world, as well as this great Saint? Why should I not detach my heart from earthly trifles which pass away? I am in this world only to work out my salvation ; everything that seeks to withdraw me from this my one only end, or is not referred to it, is worthy of nothing but supreme contempt.

2nd Point. The means of ensuring salvation.

As soon as the light of Heaven shone before the eyes of St. Francis Xavier, he determined to walk in it. The world had thought to drag him into the broad road of perdition ; he broke with it generously. But this first sacrifice was the prelude only to those sacrifices which his fervour soon after inspired him to make. Attentive to combat and immolate his evil inclinations, he thrust the sword of Christian mortification into his innermost soul. He had loved praise, but now sought only for contempt ; the hope of making a fortune in the world had had charms for him, he now devoted himself, for his entire life, to voluntary poverty; a natural haughtiness and love of independence had, up to that time, signalised his character; by the vow of obedience he placed fetters on his liberty, and was unto death faithful to his holy compact. If I wish to walk in the footsteps of this great Saint, and thus make sure my rights to my heavenly inheritance, I also must combat my favourite passions, and erect the edifice of my sanctification on the ruins of my natural inclinations. If I am given to pride, I must attach myself to humility, seek obscurity, and to be forgotten by creatures, choosing always what may lower me in their esteem; if thoughtlessness and giddiness deter me from the service of God, I must impose on my senses rigid rules of self-restraint and recollection; if I am tyrannised over by a love of my own ease, and of the conveniences of life, Christian mortification must become my daily practice. In a word, I must sacrifice myself to God with the most complete generosity. Such sacrifices may seem to be formidable, but they are the only means of meriting a crown of glory; even in this life, they alone can procure me that solid peace and interior joy of soul which our Lord communicates to His true friends, and which all the combined honours, pleasures, and goods of this world could never give me.

Colloquy with Jesus Christ. Let us offer Him the merits of St. Francis Xavier, thanking Him for the special graces He has granted to the fidelity of this Saint. Let us ask our Blessed Lord, through the intercession of St. Francis, to give us so strong a light as may disabuse us of the delusions of the world, together with the strength necessary to enable us to triumph over ourselves and to serve Him with a generous heart.

Resolutions. To labour seriously to overcome myself in whatsoever costs me most.

Offering of the Resolutions, page 3.

Spiritual Bouquet. "What shall it profit a man if he gain the whole world and lose his own soul?"
Prayer. Receive, O Lord, etc., page 18.
Examen of the Meditation, page 4.

MEDITATION FOR THE FEAST OF ST. THOMAS, THE APOSTLE.

(21st December.)

"Thomas, thou hast believed because thou hast seen; blessed are they that have not seen, yet have believed."

Preparatory Prayer, page 1.
1st Prelude. Represent to yourself St. Thomas, prostrate at the feet of his risen Lord, exclaiming, in sentiments of faith and love: "My Lord and my God!"
2nd Prelude. Holy Apostle, who didst doubt for an instant the resurrection of thy Divine Lord, but didst afterwards witness to it for this reason in a more glorious manner, obtain for me, through the merits of His Sacred Wounds, which He commanded thee to touch, a firm, unshaken, lively, and practical faith.

1st Point. We ought to labour without ceasing to quicken our faith.

The doubt of St. Thomas, in the opinion of St. Gregory the Great, is more calculated to strengthen our faith than the ready credence of all the other Apostles put together. I cannot more fittingly celebrate the feast of this Saint than in meditating on this fundamental virtue of Christianity. "Without faith," says St. Paul, "it is impossible to please God." I ought, therefore, to be penetrated with gratitude towards God, Who has bestowed on me this precious gift from my earliest years; I ought to esteem it more than any earthly advantage, to guard it with extreme care, and, if necessary, at the price of every sacrifice.

But faith which is not fruitful by charity, and which does not produce good works, is a dead faith, according to the words of the Apostle St. James. Not only must faith enlighten our mind, but it must take root in our heart, through sanctifying grace, and must become the principle of all our actions. I ought, then, carefully to preserve purity of conscience, and to penetrate myself more and more with the spirit and maxims of the Gospel, by patient meditation, causing them to pass from my mind and heart into my conduct, animating each one of my actions by supernatural motives, and by that interior spirit which can alone render them valuable before God. What merit might I not acquire each day by a faithful use of these means! On the other hand, what graces I lose when I neglect these means! O Sacred Heart of my Jesus! grant that from this day I may so fully understand the importance of doing this, that I may never lose any merit or grace through my own fault.

2nd Point. Zeal for the glory of God and the good of my neighbour ought to animate me, more and more, to excite my faith.

The inestimable treasure of faith is not known, or appreciated, or sought after by the greater portion of mankind: impiety, heresy, and, still more, a fatal indifference, are destroying it on every side. Countless souls forget their eternal interests, precipitate themselves into hell, and wound the Sacred Heart of Jesus most severely. With what zeal ought not this sight to fill me, who have been prevented with so many graces by my Saviour, who have received so many interior solicitations to give myself unreservedly to Him! My dearest Saviour desires that, sensibly affected by the blindness and loss of so many souls who withdraw themselves from Him and suffer the sacred light of faith to become extinct in their souls, I should devote myself to rekindle the light by every means which an industrious charity can suggest to me; above all, Jesus desires that I should exert myself to cause the light of faith to shine brightly in the souls of those over whom my social position may give me any influence. But I shall not be able to produce such happy fruits in others unless I am myself deeply rooted in these same virtues. A lively faith should penetrate me thoroughly with the important truth that God is all, and all the rest nothing; this truth should raise me above the weaknesses of nature, above the touchiness and meanness of self-love, and should make me sensitive to nothing so much as to the glory of God, and the honour of the Sacred Heart of Jesus Christ. This same disposition, animating all my prayers, ought to render me all-powerful with the Sacred Heart, and obtain from It all that I shall ask for the glory of God and the salvation of souls. These two great interests depend, in some way, on the liveliness of my faith and the fervour of my zeal. How much, therefore, ought not this thought to inspire me with courage and devotedness!

Colloquy with Jesus Christ. Let us thank Him for the precious gift of faith, with which He has favoured us from our earliest years. Let us ask His pardon for the little zeal we have had, up to the present time, to keep our faith alive by our fidelity to it. Let us beg His grace to repair the past, by labouring not only to strengthen our faith within our own soul, but also to establish it in the soul of others.

Resolutions. To perform all my actions in a spirit of faith, in order to procure the glory of the Sacred Heart of Jesus, and the salvation of souls.

Offering of the Resolutions, page 3.

Spiritual Bouquet. "Blessed are they who have not seen, yet have believed."

Prayer. Soul of Christ, etc.

Examen of the Meditation, page 4.

MEDITATION FOR THE FEAST OF ST. STEPHEN, THE FIRST MARTYR.

(26TH DECEMBER.)

"When the Paraclete shall come, He shall give testimony of Me, and you also shall give testimony of Me."

Preparatory Prayer, page 1.

1st Prelude. Represent to yourself St. Stephen giving testimony to the divinity of Jesus, in the midst of the assembly of the Jews.

2nd Prelude. Glorious Martyr, to whom was given the honour of being the first to shed his blood for Jesus Christ, obtain for me also the grace to give testimony to Him, by braving the fear of men, and by doing good, in spite of the contradictions of the world.

1st Point. How glorious to Jesus Christ was the testimony of the Martyrs.

Our Divine Lord, promising His Apostles to send them the Holy Spirit, said to them: "When the Spirit of truth shall come, He shall give testimony of Me, and you also shall give testimony of Me". The Holy Spirit could alone inspire weak creatures with the strength to sacrifice their lives with joy for the glory of God; and the gifts of this same Holy Spirit could be merited for man through the Blood of a God alone. The constancy and generosity of the Martyrs in confronting the horrors of death gave, consequently, one of the strongest proofs of the divinity of Jesus Christ. It was, at the same time, the greatest proof of love that staunch disciples of His could show Him. Our adorable Lord had said: "No man hath greater love than to lay down his life for his friends". The Martyrs, in dying for Him, as He had died for them, returned sacrifice for sacrifice, and responded to His love by a reciprocal love, in so far as creatures could when God is in question. How greatly to be venerated, then, ought not these generous champions of the Lord to appear to me! Above all, what homage does not the Saint deserve who is honoured by the Church to-day! He was the first to enter the glorious but painful lists; he renewed in his death that of his Divine Lord, becoming, like Him, a victim to the fury of the Jews, and praying, after His example, for his murderers. How greatly should I not honour him! What ought not my confidence to be in his powerful intercession!

2nd Point. I ought, likewise, to render glorious testimony to Jesus Christ by my courage in braving human respect.

When meditating on the sufferings and combats of the martyrs, if my heart is touched with love for Jesus, it ought to be inflamed with ardour, and bear a holy envy towards those generous souls who evinced so much love for Him, and procured Him so much glory. This sentiment will never be fruitless for the honour of my Divine Lord; for, if I am not called upon to bear testimony to Him at the price of my life, He asks of me another kind of sacrifice, from which He wishes also to derive glory. This is the daily and constant sacrifice of all human fear, and of every motive foreign to the love of God. If Christian prudence, and a regard for the charity I owe certain persons; if even the cautious behaviour of an enlightened zeal sometimes requires of me the sacrifice of certain exterior practices, and of certain desires of which piety appears to me to be the source; if, even under circumstances where a holy firmness becomes necessary, I must always show gentleness and submission, I ought never to forget that there are principles laid down in the Christian life, from which it is never permitted to depart, though, in order to be faithful to them, we must sacrifice repose, the esteem of others and even the affection of our dearest friends. "He who loves father or mother more than Me is not worthy of Me," our Lord has said. If ever I am placed by God in circumstances which enable me to offer some similar sacrifice, so wounding and painful to the heart, I must remember that, in bearing witness to God at such a cost, I am sharing, in some sort, the combats of the Martyrs, and acquiring a title to wear their crown.

Colloquy with St. Stephen. Let us congratulate him on the glory that was reserved to him in being the first to give his life for Jesus Christ. Let us beg of him to obtain for us the grace to sacrifice ourselves without reserve for the glory of so good a God, by braving generously the contradictions of the world, and the evil propensities of our nature, in order to be faithful to Him.

Resolutions. To brave human respect with generosity. To discharge faithfully the daily duties of my position, with a view to bearing witness to Jesus Christ by a holy and exemplary life.

Offering of the Resolutions, page 3.

Spiritual Bouquet. "All for the greater glory of God."

Prayer. Receive, O Lord, etc., page 18.

Examen of the Meditation, page 4.

MEDITATION FOR THE FEAST OF ST. JOHN THE EVANGELIST.

(27TH DECEMBER.)

"He who loves purity shall have the King for his friend."

Preparatory Prayer, page 1.

1st Prelude. Represent to yourself the room of the Last Supper, and behold St. John leaning on the bosom of his Divine Master.

2nd Prelude. Beloved Apostle of my Saviour, obtain for me the grace to merit, as thou didst, this sweet sign of special love, by the purity of my heart, the fervour of my love, and the earnestness of my zeal.

1st Point. What the causes were of the special love with which Jesus honoured St. John.

St. John the Evangelist is called, by excellence, the "disciple that Jesus loved". Whence arose this preference, which could not be a blind one, or without foundation? St. Augustine assigns three principal reasons. The first was the burning love which this fervent disciple bore to his Divine Master: "I love those who love Me," said the Uncreated Wisdom. There is no surer means of winning the affection of the Sacred Heart of Jesus than that of loving Him with a tender, constant, and generous love. Secondly, St. John possessed the advantage over the other disciples of being a Virgin, which precious prerogative rendered him dear to the Saint of Saints, to Him "that feedeth among the lilies," Who had willed to be born of a Virgin Mother, and Whose Precursor, chosen from among the children of men, equalled the purity of the Angels, according to the words of the Scripture: "I will send My Angel before Thee to prepare the way". Thirdly, and lastly, the meekness of the Beloved Disciple was the remaining cause which merited for him his august title. Jesus is called the Prince of Peace, and He loves those souls in whom He finds His peace, for such are meek and gentle. What important lessons are offered me in the example of this blessed disciple! Like him, I ought to have an ardent and generous love for Jesus, since my dear Lord has prevented me with so many graces, and wishes to indemnify Himself through my love for the ingratitude of mankind. I ought also to practise, according to my state, that perfect purity without which it is impossible to please the Spouse of Virgins; and, lastly, I ought to show forth His incomparable meekness, since He invites me to cause His empire to be loved, to win others to Him, and to make as many as I can love the sweetness of His yoke and the lightness of His burden. O Sacred Heart of Jesus, grant me these precious graces, I beg of Thee, through the merits of Thy holy infancy, and the intercession of Thy beloved disciple!

2nd Point. Special favours accompanied the predilection of Jesus for St. John.

To the three motives which caused our Divine Lord to honour St. John with a special affection answered three sorts of graces, of inestimable value. The tender love of the faithful disciple gained for him the signal favour of a sweet and intimate familiarity with Jesus; he was with Jesus on Mount Thabor; he followed Him to the Garden of Olives; during the Last Supper he reposed on His bosom; on Cavalry he received the most touching and most priceless proofs of His tenderness; Mary was given to him for a mother, and this inestimable gift became for him, at the same time, the reward of his perfect purity. This beautiful virtue was rewarded with another recompense; it was purity that disposed his soul for the sublime illuminations with which he was favoured—lights which enabled him to penetrate into the most sublime mysteries, and revealed to him that divine theology which unveils to us all the glories of Jesus. And, last of all, his unalterable meekness ensured the success of his Apostolic labours; he made himself dear to all, and the contrivances of his charity triumphed over the obduracy of the greatest sinners. If my Divine Lord beholds in me dispositions similar to those of His beloved disciple, He will honour me also with His holy familiarity; He will reveal to me His secrets, and will employ me for His glory, and for the salvation of souls. Oh! what powerful motives are these for my fervour and fidelity!

Colloquy with the Sacred Heart of Jesus. Let us ask for His holy love, through the intercession of St. John, for perfect purity of heart, for an unalterable meekness, and for every virtue necessary to make us pleasing to Him, and to enable us to labour efficaciously for His glory.

Resolutions. To watch over every movement of my heart, in order to preserve its purity; and to produce as many interior and exterior acts of charity as I possibly can.

Offering of the Resolutions, page 3.

Spiritual Bouquet. "He that loves purity shall have the King for his friend."

Prayer. Soul of Christ, etc.

Examen of the Meditation, page 4.